'If you are involved with [...] comprehensive compendium [...] Charity governance and practi[...] needs a fresh map. Heather W[...] her own experience, as well [...] practical advice and numerous examples, so that charities can be more fruitful and accountable. Theological precedent is also explored using the examples of Nehemiah and Daniel in particular.'
Rev Canon David Casswell, One Voice York

'The responsibilities and challenges for those who are trustees of churches and charities can seem to be increasingly onerous. Good governance requires attention to dimensions of charity law as diverse as financial probity, safeguarding and the monitoring of five-year plans and strategic aims – these in addition to the spiritual demands of Christian leadership. No wonder many ask, "Who is sufficient to these things?" Well, becoming equal to such a task has just been made easier by Heather Wraight's overview of the role and work of trustees in a Christian context. Every charity trustee – Baptist deacon, Anglican PCC member and their equivalents, whether new to the task or an "old hand" – will benefit enormously from reading this book and implementing its wisdom.'
Rev Dr Paul Goodliff, General Secretary, Churches Together in England

'I can remember Heather Wraight's frequent observation, as Christian Research published its *UK Christian Handbook*, that there were so many new but poorly run charities which had poor capacity and weak governance. Heather has answered this thoroughly with a helpful and accessible overview of what it takes to run a charity with integrity and efficiency. The major issues are covered with appropriate biblical input and examples, written in a winsome and non-critical style but compiling the insights from many interviewees who have been at the forefront of running charities. A helpful, non-technical resource for us all.'

Dr Chris Wigram, former International Director, European Christian Mission, OMF UK National Director and Chair of Board of Global Connections

Tracks of
Trustworthiness

Biblical and Contemporary Insights for
Trustees of Churches and Christian
Charities

Heather Wraight MTh

instant
apostle

First published in Great Britain in 2020

Instant Apostle
The Barn
1 Watford House Lane
Watford
Herts
WD17 1BJ

British Library Cataloguing-in-Publication Data

A catalogue record for this book is available from the British Library.

This book and all other Instant Apostle books are available from Instant Apostle:

Website: www.instantapostle.com

Email: info@instantapostle.com

ISBN 978-1-912726-29-5

Printed in Great Britain.

They could find no corruption in him, because he was trustworthy and neither corrupt nor negligent.
(Daniel 6:4)

They realised that this work had been done with the help of our God.
(Nehemiah 6:16)

Contents

Foreword

Over half a lifetime of Christian leadership I have been an elder and minister in three Baptist churches, on the Board of Trustees of some Christian organisations, served as director of a company that is also a charity, and as a member of staff attended the Trustee Board for a major Christian denomination. I currently serve as secretary to the Board of Trustees of Churches Together in England. For many ministers this is not untypical. As an adjunct to their pastoral ministry they may be a governor in the local school, serve on the parish council and support the boards of local charities. Lay members of churches will often do much more, serving on church and local councils and charity boards as trustees and leaders. Almost the only church where I have never been in any leadership role or trusteeship is where my current membership lies, although my wife, Gill, served it as an elder until a couple of years ago. My first experience of these kinds of roles was as an eighteen-year-old invited to become a member, briefly, of the Parochial Church Council (PCC) of the Anglican church where I had grown up before moving away to London and university. Then, I fear, I knew nothing at all about the responsibilities of being a trustee, and I suspect that ignorance was shared by some of my fellow PCC members of considerably older vintage. How I wish that a book like this one written by my friend Heather Wraight had been available then.

By the middle of the first decade of this century, Baptists were developing new resources and training for those who were serving as managing trustees of Baptist churches ('Help! I am a trustee' days for deacons and elders, for instance). The Charity Commission has developed a range of resources for trustees in general to help them in their work, but they lack the grounding in Christian thought and ethics that Heather brings to this resource. Recently, a guide to being a member of an Anglican PCC has been published by a member of the parish of St Edburg's, Bicester,[1] to good reviews in the Anglican press, and most larger denominations will provide some kind of resource for those who are trustees in their churches. However, none offers such a general and biblically literate guide to being a trustee in both church and para-church contexts, so far as I know. Here lies the enormous value in Heather's well-researched book – it has wide applicability to accompany the depth of the wisdom it conveys.

Being a trustee is far more than just following the rules, avoiding disaster and keeping the show on the road. An effective trustee will help drive the organisation forward in the midst of changing contexts, so that it remains valuable to those whom the charity or church serves. They will also provide support to those whom the charity or church employs, as staff and ministers alike, and upon whose shoulders the burden of administration and governance otherwise falls heavily. All churches and most charities rely widely upon volunteers – among whom trustees will be a particular group, of course – and good trustees will have an eye to the welfare of not only the people served by the charity, but also those who deliver much of its work on an unpaid basis, that army of volunteers whose generous service is the core of social capital in Britain. Indeed, having an effective and gifted trustee board can make or break an organisation.

Through Heather's research, conducted by interviewing a wide range of trustees in church and charity sectors alike, the challenges of being a trustee and the opportunity to serve the purposes of God's kingdom in a largely secular society are rooted in real experience, which greatly enhances the utility of the book. Here are real-life trustees giving their account. But, correspondingly, rooting the structure in biblical narratives (especially from Daniel's and Nehemiah's experiences of leadership in challenging situations) provides a much broader and almost universal horizon of revelation out of which the values and practices of governance and trusteeship are explored, making them properly Christian too.

The importance of good governance by effective trustees should not be underestimated. Upon it lies so much of the good reputation of Christian charities and churches, as well as the fruitfulness of their mission. Just as poor interpersonal relationships within a congregation can wreck the mission of a church, so incompetent governance, making ill-judged decisions, and turning a blind eye to poor practice, can make the building of the kingdom of God within a community so much more difficult, be that by a para-church organisation or a local church. It is my belief that this book, drawing upon Heather Wraight's experience as a researcher and practitioner as a trustee, will help in the provision of good governance for all who read and implement its wisdom and guidance.

Revd Dr Paul Goodliff
General Secretary of Churches Together in England

Acknowledgements

This book could not have been written without the wide experience I have had on various trustee boards and councils, especially Feba Radio, Global Connections, Spurgeon's College and York Schools and Youth Trust (YoYo). My church experience has been both wide, as a consultant alongside Dr Peter Brierley at Christian Research, and local, as PCC secretary at All Saints and St Andrew's, York. Particularly in my early days as a trustee, I learned much from good role models, for which I am truly grateful. When I was working at Christian Research we arranged some seminars for church and charity leaders, which were led by Paul Martin. Those helped to shape my understanding of governance, while I have referred to his books on charity law many times.[1] I am grateful to him for checking this book for compliance (as of January 2020).

My thanks go to those who helped guide the research and the people I interviewed, all of whom I have quoted anonymously to protect them and their organisations. My thanks, also, to the friend who proofread the manuscript and made helpful suggestions on content. I am blessed to have had a mother who had twenty books published and who taught me to write as a child, and a father who passed on his understanding of leadership and management. Finally, my thanks go to Instant Apostle for publishing this book when bigger publishers felt the market was too specific.

Introduction

It was a beautiful, clear, sunny morning high up in the Alps. Banks of snow lined the road on either side and here and there tracks went up a bank and headed off across the nearby fields or into the woods. One set had been made by a rabbit, another by some kind of deer, and others by human beings in boots or on skis. By looking at those marks it was possible to create a mental picture of what or who had passed that way since it last snowed. Similarly, how people behave leaves tracks which reveal how they approach life. This book is specifically for those with particular responsibilities as trustees in churches and Christian charities. What tracks do they leave in the work and ministry, community and congregations they are involved in?

The Bible book of Daniel makes it very clear that he was an excellent administrator. He served under King Nebuchadnezzar and his son Belshazzar. When Darius conquered Belshazzar:

> It pleased Darius to appoint 120 satraps to rule throughout the kingdom, with three chief ministers over them, one of whom was Daniel ... Daniel so distinguished himself among the chief ministers and the satraps by his exceptional qualities that the king planned to set him over the whole kingdom. At this, the chief ministers and the satraps tried to find grounds for charges against Daniel in his conduct of government affairs, but they were unable to do so. *They could find no corruption in him, because he was trustworthy and neither corrupt nor negligent.* Finally these men said, 'We will never find any basis for charges against this

man Daniel unless it has something to do with the law of his God.'
(Daniel 6:1-5, emphasis mine)

What a remarkable thing to be said about a foreigner who had been brought from his home country as a captive. And what a reputation Daniel must have had, not only for his administrative ability but, perhaps more importantly, for the godly and upright way in which he carried out his duties.

Nehemiah was also an Israelite in exile. He earned the trust of King Artaxerxes to such an extent that the king allowed him to return to Jerusalem to rebuild the walls, even providing some of the resources Nehemiah would need. Nehemiah faced massive logistical problems and determined opposition, yet he came through them all:

> So the wall was completed ... When all our enemies heard about this, all the surrounding nations were afraid and lost their self-confidence, because they realised that *this work had been done with the help of our God.*
> (Nehemiah 6:15-16, emphasis mine)

Administration and governance are demanding responsibilities, including for the trustees of churches and Christian charities. We can learn a great deal from Daniel and Nehemiah, as well as from other parts of the Bible and contemporary stories and insights, about how to fulfil those responsibilities in a way which honours God. The purpose of this book is to help charity trustees to be 'trustworthy and neither corrupt nor negligent' so that whatever their work is, it is done with the help of our God. But before we consider what being trustworthy can look like in practice, let's look at a few preliminary considerations.

What is a charity?

An organisation can register as a charity if it was established for charitable purposes, provides a public benefit and meets the financial criterion of £5,000+ a year income. The organisation's work must clearly benefit people, which may have to be proved by external evidence if it is not immediately obvious. Charity law lists thirteen purposes which are charitable. The 2011 Charities Act clarified definitions and also required that churches with an income of more than £100,000 and which belong to a denomination which was previously excepted must also register as individual charities.

How many are there?

At the end of 2017 there were more than 168,000 charities in England and Wales registered with the Charity Commission, more than 24,000 on the Scottish Charity Register, and several thousand more registered with the Voluntary Activity Unit in Northern Ireland. A report by New Philanthropy Capital in June 2016[1] estimated that there were around 30,000 Christian-based charities in England and Wales, although because of the income threshold the National Audit Office estimates there may be 100,000 religious groups doing charitable work but which are too small to be required to register. As the requirement for churches with smaller incomes to register individually is rolled out, this number will increase, as the estimate for 2020 is 44,000 churches in England and Wales.[2] In Scotland and Northern Ireland all churches, regardless of income, have to register separately, as do all charities.

For many years before the internet took over, the *UK Christian Handbook* listed around 5,000 Christian organisations across the country, about half of which were registered charities. They were only included if they had a regional or national scope. In York, where I live, at the time of writing there are eighteen to twenty local Christian charities, only two or three of which would have been listed in the *Handbook*. All these groups have to meet legal requirements. Add these to the churches and it is clear that we are talking about large numbers of registered churches and Christian charities, all of which are required by law to have trustees.

Why does it matter?

As editor for six editions of the *Handbook* I saw first-hand the widespread challenges Christian organisations and charities wrestled with. In one edition we found a large proportion of small Christian conference centres had closed since the previous edition two years before. Why? It turned out that new fire safety regulations were either too expensive or impossible to implement in the often-rambling old houses which had been their base. Their trustees had no option but to close, no doubt with heavy hearts. The difficulties in the book trade were clear when not only individual Christian bookshops but large chains were forced into closure, while some publishers closed and others were taken over by larger companies. And in every update there were many small organisations, which were perhaps twenty years old and had always been run by the founder, that had closed, almost certainly because the vision had not been passed on to a successor who could continue the work. If they were a registered charity, that succession would have been the responsibility of the trustees. Decisions that trustees make have far-reaching implications for the viability and success of Christian ministries.

In contrast there were multiple new organisations where my immediate thought as I put their new entry in the *Handbook* was: 'Don't they know that such-and-such an organisation is doing the same thing? Why don't they join forces with them rather than reinventing the wheel by setting up on their own?' There were also joys, such as seeing a group of residential homes for the elderly open up nursing and dementia care facilities in response to requests from their residents. These examples illustrate the challenges of new legislation, trends in society, succession planning, future vision and responding to change. Most trustee boards, whether churches or charities, have to wrestle with these issues from time to time.

Trustees

One of the requirements of registering as a charity is that it must have trustees, so those appointed know right from the beginning that they are trustees. Church governance teams, whether a PCC, a board of deacons, an eldership or whatever, are not always aware that they are also trustees. As part of my work with Dr Peter Brierley at Christian Research, we did quite a lot of consultancy as well as research with Church of England deaneries, the Church of Scotland and local churches of various denominations as well as very varied Christian organisations. Whatever kind of governance the church had, the group was likely to have a fairly clear idea of what their denomination and local congregation expected of them, though a request for help was often because they were uncertain how to achieve it. However, they were not necessarily aware of the wider demands made on them by charity law and government requirements. It has sometimes come as a shock for church leaders to realise the extra demands that being a trustee places on them: talking to some at a weekly leaders' prayer meeting it seems many of their members are either unaware of, or scared by, these additional responsibilities. When trying to recruit trustees myself, fear of what is involved is one reason why people I approached have said 'No', while another is that Christians do not always perceive the role of trustee as being 'ministry'.

Then there are national concerns, such as overzealous fund-raising and sexual and safeguarding issues, which have raised their ugly heads in recent times. Sadly, individual churches, denominations and Christian organisations are not immune. These events can, and often do, lead to yet more legislation as well as loss of trust by the general public. When such things happen, it is the trustees who are held to account and who also have to implement the new laws. The Charity Commission also sometimes investigates groups that are not registered as charities, but they consider should be – and they measure those groups against charity law.

Why write this book?

I was coming to the end of nine years as a trustee of a local charity, seven of them as chair. As it became known that I would soon have to step down, three other local charities approached me asking if I would join their board or, in one case, become their chair. Essentially, they all made the same request: please could I sort them out? Over my thirty plus years as a trustee of various types of Christian charities, including being chair of three, I have become increasingly aware how many feel they need to be 'sorted out'. Others do not even realise they ought to feel that way, as well-meaning but out-of-touch trustees carry on as they always have in spite of rapidly increasing legal and ethical demands on their work.

The more I thought and prayed about these various situations, the more convinced I became that rather than seek to help one or two more local charities I should share some of my own and other people's experiences to alert trustees to good practice and the potential pitfalls of poor governance. I have based my thoughts around biblical examples of excellent leadership and administration to assist boards, PCCs and their like to apply their faith to their role. Hence this book tells stories of success and failure and looks at what we can learn from the lives of biblical characters, particularly Nehemiah and Daniel.

There is plenty of Christian material – books, courses and conferences, websites etc – about leadership in general and leading churches in particular, but few resources on leading charities and organisations. There are many similarities; however, there are also distinct issues which arise in non-church (or para-church) contexts, as well as fresh things for churches to wrestle with when they register as charities. Much of what I have learned has come from serving on a range of well-governed boards with experienced trustees and chairs. My research for this book revealed that many trustees and chairs, especially in small charities, take on their roles without any previous experience and would find it helpful to have somewhere to turn.

Methodology

To explore some of these issues I initially drew up a summary of matters my own experience had shown me to be important for trustees. I sent this to six people with a wide range of relevant experience. Their responses enabled me to sharpen up the original summary and to shape a questionnaire. I then undertook in-depth interviews with trustees from a wide variety of backgrounds, types of organisations and different denominations, most of whom had both charity and church experience. Alongside this more formal research I also had numerous conversations with a wide range of people with trustee experience. I am immensely grateful for everyone's insights and stories, which you will find quoted throughout the book. The quotes are anonymous as some of those interviewed did not want negative stories to be associated with them in case that jeopardised their position as a trustee or because they did not want to publicly criticise a person with whom they still worked or had contact. However, the people I formally approached had between them the following experience of boards, most with two or three of these:

Advisor/trainer of trustees (3 interviewees)
Archdeacon (1)
Baptist church deacon (3)
Baptist minister (1)
Chair of trustees (4)
Church of England PCC and churchwarden (1)
Church of England vicar (2)
Church treasurer (1)
City-wide local charity (5)
College governor (2)
Company Secretary to large Trust (1)
Diocesan Secretary (1)
Employed by a charity (12)
Independent church trustee (3)
Methodist minister (1)

Nationwide charity or mission agency trustee (3)
School governor (1)
UK board of UK-based international mission agency (2)
UK board of international mission with a trading company (1)
UK board of non-UK-based overseas mission (2)

All those formally interviewed were offered the opportunity to read the book and asked to confirm that they were happy with the way I have used their material. Several asked for amendments and these have been made. As well as not naming individuals I have also not named churches or charities except those I have personally been involved in or where I quote a published source.

The legal aspects of this book were checked for compliance and were correct in January 2020. New laws or changes to guidelines after that date, say from the Charity Commission, are not included.

The importance and relevance of having good trustees

It is often said that there are two sorts of experts, those who know and those who know where to find out. I am not an expert in legal affairs; I leave that to the likes of Paul Martin, whose excellent book *Faith, Hope & Charity: The A to Z of governing a charitable organisation*,[3] I heartily recommend for the insight and understanding he gives into the increasing legal requirements placed on charities and churches (listed in Appendix 2 along with other resources). But it is vital that all trustees should know what the issues are for their organisation or church so that they can then proceed to find out what they should do. Above all, they need to reflect on how their Christian faith makes a difference, not only in the Christian ministry or outreach they undertake, but also in how they organise and govern their church or charity.

These days trust has to be earned; it is not given by right to anyone, whatever their role. Daniel was declared trustworthy because of the way he carried out his administrative role. His attitudes and values were markers, or if you like, tracks, which revealed his trustworthiness. Following animal tracks in the snow is a delightful way of discovering what creatures have been around. Trustworthiness leaves such tracks which the discerning onlooker can identify. My hope and prayer is that these pages will be both a challenge and an encouragement to all Christian charity trustees, whether of local, national or international organisations or individual churches, and especially their chairs, so enabling ministry to be effective in contributing to the advance of the kingdom of God. It may also be of value to others in similar roles, such as school governors, or to Christians who are a trustee of a charity which does not consider itself to be Christian.

May Christian trustees be trustworthy ones!

Note: *Direct quotes from interviewees are in italics.*

SECTION 1

GODLY TRACKS

1
Do it Well
Good Governance Matters

*We will never find any basis for charges against this
man Daniel unless it has something to do with the law
of his God.
(Daniel 6:5)*

*Things need to be done well so that there is honour to the name of Christ
publicly.*

Governance is an awkward-sounding word: it does not trip
easily off the tongue, and it even sounds a little threatening. It
can feel that way too, especially when there are regular news
items about something going wrong. But done well, governance
can honour God, enable a ministry or church's mission to be
fulfilled and focus energy and resources on what really matters.

The word means different things in different contexts but
for registered charities, whether organisations or churches, it is
about the role of a board of trustees and what is expected of
them. It is not exactly the same as leadership, though it does
include some aspects of it, such as finding vision and developing
the strategy necessary to carry it out. Neither is it exactly the
same as management, though it also includes aspects of that, for
example, appointing staff and overseeing finances. Nor is it

about doing the day-to-day work of the charity. Most so-called Third Sector organisations have a different governance system to industry and businesses but while many corporations call their governing board a board of trustees, their role is different to that of charity trustees. Governance happens at all levels of society, from the small local organisation to the national. It's the approach that is taken to managing the organisation and the methods used for doing it. For a church or Christian charity, governance is about putting in place the policies and procedures necessary for its ministry to flourish. These are decided when the charity is registered and form the major part of the governing document which is what the Charity Commission actually registers.

> *A basic responsibility of trustees is to make sure the resources are being utilised for the purpose for which the church* [or charity] *came into being, to ensure a context in which the resources and the energies of the church are brought together and that people work together.*

Establishing a separate charity can enable something to be achieved which no one church could do on its own.

> *For me the common theme through all of these* [charities I've been involved in setting up] *has been about enabling the church to work together to serve the community – and to work together in a way which wouldn't be possible or even desirable for any one church to do on its own. For example with YoYo's* [York Schools & Youth Trust] *work in schools I think there's a tremendous strength in the churches in York coming together to offer that resource to schools and it could never be the same thing if any one church set out to do it – I don't think any one church could do it, and it wouldn't be a desirable thing for one church to do it. Setting up something that's extra to church structures inevitably means setting up some form of governance, which usually involves trustees.*

This book focuses on the particular governance required for charities and specifically Christian charities. That includes the bodies in churches which make governance decisions, whether an Anglican PCC, a Church of Scotland eldership, or a nonconformist or independent church's deacons or elders. The first four chapters, the section on godly tracks, considers why it is important that they carry out their duties well. But first, what are the advantages and disadvantages of being a registered charity?

What is a charity?

The Charities Act 2011 says that a 'charity' is an institution which:

- is established for charitable purposes only and
- is subject to the control of the High Court's charity law jurisdiction.[1]

Charities exist to benefit the public or a certain section of it, not to make profits for shareholders as business and industry do. The Charities Act 2011 lists thirteen charitable Objects, one of which is 'The advancement of religion'. For churches that is taken as given, but other organisations, especially new ones, have to think about what sort of governance will suit them, including whether registering as a charity is the right course of action for them, and if so, what kind of charity they will apply to become. There are different kinds of charities, the most common of which are a Trust only, a Trust which is also a limited liability company registered with Companies House, and a Charitable Incorporated Organisation (CIO).[2] There are pluses and minuses to each of them and there is guidance about this on the Charity Commission's website, along with much other information which will help in the application process. An organisation considering registering would be wise to seek advice on what would suit them best.

A group applying to register as a charity has to demonstrate that its work or ministry will benefit the public in specific ways. The overall purpose for which a charity exists is termed its Object and what it proposes to do its Aims (so the phrase 'Aims and Objects' is often used). 'Promoting the Christian faith' is not a sufficient Object in itself: how will that be done, in what geographical location or for which group in society? In other words, who will actually benefit from it, and how? These are important questions to answer, as they help shape the vision and ministry, which we will look at in more detail later. I was most recently chair of YoYo. Some years before, YoYo's Trust Deed had set out the charity's Object:

> To advance the Christian religion in schools and youth clubs and to promote any other charitable purpose for the benefit of young people in York and the surrounding areas.

As trustees we found it necessary to define what we meant by 'surrounding areas' and decided that it should include the villages surrounding York, where at least some of the children from the primary school moved up to one of York's secondary schools. However, to start working regularly in, say, Leeds or Hull, would be outside our Object and therefore could not be considered unless we wanted to ask the Charity Commission's permission, or change our Trust Deed (which would have to be approved by the Charity Commission).

Registering as a charity has become more demanding since the 2011 Act, but that can be a good thing:

> *The Charity Commission application and the new documentation for CIOs involve a lot more questions and the trustees have to have a clearer idea of what they're doing. The charity application is so much more complicated than it used to be, so trustees of a new Trust now have to think through a lot more what the charity is about and what they have to do. That means the new Trusts are much better at understanding what's involved.*

If it is a complicated process, why bother? There are several advantages to being a registered charity. Perhaps the most valuable is that various tax reliefs apply to charities, the best known one being the recovery of income tax from HMRC on gifts made under the Give As You Earn and Gift Aid schemes.

Grant-making Trusts and local and national government are often more open to approaches from charities than from non-charitable groups, so being a registered charity can make a significant difference to income and is therefore financially worthwhile as well as being good stewardship.

What governance involves

The first place to go for guidance about starting or running a charity is the Charity Commission.[3] Their website holds many resources, which clearly spell out what charities *must* do – things that are a legal requirement – compared with those things charities *should* do, which are strongly advised and good practice. There is also a Charity Governance Code,[4] which was created by people involved in charities and is acknowledged by the Charity Commission. Much of it is helpful in encouraging good practice and helping trustees to think through issues, but some sections have ambiguous wording which needs careful reading. It is worth looking at and can be very helpful, but it is important to remember that it is not legally binding.

Charity trustees

The word 'trustee' was first recorded in about 1640 so it has been around for a long time. It is a legal term for someone in a position of trust, and in its widest sense refers to a person who holds property, authority or a position of trust or responsibility for the benefit of someone else. Registered charities are required by law to have trustees. For the purposes of this book, 'trustee' is the term used for people who serve on the board of trustees of an institution that operates as a charity and which therefore exists for the benefit of the general public rather than for the benefit of the individuals themselves or to make a profit for shareholders. They are usually elected, though may be appointed in some other way or become trustees by nature of the job or role they hold, an example being the minister of a church who is almost always automatically a trustee even though in the wider charity world the person employed to lead the organisation is not normally a trustee. The founding document (which can have a variety of names – see the definitions in Appendix 1) will set out how trustees are appointed and may include how long they can serve for and other related matters.

Trustees have certain duties, some of which are fiduciary, that is, the legal requirement that they act on behalf of and for the benefit of other people rather than themselves. It was Archbishop William Temple who said, 'The Church is the only society that exists for the benefit of those who are not its members',[5] so acting for the benefit of others should be part of the DNA of a church or Christian organisation. Nehemiah's primary aim in rebuilding the walls of Jerusalem was the honour of God, but he didn't benefit from it personally. When the wall was completed he returned to the service of King Artaxerxes, which meant that he did not live for any length of time within the city he had been instrumental in making secure. Working for the benefit of others is not only a legal (fiduciary) requirement, but should be almost second nature to Christians.

Integrity and Trustworthiness

There are other benefits to being a charity, particularly in public confidence and image, though sadly some of this has been damaged by high-profile cases in recent years. Nevertheless, people are still more likely to offer time, energy or money to a registered charity than to a non-charitable organisation doing similar work because they expect it to be honest and have integrity. That applies to churches also – the general public has expectations about what a church should and shouldn't do: it can be high-profile local news if a vicar or church treasurer misappropriates funds, but not nearly so likely if the manager of a local shop does the same! As Christians, integrity should be one of the things that characterises all aspects of what we do, including how we run and manage our churches and organisations.

'Integrity is doing the right thing even if no one is watching'[6] is a statement often incorrectly accredited to C S Lewis, but whoever did say it caught the essence of integrity. Showing integrity in what we do and how we do it is a biblical characteristic. When Nehemiah had completed the building of the wall around Jerusalem, he appointed Hananiah as:

> the commander of the citadel, because he was a man of integrity and feared God more than most people do.
> (Nehemiah 7:2)

King David recognised his personal need for integrity and asked God for it at one of the times when he was facing many enemies:

> May integrity and uprightness protect me, because my hope, LORD, is in you.
> (Psalm 25:21)

A later psalmist, Asaph, recognised that God had answered that prayer of David's:

> David shepherded them with integrity of heart.
> (Psalm 78:72)

The book of Proverbs also acknowledges the importance of integrity:

> Whoever walks in integrity walks securely.
> (Proverbs 10:9)

> The integrity of the upright guides them.
> (Proverbs 11:3)

> Righteousness guards the person of integrity.
> (Proverbs 13:6)

The very word trustee implies that the role should be carried out in a trustworthy way. It was certainly what marked Daniel out and summed up his characteristics. When King Belshazzar saw the writing on the wall and was desperate to find someone who could interpret it, his mother suggested Daniel, with the most amazing commendation:

> There is a man in your kingdom who has the spirit of the holy gods in him. In the time of your father he was found to have insight and intelligence and wisdom like that of the gods. Your father, King Nebuchadnezzar, appointed him chief of the magicians, enchanters, astrologers and diviners. He did this because Daniel, whom the king called Belteshazzar, was found to have a keen mind and knowledge and understanding, and also the ability to interpret dreams, explain riddles and solve difficult problems. Call for Daniel, and he will tell you what the writing means.
> (Daniel 5:11-12)

Insight, intelligence, wisdom, a keen mind, knowledge, understanding, the ability to interpret dreams, explain riddles and solve difficult problems – wow! What an amazing list. What is more, King Belshazzar's mother recognised that the source of these abilities and characteristics was the 'spirit of the holy gods' – even though she quite likely did not know which God Daniel worshipped.

I doubt whether Daniel would have claimed those characteristics for himself! The reason he was able to serve different dynasties over many years, perhaps until he was in his eighties, was the way other people saw him. Daniel did interpret the meaning of the writing, but that very night Darius the Mede conquered the Babylonians, killed Belshazzar and took over the kingdom. Darius must have heard about Daniel's reputation because when he appointed 120 people to rule on his behalf across the kingdom, Daniel was one of three administrators put in charge of them. No wonder those 120 became jealous of him when 'his exceptional qualities' (Daniel 6:3) meant Darius wanted to set him over the whole kingdom. It was at that point when they

> ... tried to find grounds for charges against Daniel in his conduct of government affairs, but they were unable to do so.
> (Daniel 6:4)

They realised that they could not find fault with Daniel unless it was to do with the law of his God. That led to them pushing for a new law that no one should pray to anyone except the king for thirty days. Daniel broke that law and so ended up in the lions' den. Peter said something similar when writing about the attitudes Christian slaves should have towards their masters:

> How is it to your credit if you receive a beating for doing wrong and endure it? But if you suffer for doing good and you endure it, this is commendable before God.
> (1 Peter 2:20)

Biblically we've got models of excellence in how we should be and how we work and operate. The kingdom of God is one of order and not disorder. One of the examples I use is to look at how slaves were told they should approach working for their masters: it wasn't do the bare minimum, but glorify God through the way they operated. So very much from my perspective, especially as a church charity, we need to be working from a basis of excellence because it's a kingdom principle in my opinion.

Nehemiah also recognised the importance of trustworthiness. Before he left Jerusalem for the last time, he appointed people to a variety of roles, one group of whom he considered trustworthy (Nehemiah 13:13).

A prophetic dimension

For Christians, being of benefit to others may have a prophetic dimension to it.

In governance and leadership terms, one or two people need to be a shaker, without wanting to create division: it's not my view against somebody else's, but it's trying to create the dynamic to make the changes that are necessary – there's a sort of prophetic voice in it.

I am old enough to remember when evangelism and social action were considered polar opposites by Christians: liberals did social action, evangelicals focused on evangelism, and whichever 'side' you were on, you were likely to look down on the other. In 1974 the Lausanne Covenant was agreed by a large international group of evangelicals brought together by Dr Billy Graham.[7] The Covenant itself was mainly shaped by Rev Dr John Stott. It had a major impact in convincing evangelicals in particular that social action was biblical and something they should be involved in. More than forty years later, data gathered by the Church of England and published in 2018 from some 13,000 churches found that 80% of them were involved in one or more forms of social action. This totalled more than 33,000 social action projects which were acting as a social lifeline to their communities.[8]

That is prophetic. It says to the community, 'We care about you.' It says to local authorities and government, 'We will do what we can to meet the needs.' Above all it demonstrates the love of God in practical ways. The decisions necessary to start such projects are very often made by trustees, or those who will become trustees as and when a charity is formed.

It can also be prophetic for a church when trustees ask the right questions, even though they may be difficult or challenging questions to ask. Trustees ought to confront the kind of attitude which seeks to maintain the status quo because it is too demanding or threatening not to.

Sometimes PCCs get so weighed down by the money and the buildings that they feel strangled and not able to engage with the bigger issues. A prime example of that has been in one of the vacant benefices. There is one lady who, in the middle of a PCC who are getting obsessed about everything else, consistently reminds them about the importance of spreading the gospel, to the extent that sometimes she gets so frustrated that she has to leave the room. She's left the room three times when I've been there because she's got so irate about some of the behaviours around her. But her voice is really important in that meeting because she tells them that what's really important is that they tell people about the love of God, not that they just keep everything to themselves. There is a feeling in that particular setting that the church is for people who currently go to it and there's no responsibility towards or interest in anybody else knowing about the gospel. This one woman has made it her mission to make sure that that is a significant part of their discussions every time.

One interviewee, when asked why he became a trustee of a charity, put it this way:

I would need to feel I could make a difference. It's taken me a lifetime to accept what my gifting is, but I think strategic thinking and forward thinking, and encouraging people to plan ahead and understand the challenges they face rather than skirt round things — that interests me a lot: organisational development, spiritual development, personal development going together.

It is all too easy to separate organisational, spiritual and personal development and focus so much on one that the others get lost. I have come across charities and churches which are very well organised but have poor personal relationships, as well as those where there are excellent relationships but they have lost sight of why they exist. Both are likely to have lost their cutting edge, to no longer be prophetic in their situation, and to be unable to fulfil their ministry as well as they could.

When things go wrong

Unfortunately, things do go wrong in churches and charities. Good governance can sometimes forestall such events and can often minimise the impact when something does happen. I had to handle an accusation related to safeguarding. We had a safeguarding officer and he and I worked hard on understanding the implications of the accusation. We were able to demonstrate that we had appropriate policies in place and explain how we were implementing them. In response, the trustees clarified our position about volunteers and put in place extra training for them. What turned the situation around was when the person who had put the accusation to us, on hearing what action we had taken, was able to say, 'You know what you are doing, don't you?' He then worked to resolve things at his end. Clearly it is easier to take that kind of action in a local charity where face-to-face interaction is possible. For larger, especially international, charities, if something goes wrong it can easily be hidden from trustees, who may not know about it unless a whistle-blower speaks up or the media unearth a situation. The response by charities such as Tearfund to scandals which have hit other charities in similar situations has been to look carefully themselves at what is taking place in their organisation and to make sure they have strong policies in place and relevant procedures to ensure that appropriate action is taken when necessary.[9]

Good governance is about knowing what you are doing as far as you possibly can:

> *Know the rules for governing the charity or church, as per the founding governance document. It's important to always function within those rules — not to simply become legalistic, but function within the spirit of the rules.*

Alongside that, trustees need to know, or have good advice available to them, about laws and regulations which apply to them, especially new ones, or particular issues which are of concern to the Charity Commission or the wider charity world. That means

> *... a lot of reading. There are plenty of training courses and I think it's a really good thing to aspire to good governance and for people to go on these courses. They're run by secular people but there are plenty of very well-run courses. You should pick up the Charity Commission*

newsletters and read the test cases of things the Charity Commission is doing, to understand the principles. There are governance magazines that are really, really helpful, that pick up on latest cases where the Charity Commission has challenged something and help you understand the principles. They're good magazines for disseminating the news and analysing it.

There is a list of resources in Appendix 2 which will help with following up on this. In addition to these widely available resources, denominations may provide resources and training at local or national level, while local groups, such as Community Service Volunteers, may put on training.

Summary of the trustee's role

I believe it is really important that trustees understand what is expected of them. How else can they exercise good governance? When I have been looking for new trustees, I have summarised the key dimensions of our responsibilities as embracing three aspects – vision, compliance and resources:

- **Vision** is what enables trustees to fulfil the Object of a charity or the purpose of a church in the way God wants them to at this point in time, in this context and on into the future.

- **Compliance** is ensuring that all relevant laws are kept and best-practice guidelines are followed.

- Responsibility for **resources** involves establishing what resources are needed for what you believe you should be doing, finding those resources – whether money, people, buildings etc – then using them in the most effective way.

We will look at each of these in more detail later. It seems daunting, but with God's help:

Do the best you can to comply with good practice, regulations, the rules that apply, with common sense.

The resulting tracks of trustworthiness will honour God and play a significant part in enabling your church or charity to fulfil what you exist for and what you believe He wants you to do to build His kingdom.

Questions

Have you ever seen your charity/church's governing document? Do you know what your Objects are?

What is it about the idea of being a trustee that made or makes you or others scared of taking on the role?

In what ways do you, or would you like to, see integrity and trustworthiness modelled in your context?

2
Seeing the Big Picture
Vision and Goals

*I answered the king, 'If it pleases the king … let him
send me to the city in Judah where my ancestors are
buried so that I can rebuild it.'
(Nehemiah 2:5)*

*It's really important for any Christian charity to be thinking about where
they fit within the bigger scheme of things.*

I listened with growing dismay to two people talking about their
charity. They described how it had been set up to do this, that
and the other, but now legislation made it difficult or impossible
to do most of those things in the way they'd always done them.
For ten minutes or more they talked about what they could do,
and mostly what they could no longer, do, with no more than a
passing mention of who they wanted to serve. I wanted to ask
them who used to come to their facilities and what difference
they hoped to make to those people's lives, and to challenge
them to think about ways in which they could still serve those
people, using their facilities and within the current law. They
seemed to have lost sight of the vision which had set up the
charity and become completely focused on the nuts and bolts,
seeing only obstacles rather than opportunities.

A large church with a student ministry asked us at Christian Research to find out why as many people left their church as joined it. Questionnaires, interviews and focus groups revealed that the church was doing well at challenging students to become Christians and discipling them in their early days of faith. But when those young people asked the question 'What next?', there was no 'what next'. The church's vision to see students become Christians was effective, but they hadn't looked at the bigger picture of how to help those converts mature in the faith and get involved in some kind of Christian service, whether within the church or outside it. With no answer from the church as to 'What next?', many looked elsewhere, often moving to other churches in the area, though sadly some stopped going to any church.

A key responsibility for charity trustees is to ensure that the charity fulfils the purpose for which it was set up as laid out in its governing document. That will say why the charity exists, its purpose, the reason it was established and who will benefit from its existence. What that document (or Trust Deed, Constitution, or whatever it is called) doesn't usually say is how that should be done, either at the time the charity was set up or in its future. Simply carrying on 'doing what we've always done' without reviewing and reimagining ministry and mission in line with current needs and resources could be deemed negligent. It demands vision to perceive how God wants the original intention to be fulfilled in a relevant and up-to-date way and what that could look like over the next few years:

> *Good governance in the twenty-first century, as defined by things like the Governance Code, includes the ability to see things in the round and to be able to ask sensible questions. Why is this being undertaken? Who will benefit? What is the long-term outcome likely to be if this course of action is pursued? Can we measure its success? Do we have any objective evidence that this proposed action will work? What will be the result if it is a total disaster? Not everyone is willing to ask, or able to answer, such questions or has the confidence to do so.*

Vision

'Vision' is a word some people shy away from because for them it sounds too demanding or too much like business language rather than spiritual language. One of the many research projects I undertook at Christian Research was to investigate churches which had been on the brink of closure, but which had been turned around so that they began to grow and flourish. In every place I found there was at least one person who, as one of them put it, believed 'things could be different around here'.[1] Vision need not, and indeed should not, be seen as a threat, but as an opportunity. In practice it is believing things could be different: that this slowly declining church could grow; a local charity could serve more people; an overseas mission could take the Christian message to a people group who have never heard it; a deprived community could find support and encouragement as part of a church family.

Lesslie Newbiggin wrote that 'It is hard to find people in our society who have any strong sense of a worthwhile future'.[2] As Christians we have a future hope, set out most clearly in Hebrews chapter 11, which begins:

> Now faith is confidence in what we hope for and assurance about what we do not see.
> (Hebrews 11:1)

> Hope that is seen is no hope at all. Who hopes for what they already have? But if we hope for what we do not yet have, we wait for it patiently.
> (Romans 8:24-25)

Lesslie Newbiggin went on to say that this hope should apply to our lives and ministries now, not only to our long-term future in God's kingdom: 'Action is only meaningful when it is directed to some goal ... this is what gives its distinctive character to the Christian hope.' Finding that goal is vitally important to having a sense of a 'worthwhile future' for our church or ministry. It makes a difference to our present situation and helps us move positively towards the future.

Finding vision

How does a church or ministry (or for that matter, an individual) find a vision? There are many different ways. Here are some.

Revealed from God
This is how Nehemiah received his vision to rebuild the walls of Jerusalem:

> While I was in the citadel of Susa, Hanani, one of my brothers, came from Judah with some other men, and I questioned them about the Jewish remnant that had survived the exile, and also about Jerusalem.
> They said to me, 'Those who survived the exile and are back in the province are in great trouble and disgrace. The wall of Jerusalem is broken down, and its gates have been burned with fire.'
> (Nehemiah 1:1-3)

Nehemiah's response was initially deep sorrow, then to turn to prayer, and through those processes to realise he was the one to do something about the situation. He recognised that he had the vision and determination to go and rebuild the wall. There were plenty of other people who potentially could have taken up the challenge, his brother Hanani for a start, as well as those who had already returned to Jerusalem, some of them with Ezra the priest. But God gave Nehemiah the vision and gave him such confidence in that vision that he had the courage, at the right time, to ask the king to whom he was cupbearer for the permission and the resources to take action.

Some trustee bodies are highly focused on seeking vision in what they would term 'spiritual' ways, for example, primarily through prayer:

'Where there is no vision, the people perish' [Proverbs 29:18, KJV], *which might be better translated 'prophetic vision', that sense of ensuring we listen to God's voice. At the charity I'm involved with we do this practically by spending time in the local House of Prayer, just sitting quietly, listening to the Lord. We are looking for a number of us to confirm the accuracy of what we sense Jesus might be saying to us. Our move to extend geographically came from these times, and we have seen many miraculous blessings from that move in both new locations. 'Commit to the LORD whatever you do, and he will establish your plans'* [Proverbs 16:3]. *To commit to the Lord means to consult Him and discuss your plans with Him and seek His wisdom and advice. With major decisions a wise person will consult others to check the accuracy of what they heard from the Lord; there is strength in knowing others have heard the same thing.*

Especially when the way forward is not clear, or there are conflicting ideas in a trustee board, praying together, whether or not in the way just described, can bring clarity about vision as well as other matters under consideration.

I have been in meetings of trustee bodies in both churches and charities where the meeting will open with prayer and close with prayer and we have paused at times in the middle for prayer when things have got particularly unclear or emotions are rising or it just feels we don't have the tools to resolve this. The opening and closing prayer is common but I think we rely on the fact that when we open in prayer we invite the Holy Spirit to guide us, and we assume the Holy Spirit does what we've asked and is speaking through us and moving people to speak and listen.

Developed by review and discussion

This is quite often how vision either originates or is shaped in a church with some form of congregational government. I have been a member of two Baptist churches which did significant redevelopment work on their buildings. In one of them in particular, the first tentative ideas were brought to a meeting of church members to test their reaction and seek their support. Ideas were tossed into the discussion, pros and cons debated and potential ways forward considered. What came to the meeting as a tentative suggestion was taken away as a clear decision to move to the next stage, plan what would be involved, get a reasonable idea of costs and think about where the money might come from. A small group worked on the detail but at each major stage they came to a church meeting where they asked members for their input as well as approval to move on. What started out as a plan to cover the outside corridor between the church and the hall eventually led to buying the adjacent house and expanding into it to create offices, further meeting rooms and a small prayer chapel.

Initiated by one individual

I seem to have been dogged by redevelopment programmes! When I became leader of Radio Worldwide, we had recently been able to buy the freehold of the large Victorian house we lived and worked in. To make it more accommodating, especially for families, it needed a lot of work, which became one of the major projects during my years in charge.

My current church has two buildings, one of which used to have unused spaces and poor facilities. A retired man with considerable building experience saw the potential for upgrading the building, but right from the start he said again and again, 'This is an outreach project, not a building project.' His vision for the building to be adapted so it could be used for the community shaped the decisions that were made about altering spaces, for example putting in a catering-standard kitchen so meals could be served to the public, and opening up the roof space to allow more light into an area which is now used for drop-ins: one for young people at the secondary school across the road, and one for elderly people in the community. Yes, decisions had to be made by the PCC/trustees, and considerable fund-raising and giving taken up as a challenge by the whole church. But without his vision and enthusiasm – and expertise which saved us thousands of pounds – the building would have remained unsuitable for such outreach activities.

Completing the renovations was a significant goal, but the vision was to see the building being used to serve the community, not just the regular worshippers.

Shared with others

There have been a number of programmes over the years which have been designed to help churches think about what they are doing. Working through one of these, either as an individual church or in company with others, often leads to fresh vision of how things 'could be different round here'. One which has been running since the early 1990s is Leading Your Church Into Growth (LYCIG).[3] On their website LYCIG is described as 'serving the local church across the country with a vision to encourage and equip churches to grow both numerically and spiritually'. They 'run residential courses, provide training days and resources as well as supporting dioceses in developing their own growth programmes, in all kinds of churches, Catholic or Charismatic, Evangelical or Liberal, Rural or Urban, Big or Small'. LYCIG provides all the materials, and where a diocese or group of churches takes up the programme, doing it together can provide the encouragement and incentive to keep going.

When a local church works through the process, the outcome can be anything from coming up with more effective ways to do what they are already doing to a vision for a completely new outreach or ministry. In my own church it gave us the incentive to move forward with a goal we'd had for a while, of developing a new congregation in a more deprived part of the parish. That fresh impetus can be infectious, encouraging people in the congregation to engage with it and becoming a catalyst for other churches to consider similar possibilities:

> I've been involved in LYCIG for years – I think I've been to seven LYCIG conferences with different parishes and dioceses and the impact is considerable in terms of the thinking going on in a church. As part of LYCIG, for instance, churches are encouraged to have a small group of people who are thinking specifically about the strategic issues. Often it's good to have a small group of people rather than try

to do everything by a large committee. That small group might include people who have interesting things to contribute but aren't on the PCC. But you have to have your PCC, your clergy and lay leaders on board, otherwise there is going to be a battle. I've seen it work well and I've seen it not working well – more working well than not, to be honest. I see people really up against it in a vacancy and we really see how their thinking is being impacted by LYCIG. That makes a significant difference to their missional thinking, their thinking about the future of the church, their realism and willingness to express the fact that everything in the garden might not be perfect, so that they can really think clearly about the leadership that they need.

There are many other effective church growth programmes – google the topic and you will find them! Which one might be right for your church is a decision the leaders and trustee board (PCC etc) need to think carefully about, but then working through it as a whole church can provide fresh vision, the incentive to make the effort involved, and a sense of expectation that God is at work among you.

Response to a crisis

I was on the board of Feba Radio when we saw that before too long we would have to make the decision to close the broadcasting station in the Seychelles. Up to that time pictures of the transmitters set in the sea next to a beautiful tropical island were the image the Christian public had of the mission agency. The situation in the Seychelles was changing and the government stated that the transmitters, which were offshore in a shallow sea area, were not compatible with its land reclamation plans. Developments in technology also meant that increasingly broadcasters were moving away from short wave to local stations. These factors were having a significant impact on the effectiveness of the ministry, so they had to be addressed. Within a year or two those then on the board realised it was the right time to close the station, but what next?

When Seychelles closed down, the vision was fairly fuzzy and it was difficult to pull together a new vision, and that was one of the struggles that we had as a board – trying to develop a new vision in the post-Seychelles era. We had to find a new ministry, a new way of doing what we'd always done, reaching people with the gospel but using new methods such as local community radio, and vehicles such as using people within communities to reach their own people, to de-Westernise its message.

That decision, which has been described as 'moving an ocean liner by 90 degrees', was a tough one to carry through:

Associates and supporters intellectually understood that we were no longer transmitting from the Seychelles, but it hadn't reached their hearts, there was still an emotional attachment to the transmitters – the pictures of them were so iconic, they were Feba. There was a very painful AGM where a lot of accusations were thrown at the board because although we had tried to communicate what was happening and why, people did not clearly understand what we had been trying to do. Because it was a change process, some staff unfortunately lost their jobs and some roles changed – there was a fair bit of anger about some of the former staff who had been moved on, whom supporters were emotionally committed to.

Over time, that 'new way of doing what they'd always done' became reality, with teams of radio producers from the area using local and national radio stations to broadcast their programmes and, in the case of some local stations, owning and running them. The UK team provided training, technical support and in some cases finance to these local teams, and total audiences grew. The overall vision remained but it was interpreted differently for a new situation.

Grown through experience

Situations sometimes arise where the experience of one or more trustees suggests that the current *modus operandi* isn't working as effectively as it used to. Asking the question about whether there is another way of achieving the same vision can lead to significant new ministry.

> *The big change that happened was when we decided not to be a campus-based college, which was huge because everybody thinks a college should be campus-based. But we went back to vision and values: we are a multicultural college, offering culturally appropriate and accessible theological training. The decision came out of thinking about what we were trying to do. We were trying to resource the worldwide mission force and that wasn't necessarily best done by bringing people to the UK to be trained in the UK by mostly UK people. The different strategy was to have a smaller hub but greater reach. We had had a big hub to which people came but now we were going to have a smaller hub from which people went to train elsewhere in culturally appropriate ways in other contexts.*
>
> *In a sense it evolved – we'd had the idea for a long time, which was that we wanted to plant hubs around the world and partner with existing organisations there using the materials we had. We had a very good relationship with a university which made that possible because we wanted to still be academically rigorous in what we offered. That was proceeding and then there was a moment when we started to move more quickly. We were looking at investments: we had a lot of money invested in a big building, but was that the best use of the money, to have a building that was used for three terms of the year plus letting it out to conferences? We didn't really want to have commercial things … we're not about bricks and mortar, we're about kingdom and how to best do the things we actually do. If we can go to Africa, if we can go to Asia, if we can go to Australia and do our thing there, that's kingdom stuff.*

Tools for finding vision

There are several ways a vision can be developed. Perhaps the best known is a SWOT analysis, asking the questions: what are our church's or charity's Strengths and Weaknesses, and what Opportunities and Threats do we face?

Another source of helpful questions is the ones God asked:

- He asked Adam and Eve in the Garden of Eden 'Where are you?' (Genesis 3:9), in other words, what is your current situation?

- The question to Moses from the burning bush was 'What is that in your hand?' (Exodus 4:2). What resources and gifts do you have?

- The challenge to Elijah when he had run away from Queen Jezebel was 'What are you doing here ...?' (1 Kings 19:9), which helps to evaluate current activities and priorities.

- Ezekiel was asked 'Can these bones live?' (Ezekiel 37:3), which challenged the prophet to have faith to believe God could change what looked like an impossible situation.

- Three prophets, Jeremiah (1:11,13) Amos (7:8; 8:2) and Zechariah (4:2; 5:2) were asked 'What do you see ...?', which every time had implications for the future:

    They all saw concrete items, and most of the timescales were relatively short, say five years (Jesus' time scale was only three years). None of this 'Let's help as many as possible', but rather something specific, 'aim to feed 500 with a meal every day' – that was the vision Mary's Meals[4] began with.

By 2020 Mary's Meals was feeding 1.6 million children every day with one square meal!

Both these methods start in the present and look forward to what could be a different future. A different approach starts in the future and works back to the present. It is known as Horizon Mission Methodology. It is essentially values-based and seeks to establish how values that are currently held by a congregation or charity could be worked out, perhaps very differently, in the future.[5]

Constraints on vision

Vision is not a free-for-all to do whatever new idea is presented to a charity board. New developments need to be measured against a number of factors. The first one is the purpose, or Objects, for which the charity exists:

> Objects set out in the governing document need to capture the scope and location of your charitable activities or ministries. The danger for churches in pursuing their ministries, and any subsidiary companies that they might have set up, is that there can be a tendency to pick up any good idea and assume that because the church or charitable entity is a charity and a Christian ministry, the idea is bound to be acceptable. This generalised thinking needs to be challenged, and new developments need testing against the Objects – external advice may be required to confirm whether the proposed activity is technically acceptable within that charity.

> There was one member of the board who was very hot on 'mission drift' and making sure that when we were looking at new projects we were sticking very clearly with our statement of faith, and our purposes. That was very helpful.

It is surprisingly easy to drift away from the Objects for which the charity was set up:

> Some Trusts doing schools work have drifted into certain types of work that the schools have wanted and over perhaps three or four years they've stopped doing the direct faith-based stuff and done more educational stuff because that's what the schools have asked for. It's seemed like an easy win and they've been carried along, but they've finished up ticking the school's boxes rather than making it faith-based. Some of them haven't even noticed that they've drifted from what their governing document states; they can see a destination but they haven't realised it's not the destination they started off to reach. It's a weakness by the trustees to not say, 'This is not what the Trust was set up to do.'

Trustees need to be very clear on the scope and limitations of the charity, where there is flexibility, and their role as a trustee. A lot of time can be spent trying to understand whether we are allowed to do something!

Vision also needs to fit in with the whole ethos of the church or charity. We will consider values and the role of statements of faith in the next chapter, but they can help trustees to assess what is appropriate to consider:

The whole statement of vision and values and faith is vital because everything you do has to tie back to that. If what you're doing doesn't match with your values or synchronise with your faith, then there's an obvious red flag and you're not going to do it. They're where you go to, to judge that. Some things are obvious, you don't really have to go to anything, but others are more difficult: perhaps you're asked to be in partnership with another group, then you really have to see if there's any sort of mismatch in faith values and vision.

Maintaining and passing on vision

In the introduction I said, 'In every update [of the *UK Christian Handbook*] there were many small organisations, which were perhaps twenty years old and had always been run by the founder, that had closed, almost certainly because the vision had not been passed on to a successor who could carry on the work.' Founders need to pass on their vision if a charity is to continue, and so do trustees. Accepted good practice is that trustees should serve for no more than nine years except in special circumstances. The first generation of trustees of a new charity are likely to be enthusiastic about the vision, as are the members of a church trustee board who develop a new vision. But that vision needs to be passed on to the next generation of trustees:

[It] began with the enthusiasm and vision of the first generation of trustees who owned the vision, but in the course of time – I think particularly because it was an interdenominational body and from the outset it was people in senior positions within those denominations

who came together to see it off the ground. It was chaired by the bishop but with the local Methodist chair and other significant individuals. Over time they retired or moved on to other posts and then there was a kind of expectation that their successor will pick this up, in an already busy diary, and they may well have other initiatives they want to pursue. So that's a very good example of second- and third-generation trustees who don't share the original vision, particularly if they are just doing this as some kind of ex officio role – 'I'm here to represent the Methodist Church', for example, rather than 'I'm here to see this work thrive'! There's a big difference – if I'm simply representing my denomination in this charity I'm not necessarily investing in it, I haven't necessarily caught the vision of it – they just turn up when there is a meeting because it's in the diary, and they turn up like they turn up at so many other meetings they have to be part of.

That particular charity closed precisely because the vision for its ministry was not passed on to new trustees and the whole governance ground to a halt. To keep vision fresh, it needs to be embraced by successive generations of trustees, and ideally reviewed and reimagined by them so that they own it. The vision which led to the establishment of a charity or the decision to go ahead with a new initiative in a church will grow tired and old if it is not kept at the centre of every decision. The vision also needs to be passed on to new people, whether staff, volunteers or new attenders at a church. Jesus spent three years teaching and demonstrating the kingdom of God to His disciples, while Elisha seems to have spent several years watching Elijah at work (1 Kings 19:16-21; 2 Kings 3:11). On the other hand, if the vision has been fulfilled, perhaps it is time to call a halt.

Nehemiah's vision and strategy

Nehemiah not only had the vision to go and rebuild the wall, he also had to develop a strategy to make it happen. As he prayed, repented and sought to know what God wanted, the way forward became clear. When he had the opportunity he asked King Artaxerxes for three things: permission to go, protection along the way and the resources to accomplish the work (Nehemiah 2:5-8). The detail of the strategy was worked out after he arrived in Jerusalem and he saw for himself the situation. In spite of all kinds of problems and opposition, some of which we will look at in more detail in later chapters, he succeeded in rebuilding the wall and was then able to return to his post back in King Artaxerxes' palace. He had proved himself worthy of the trust that the king and the Jewish people had placed in him.

May God grant your church or charity similarly clear vision to accomplish what He wants you to do as part of the bigger picture of building His kingdom.

Questions

Is the charity of which you are a trustee fulfilling the Objects set out in your foundation document?

Does your church or charity have a clear vision of what you believe you should be working towards for, say, the next five years?

If you don't have a clear vision, how will you go about finding one? If you have, how recently did you review it to make sure you are still on track?

Is your vision focused inwardly, or does it take into account the bigger picture of what God might want to do in your community, town or city?

3
Who Do They Think You Are?
Values, Image and Reputation

All our enemies … realised that this work had been
done with the help of our God.
(Nehemiah 6:16)

As people look at what we are saying, what we are resourcing, can they
see Christ in it?

Kids Company collapsed spectacularly in August 2015.[1] It had been providing support for many thousands of deprived and vulnerable inner-city children and young people and employed more than 600 people. Just a week earlier it had received a £3 million grant from the government. Immediately questions were asked about what had gone wrong and it soon emerged that two issues lay behind the collapse. The first was concerns about mismanagement of funds, which had first been raised with trustees as long ago as 2002 – reports which had so alarmed donors that they had been gradually withdrawing support for some time. The situation was compounded by the revelation that summer of a Metropolitan Police investigation into allegations by former staff of serious incidents including sexual abuse. That resulted in a major donor who was expected to match the government funding withdrawing. Six months later the police investigation closed without finding any evidence of criminality, but the damage to Kids Company's reputation was already done.

The scandal which engulfed Oxfam in early 2018, when whistle-blowers told of sexual abuse being perpetrated in Haiti, was similarly met by a drop in donations.[2] Within weeks 7,000 donors withdrew support and 100 staff were made redundant. A poll by ICM and *The Guardian*[3] revealed that as a result 52% of people said they would be less likely to give to humanitarian causes. The damage to reputations spread far beyond Oxfam.

Charities have been lambasted for taking sides in political debates, some larger ones criticised for paying their senior leaders six-figure salaries, and fund-raising methods scrutinised for overwhelming vulnerable potential givers. Several denominations have been accused of covering up sexual abuse. Some Christian youth charities were publicly 'named and shamed' for so-called proselytising in schools, while Charity Commission investigations of several high-profile Christian charities and churches have caused concern.

Whether churches and charities like it or not, and whether or not there is any whiff of scandal, what supporters, donors, local communities and the people whom churches and charities serve think about us matters very much indeed. In our postmodern society, trust has to be earned, whether by individuals such as church leaders or organisations such as charities. It cannot be taken for granted as perhaps it once could. When it is lost it can have significant implications, cutting off financial support and closing doors to ministry. Trust is hard to recover.

Writing in *The Yorkshire Post* about the Oxfam revelations, Bill Carmichael commented, 'I believe the big charities, including Oxfam, need a major rethink of their strategies if they are to regain public trust. They should ... return to the values – mainly Christ-inspired – of their founders.'[4]

About the same time, a former charities minister wrote that

… many other public and private organisations are just as preoccupied as big charities with protecting their image, even to the point of covering up terrible mistakes. The fact that others are as bad, or worse in some cases, is not an excuse. The difference is that charities must have higher ethical standards than other organisations to retain the good will and trust of the public.[5]

The importance of image and values

The underlying values of an organisation are revealed in a number of ways, but the one the public see most readily is the outward image.

What image are we projecting? What values does our organisation wish to project? Are we being consistent in those values? Should not the governing body debate those? We did that in one of our meetings and now ask every new staff member, potential new trustee, and every renewing trustee (we serve for three years) if they accept them (or continue to). What image does your website convey? Does your building mirror your values; is it a living example of your image?

What people think about churches and charities is not based only on what they do or say, but on a wide range of factors, including what the building looks like, how well the website works and what family and friends think. The church I attend used to have a hedge and an unattractive tree along the road frontage. After we took them down, laid grass and tidied up the area, several local people commented that they hadn't realised it was a church; one person had even thought it was a warehouse! Image affects our reputation, and both of these should reflect the values. Values themselves are an outcome of vision. However, even if they have a clear vision, surprisingly few organisations have given sufficient thought to what their values are, and churches are not necessarily any better:

I think the majority of our partner organisations assume their values, which is a weakness. Looking at their values should be part of their review and a challenge for those who haven't actually thought about their values, or haven't written them down. They need to ask themselves, 'What is it that we value?' They should write them down, and put them on their website so that people can see what their values are. When they say, 'This is our vision, this is what we were set up to do,' they need to add their values: 'This is the way we go about it.' If they just assume what their values are without writing them down, one trustee may assume one thing and someone else assume another and so they're not in agreement about what their values are but they may not realise that.

Values ... are mainly assumed, and I'm not sure that organisations are very good at writing them down properly and holding on to them. So their values don't sufficiently inform their decision-making. Of all the trustee bodies I've worked with, I've only found two or three that have very clear value statements which they could then use as a basis for developing their governing principles.

Having clear values is not simply so that you can list them on your website or put them in a grant application. They play a significant role in shaping how to go about activity and ministry:

You examine what you do in the light of your values, so if your values are not clear then you can fudge what you do. When you ask what people believe, we always say, 'Don't ask what they believe, watch what they do.' We act out of our values, so if we're saying something is a value but we're not acting on it then we've got to question the value statements or we've got to ditch something of our activities.

There is nothing specifically Christian about most of these comments on the importance of image and values. Organisations and churches are only able to register as charities because they provide benefit to the public, but is that benefit any different because we define ourselves as Christian? Should it be, and if so, in what ways? It is therefore important to ask the question: what are those Christian values which are relevant to the ministry of our particular church or charity? Are they demonstrated in a way which the public can see? Let us take a look at how Nehemiah's actions revealed what his values were.

Nehemiah's values

One could say that Nehemiah's basic values were those of any good Jew of his time: a concern about the honour of God's name, a longing to return from exile and a desire to be able to worship in Jerusalem. However, a look at the way he carried out the rebuilding of the wall reveals other things that were important to him.

Prayer

Again and again we read that Nehemiah prayed. Much of chapter 1 is his prayer of repentance on behalf of his nation and pleading with God to keep his promise:

> Even if your exiled people are at the farthest horizon, I will gather them from there and bring them to the place I have chosen as a dwelling for my Name.
> (Nehemiah 1:9)

He ends that prayer with a very specific request to God:

> Give your servant success today by granting him favour in the presence of this man.
> (Nehemiah 1:11)

'This man' was King Artaxerxes, to whom Nehemiah was a cupbearer. When God gave him an opportunity to speak to the king, his reaction was a quick prayer before he spoke. When he got to Jerusalem, we see him praying very practical prayers when there is opposition (4:4-5; 6:9,14) and encouraging the people to pray too:

> We prayed to our God and posted a guard day and night to meet this threat.
> (Nehemiah 4:9)

Clear thinking

By the time he had the opportunity to speak to King Artaxerxes, Nehemiah knew exactly what he would need. He asked for specific things: letters to the governors of the provinces he would pass through so he could have safe passage and a letter authorising him to ask for timber for building. He also told the king how long he expected to be away to complete the work (Nehemiah 2:6-8). Once he arrived in Jerusalem, he went out at night to find out exactly what the situation was so that when he spoke to the leaders there he knew what needed to be done (Nehemiah 2:13-16).

Individuals mattered

At first glance chapter 3 looks like simply a list of names and places, but it reveals that everybody (except the nobles from Tekoa!) worked on rebuilding the wall. Nehemiah named individuals and where they lived, often along with a comment about them, so we know that goldsmiths, perfume-makers, Shallum's daughters, priests and merchants all played their part (Nehemiah 3:8,12,22,32). He didn't see the people simply as labourers but as individuals whose backgrounds he knew. Later, when he had to return to King Artaxerxes, he appointed people to positions of responsibility and it is clear that he knew them well and so was able to appoint individuals who were suitable for different roles (Nehemiah 13:13).

Willingness to confront opposition

Those who had been running the area while the Israelites were in exile were not at all happy about people returning and reclaiming their city and land. The opposition started with mocking and ridicule (Nehemiah 2:19), brewed into anger and insults (Nehemiah 4:1-3), became plotting to fight (Nehemiah 4:8), involved intimidation (Nehemiah 4:11,12) and challenged Nehemiah personally (Nehemiah 6:1-13). Each time, Nehemiah took action: he responded with the assertion that God would give them success (Nehemiah 2:20), encouraged the people to work wholeheartedly to get the wall built as soon as possible (Nehemiah 4:6), 'posted a guard day and night' (Nehemiah 4:9,13) and made plans for how to respond if there was an attack (Nehemiah 4:19-20). Each time, people trusted him enough to respond as he asked and the outcome was positive:

> When all our enemies heard about this, all the surrounding nations were afraid and lost their self-confidence, because they realised that this work had been done with the help of our God.
> (Nehemiah 6:16)

Integrity

The opposition to Nehemiah grew stronger and more intimidating as the work progressed. One day he was asked to meet someone in the temple, ostensibly because they would be safe from attack there (Nehemiah 6:10). However, Nehemiah was a servant of King Artaxerxes and therefore would have been subjected to castration so that he was no threat to the king's harem. The Law of Moses decreed that eunuchs could not enter the assembly of the Lord (Deuteronomy 23:1) so Nehemiah's response was one of real integrity:

> 'Should someone like me go into the temple to save his life? I will not go!' I realised that God had not sent him ... He had been hired to intimidate me so that I would commit a sin by doing this, and then they would give me a bad name to discredit me.
> (Nehemiah 6:11-13)

Care for the poor

Most of chapter 5 is given over to describing how Nehemiah responded when there was an outcry that people did not have enough to eat, and the reasons behind it. He not only confronted those who were taking advantage of the situation to line their own pockets, but he personally fed 150 people at his own expense (Nehemiah 5:17).

Justice

He was deeply moved by unjust actions, such as people taking advantage of the poor (Nehemiah 5:6-11), an enemy being given a place to live within the temple (Nehemiah 13:4-8), the Sabbath laws being broken (Nehemiah 13:15-22) and men who had married non-Jewish wives (Nehemiah 13:23-28). Each time, he took decisive action, for example:

> I was greatly displeased and threw all Tobiah's household goods out of the room. I gave orders to purify the rooms, and then I put back into them the equipment of the house of God.
> (Nehemiah 13:8-9)

Another biblical place to look for Christian values is the Sermon on the Mount, particularly the Beatitudes (Matthew 5:3-12).

Christian values

Just as we can deduce Nehemiah's values from what he said and did, so we can work out our church or charity's values based on our vision and how we fulfil it. We did that at YoYo when we were challenged to put our values on our website and in a Case for Support we were creating to submit with grant applications. The values had not been defined previously, so we had to decide what they were. The team and trustees spent a morning doing it. We debated and prayed, then in groups of two and three we discussed and listed values which were exhibited in our ministry. Then we combined the groups' lists to include all those proposed. We talked for some time about whether to include professionalism but eventually decided that as we work in schools but most of our staff are not trained teachers, teachers in schools could be uncomfortable about us claiming to be professional. We prayed together about which values on the list were the most important, and then voted for what each of us felt were the top five. By the end of the time we agreed on six: passion, excellence, integrity, relevance, impact and discipleship.

The last one, discipleship, was eventually chosen from several possible words to express our Christian ethos and commitment. Though we cannot disciple pupils in school lessons, we can do so in other contexts including lunchtime and after-school clubs, through links with church-based youth workers, and by making known the York Christian Youth Holidays.

WEC International is a large interdenominational mission agency. An article in their magazine described their values:

> Jesus has called WEC to a great and noble task – to see Jesus known, loved and worshipped among the unreached peoples of the world ... WEC is founded on four pillars: faith, holiness, sacrifice and fellowship. These values are our DNA. They hold us together. Everything we do springs from them ... Today, the expressions of these values are as unique as each of our workers. But the four pillars remain our foundation. They encapsulate who Jesus has called us to be. They underpin what he has called us to do.[6]

> With this one vision we have six goals: engage, disciple, pray, mobilise, recruit and support.[7]

Carrubbers Christian Centre in Edinburgh has printed its values on a leaflet available at the church: 'committed to Biblical truth, a worshipping community, a praying people, equipping for life and service, reaching others, caring compassionately.' The leaflet also states their vision: 'To see lives transformed by the good news of Jesus in Edinburgh, across our nation and around the world.' Carrubbers is based on The Royal Mile in the city centre and they make the most of opportunities to demonstrate those values to the thousands of students in the city's universities as well as to the millions of visitors to the city, especially during the annual Edinburgh Festival.

Applying the values

Agreed and shared values can unite trustees, especially in a charity where board members come from different church backgrounds. They also help staff to understand and accept the ethos of the organisation. A housing charity in a large city grew out of the work of a local church. They make that quite clear in a variety of ways:

> We are very clear that we come from a church, we are based in a church building and we are a Christian charity. Donors are made aware that we are a faith-based charity. We've had funding from the National Lottery and others but we were very clear that, although we have a Christian ethos and that the history of the charity is that it came from and was started by a church, we accept and welcome and will work with people of all faiths and none. While it may not be necessary that all volunteers, staff and trustees are themselves believers, it is important that the ethos is understood and accepted by all. We weren't requiring people to be committed to the Christian faith, but we were requiring people as part of their contract to be supportive of our Christian ethos.

Shared values need to be worked out in day-to-day life and work:

> I've encouraged charities to recognise the benefit of stating their values, but more important is how do we get them lived right across the organisation? It needs to be a whole organisation process. One of the things I encourage people to do is maybe once a month in a staff meeting to take a value and unpack it: what does it mean, how do we do it, how can we ensure it remains part of our DNA?

Particularly as a charity gets larger or if the work it is doing is the same as a secular charity, its values are one of the ways of explicitly stating the Christian ethos underpinning the organisation:

> I was working with one charity recently. They are deeply Christian but they have no 'advancing the Christian faith' in their Objectives.

If you were to look at their Constitution you would not see any difference whatsoever between them and a secular charity. However, they've kept their trustee body Christian and have only recruited Christians. I led them through a discussion about what were their governance principles. Coming out of that was what did it mean for them to be Christian at all? In the end they came to something along the lines that they wanted to listen to God's voice and to follow Him in what they were doing. Immediately two of the staff who were in the room said, 'But we are not a Christian charity' and the trustees were ... shocked I think is the only word I can use. There was a very big disconnect.

There is sometimes a disconnection between what a trustee body thinks it means for them to be Christian and what the staff are implementing. It depends on the genesis of the charity: the more you are about the advance of the Christian faith, the easier it is for there to be Christian values at the centre of the charity. But if you've not got a really good understanding of integral mission there can then be a disconnection between the values of the staff and the values of the trustees. You need to get those integrated, whatever your understanding of Christian values and having a Christian ethos.

What is true for separate charities also applies to churches: their theological position should have a significant impact on what values they espouse. However, that isn't always the case:

The weight of history often has a bigger impact on the way people function. Certainly in rural areas we are still functioning in a feudal society a lot of the time, so people who are big landowners or significant people in the local community actually have more of an impact than the theological understanding or particular spiritual tradition of the church.

This can easily lead to a disconnection between the church and the community:

In a deeply rural village they've had a very unpleasant dispute over Glebe land. It's a tiny village so it really matters, people are falling out with their neighbours and real difficulties have emerged. The PCC have been very hurt by it and they've been trying to do the right thing, the good and godly thing in the middle of it all and to express their Christian values through their actions. Sadly that's not the way it's always been seen in the village and some people are really annoyed because they think the PCC should give them preferential treatment because they are their friends, whereas the PCC's Christian values lead them to a different conclusion. So I do think that image and values come into play quite considerably, especially in difficult situations. People can't always articulate what their values are or why they do what they do but when it gets difficult, particularly with contentious issues, they can articulate what it means to them.

What makes an organisation specifically Christian?

This is an interesting question for trustees to debate. Can an organisation *per se* even be 'specifically Christian' or is it not rather the nature of what they do and how they do it? For many it is very clear in the Objects of their charity. For other charities what makes them Christian is how they function, in other words, their values:

There are charities which do things in a Christian way but the things that they do would be the same things as other charities do. What makes them 'Christian' is probably the way that they look at choosing their activities and the way that they carry them out, but they might have a Public Benefit which is not related to religion. Other charities are 'Christian' because they have a religious Object and that is still, thankfully, considered to be a Public Benefit.

Charities are required to provide a benefit to the public, not only to their own members. For some churches, this is a challenge as they try to

... answer the question about what their part is in the bigger picture, what their outward looking bit is, as opposed to having just a nice club for themselves. Their values can be an area of tension. Some of the BAME[8] churches have struggled with this with the Charity

Commission: to what extent, if you're going to receive the benefits of being charitable, are you serving the wider good as against only serving those who are already inside? The brilliant thing about the Church of England is that our vision as a denomination is that we are called to serve the communities in which we are set, not just those who believe the same as us. To that end we can meet that charitable objective but we need to do it with a Christ-like heart, whether our charity is there for social action or mission or some other purpose. It's that Christ-likeness bit, as people look at what we are saying, what we are resourcing, can they see Christ in it?

Christian Research did several projects working with Church of England deaneries to help them grow together and establish a common vision which each church could contribute to in different ways. There were one or two occasions when, after visiting a church and talking with the leader, we wondered how that church was any different to a secular charity such as Age Concern. They were running various activities and projects but the Christian faith wasn't mentioned:

For me it's about its motivation, what it is seeking to do, and seeing that in the context of the kingdom of God. There are many good initiatives which have Christian origins and we could make a very long list of organisations and charities, including many well-known national and international charities, which began with a Christian initiative but over time have become more secular and the organisation would not necessarily identify itself as Christian now. I think of The Children's Society, which for a long time was known as the Church of England Children's Society but very deliberately changed its name, or an organisation such as The Samaritans – the very name suggests something about its Christian origin but today it wouldn't see itself as Christian. It would be too easy to say they began as something Christian but then they became secular. If the Church is actually meeting a need which is not being met elsewhere, but through them that need is being met, I would say that's a success.

Statement of Faith

Values based on Christian teaching, with a biblical basis and demonstrated practically in work and ministry, play a major part in a charity being seen as distinctively Christian. Another aspect underpinning that is often the theological position held. That may be described overtly in a Statement of Faith, which for some churches may be common across its denomination. For others it is specific to one church, while some denominations have decided not to have a Statement of Faith. Where they exist, they define a church or charity's theological position and in that sense they are particularly important for some. They may become increasingly important in the future if more challenges are posed about why an organisation did or did not do something, especially if the challenge relates to their Christian beliefs or values. To be able to point to a Statement of Faith, especially if it is part of the governing document, may be a vital deciding factor in their defence.

A Statement of Faith can help to unify trustees and staff in Christian charities who come from a variety of theological backgrounds:

The more evangelical and evangelistic you are, and also the more Reformed you are, the more important the Statement of Faith is in the charity. The more openly evangelical you are, the less important a Statement of Faith is. Increasingly Statements of Faith are not in the Articles of Association or Trust Deed, they are an add-on. I think that's good in the sense that you can change it without having to go to the Charity Commission for permission, but it's bad in that it is easy to drop it completely if you're not careful.

For Christian charities, it's an incredibly important document to set the groundwork for how we relate to the outside world and how we accept one another. So it's a unifying document. Those who work in those charities have had to sign up to that faith statement because they are representing a number of other people, so in most charities it's unifying a number of churches and different denominations.

A Statement of Faith can help to shape the values of a church or organisation and in some cases act as a barometer for testing whether the ethos is still upheld:

> The Statement of Faith is at the centre: out of that comes our values and out of those come our behaviour. The critical thing is that we live out what we believe, and do it with integrity. We had a theologically very old-fashioned statement of faith. We put the new statement of faith as a narrative from Genesis to Revelation to try to make it more readable and understandable to a younger generation because this goes to the very foundation of who we are. Take the analogy of a ship: if there is no clarity in this area it is like the ship is getting ripped right at the very bottom of the hull where the most water comes in and you'll sink quickly. For Christian organisations it's a big one; if there's no unity around your Statement of Faith you're on a downward trajectory eventually.

Having a Statement of Faith that trustees, and perhaps also staff, are willing to sign up to can be very unifying, but it can also have some drawbacks:

> At first sight an accepted Statement of Faith is a good protection for an organisation, so that there is a core basis for when there are changes of key personnel and dialogue can take place about what is expected and what the core values are. But it can sometimes become a difficulty for some people who are in effect forced to agree a basis of faith where they may have acceptable hesitations about it. They sometimes have to compromise their views to be accepted and I think that can be an unhealthy position. I don't think coming to an agreement about a basis of faith is therefore necessarily a protection in all circumstances, I think it can be overstated.
>
> For a range of Christian charities it is important, but managing it can be quite difficult. So ... I think when you have a well-founded Christian charity working in a very needy area of society, holding on to its Christian ethos is a challenge. For example, the chief executive who has to be professionally qualified in that area leaves and you may have a candidate who is not outwardly strong from a Christian point of view but from a professional point of view might be better – that

gives trustees a major dilemma. There is tension between faith and professionalism – I think there is a tension in good governance that way quite a lot, actually. I've been in situations where we have gone for the more highly qualified professional and it has been the right decision. So there isn't for me a legalistic formula around a Statement of Faith, I think there's some wisdom around it but it needs careful thought.

Image and values are part of good governance because the reputation of a church or charity depends on them. They are the backbone of how we go about what we do. As we seek to build the kingdom of God and (as is the expectation of the Charity Commission[9]) provide a public benefit, they are how we demonstrate that we are trustworthy and really do love our neighbour as we love ourselves (Matthew 22:39).

Questions

Has your church or organisation ever written down its values? If not, how can you go about doing so? If yes, when did you last review or discuss them?

Are the values shared by staff and volunteers across the organisation, or the congregation? How could you encourage that to happen?

Do you know what image and reputation you have locally or more widely? Do they match your values and theology/ Statement of Faith?

4
What If ...?
Risk and Faith

The God we serve is able to deliver us ... But even if he does not ... we will not serve your gods.
(Daniel 3:17-18)

If you've had someone pull a gun on you four times in your ministry, this is nothing!

An important part of governance is recognising the risks a charity or church faces and addressing how they can be managed. 'You and your co-trustees must ... avoid exposing the charity's assets, beneficiaries or reputation to undue risk.'[1] From a Christian point of view, there is an extra dimension: trustees need to consider when it is right to take a risk in faith, believing that the proposed action is in God's will for them. When is a risk not a risk because it is faith? That is part of assessing whether the risk is worth taking, though that assessment should also consider 'What if ...?' What if the money doesn't come in or something else goes wrong?

Biblical risk-takers

The verse quoted above is from the biblical story perhaps many people would think of first for the topic of risk. King Nebuchadnezzar had set up a massive image of gold and summoned the governors of his province to worship it. Famously, Daniel's three friends, Shadrach, Meshach and Abednego, refused to do so and were arrested as a result. The king gave them a second opportunity to worship the image with the threat that if they did not he would have them thrown into a blazing furnace. He taunted them by questioning which god could possibly rescue them (Daniel 3:15). The three friends heard his question as much more than a challenge to them personally: it was a challenge to their God, the Most High God. They fully believed that He was able to rescue them, but they were aware of the consequences if He did not. Amazingly, God not only rescued them but appeared in the furnace with them in such a spectacular way that the king decreed that from then on no one in his kingdom was to say anything against their God.

There are other stories of risk in the book of Daniel. The book opens with the people of Jerusalem being taken into exile, among them members of the royal family and nobility. These men were to be taught the language and literature of the Babylonians and were looked after handsomely. Daniel and his three friends were among them but Daniel believed that eating the royal food and wine was not right for them. He asked the king's chief official to provide the four of them with a much simpler diet, but while the official was sympathetic he was also worried about the negative effect that could have on the young men and therefore on him as he was responsible for them. Daniel had thought about the 'What if ...?' and so offered the official a way out: test them for ten days and then make a decision about whether they could continue. It was what we would now call a win-win offer, with the four friends allowed to do what they believed was right but doing so in a way which did not put the official in danger. It worked, too! At the end of the ten days they were healthier than the others, and after three years' training, the king found these men were

> ... ten times better than all the magicians and enchanters in his whole kingdom.
> (Daniel 1:20)

Daniel took other risks during his lifetime, confronting different kings with the challenge of his God when he interpreted their dreams (Daniel 2 and 4), and refusing to stop praying when the law said he must and so finishing up in the lions' den (Daniel 6).

In most of the Bible stories one can think of in relation to risk, God vindicated the faith of the person concerned, though not always immediately:

- Abraham risked being obedient when God asked him to sacrifice his son Isaac, even telling the boy that God would provide. At the last possible moment God did provide, with a ram caught by its horns and available to take Isaac's place (Genesis 22).

- Moses challenged Pharaoh to release the Israelites from slavery in Egypt but that did not happen until after the plagues, the last of which resulted in the death of Pharaoh's son and heir (Exodus 7:1–12:30).

- David challenged the massive Philistine, Goliath, because Goliath was defying the armies of the living God. David felled him with a well-aimed stone from his sling (1 Samuel 17).

- Elijah challenged the prophets of Baal that the god who answered by fire was the true God. When Baal did not answer, Elijah made things as difficult as possible, pouring masses of water over the altar and sacrifice. Nevertheless, God did answer by fire, consuming not only the sacrifice but the altar and the water (1 Kings 18:22-39).

Each one took a risk, either because God had directly spoken to them and told them to take a specific action, or because they were determined to honour God, particularly when others were defying Him.

Jesus told two stories which speak directly to the issue of risk. In the parable of the talents, the third servant was so afraid of his master that he dared not do anything with the talent he had been given and so buried it. When the master returned, the servant lost everything because he had done nothing with the money, not even invested it – he had not taken the risk (Matthew 25:24-29). When talking about the cost of being a disciple, Jesus gave the example of someone who wanted to build a tower, but would need to estimate the cost to see if they had enough to complete it, otherwise they would be ridiculed for beginning to build (Luke 14:28-30).

Risk versus faith

There are, of course, many other levels at which these stories can be interpreted, but they point us to a God who sometimes asks us to trust Him in a situation which humanly looks like a huge risk. But, as Jesus' stories show, burying your head in the sand hoping a situation will turn out OK, or rushing headlong into a project without thinking it through carefully are equally dangerous. The Charity Commission, as well as supporters, the public, staff and volunteers, could legitimately look on either response as negligent.

> *Faith based 'merely' on feelings would not be good enough in the eyes of the Charity Commission. If faith is based on experience, such experience needs to be noted in the minutes to help justify the decision.*

As individuals, we respond to risk in different ways:

> *I think the issue of risk is a really interesting one. I've no love of rules and regulations, so I would be a calculated risk-taker, recognising that you need to follow rules but also help people take risk.*

The level of risk a trustee board is willing to take varies enormously:

Some people find risk really difficult, while some PCCs are almost 'risk junkies', to be honest! They'll just throw everything up and go for it at any opportunity — my PCC was like that in one of my churches, they would go for anything, and if I encouraged them they'd throw everything to the wind and be off!

I've seen people respond to opportunities for renewal in the church and new ministry in the church — you could say they had no choice because everything else had failed, but actually I think there was more to it than that, it was more to do with trusting in God for the future. I've seen PCCs take some extraordinary steps of faith in terms of what they believe God is doing in their place and what that might mean for them.

For other churches and boards, risk is too dangerous or demanding:

In our church I think we're quite risk-averse, I'm not sure why that is. The church has done tremendous things in the past. We've been talking about church planting for a number of years, but nothing seems to happen and it goes round in circles; perhaps that's because of a bit of lack of direction from those who could say, 'This needs to happen.' If you don't have full-on engagement about moving forward in new ways, then it won't happen. I think it's also perhaps about loss of control.

Or perhaps the risk is too challenging to the status quo:

A lot of boards know the people who are giving them money and the last thing they want to do is upset those people by doing something different, perhaps something that churches might wonder why they did it. You need to be accountable to your supporters, but if you want to start something new, that's a bit different; you also need to be accountable to what the governing document says you're going to do. I think it comes down to the nature of the trustees because if they've had a good discussion about something — perhaps someone's brought some fresh perspective and the trustees can see it's worth doing — they've prayed about it and they know it's a risk, then they're going to go ahead in faith and do it. That usually comes from somebody who has the vision to help the other trustees to have the confidence to take a risk, who can help them think it through, pray about it, make sure it's what God wants, but then take the risk.

Good risk and bad risk

The implication in the Charity Commission's documents can easily be read that all risk is bad. That is not true! In some ways simply being a charity is in itself a risk, just as business is. Charities have to ask themselves whether the people they hope will benefit from what they will offer will want it, just as businesses have to consider whether there is a market for their products. If a church is to survive long-term it has to find ways to bring in new people and how they choose to do that may well be a risk. Charities are dependent on raising money or on individual donors or churches supporting them. Churches rely on their members giving regularly and often sacrificially, while businesses only succeed if customers are willing to pay the right price. If no one ever took a risk we would not even get out of bed in the morning – after all, there might be a lion roaming the streets as the sluggard suggested (Proverbs 26:13)!

There's good risk and bad risk. I like it when PCCs take good risks, when they're willing to step out in faith. One of the tensions we have, especially for treasurers (money is always a tension for treasurers!), is that the Charity Commission says you shouldn't hold too much in your bank, you should have a reserves policy. You're not a charity just in order to build up funds, so they ask questions about charities which build up funds. I like it when churches take risks and say, 'We believe this is of God and we will step out and take the risk.' It is a risk because there's a tension in it. There will be people who say, 'You're spending your reserves; how do you know that the money will eventually come?' We have the benefit of both Scripture and experience to tell us that, by whatever miraculous way, our God does provide, and so we can take some risks that perhaps go beyond what other charities will do. To me, that's a good risk.

On the other hand, you see charities which take risks, perhaps because they've got a bit too clever. They've built their reserves but they want more – and there are parables about that! – so perhaps they decide to use less safe investment routes and then when there's a financial crash they get burnt and what they thought was there to support them suddenly isn't. Then there's a PCC that doesn't follow good practice on money handling and then discovers that their treasurer wasn't quite as trustworthy as they thought, or don't make sure that they've done their DBS checks on all the people they should have done them on and are then surprised when something happens. It's those kinds of bad risks that people take.

When the writer to the Hebrews described faith as 'confidence in what we hope for' (Hebrews 11:1), they weren't meaning the kind of hope that would like a dry day on Saturday for the church barbecue. It was the hope that wants to please God (v6) and is determined to know what His will is in a particular situation. The latest idea, however good it may appear, is not necessarily going to honour God, so following it may be one of those bad risks. Far better to pray and discuss until there is clarity and agreement about the right way forward.

It's dangerous to have a 'gung-ho' attitude to risk-taking, backed by a suspect theology that the Lord will take care of us, whatever approach we take. That's not an honourable approach.

It can also cause considerable tension among trustees, especially if only one member or a minority of the board enthusiastically challenges the rest to 'have faith', while others have real concerns about the dangers of a proposed action.

This kind of faith is different from the faith we exercise when we accept God's gift of salvation. It is a level of faith which involves acting in line with what we believe and committing ourselves to take steps to do what God has shown us He wants us to do. For an individual, that might be following God's call to ordination, serving God overseas or moving to a deprived area to help grow a church there. For a church it might mean planting a pioneer church and starting a new congregation, developing a ministry to children and young people, reaching out to the elderly and lonely in the community or championing justice issues. For a charity it might mean extending the work to a new area geographically or a different age group, or perhaps purchasing or selling property. Is this just a desperate attempt to survive, or the latest new idea, or do we believe it is what God wants? All involve risks; all are tied closely to vision.

Different kinds of risk

Just as there are good risks and bad risks, there are also risks which are perhaps demanding but not of the level that have to be managed in detail by trustees. For nine years I ran a youth group for eleven- to fourteen-year-olds. When our church youth leader proposed restructuring all our youth work, I agreed with his plans but felt that it was the right time to step down and let him lead the new groups. One of the minor reasons why I was ready to pass it on was that I had become frustrated by the need to do a risk assessment for every event or outing. One example: I planned a bike ride for the group. A well-meaning person in the church offered to do the risk assessment: he sent me a questionnaire with forty-seven questions relating to the possible bike ride! For someone who grew up in an era when we talked about being sensible rather than taking a risk, I was exasperated. The PCC didn't want to look in detail at each risk assessment, but they did have a responsibility to have a policy about risk assessment and then to be assured that it was being adhered to. Trustees should not be involved in managing the details, but they do need to be clear about the implications of policies, however seemingly insignificant they might be:

> It's surprising how church people, including leaders, agree something but then make exceptions for themselves or turn a blind eye to folk deliberately bypassing the rule, especially in what they think of as little things, like dumping stuff near fire doors so the escape route is blocked or using fire doors like normal doors despite clear notices to the contrary.

There are some kinds of risks which all organisations face, and regular assessment of these should be routine. It sounds simple to say that, but it's not always so easy to do:

We have a financial risk assessment which looks at various things which might occur, which might prevent us using the building or incomes drying up or grants failing. We have physical risk assessments about the building, fire risks and all that stuff and event risk assessments – though we're not very good at those. If you go online you find umpteen versions of how to do risk assessments, but there's always a sense when you're doing these things of, 'Am I doing this properly?' You would like someone to guide you, but finding that guidance ... so you do your best, but you feel vulnerable.

There are considerations about risk that are specific to the Christian ethos. Choosing new trustees is one area: will they give the time needed to fulfil their responsibilities or conscientiously carry out the role they've agreed to, or are they already too busy with other church responsibilities which perhaps will take precedence over giving time to being a trustee? If they are from a different theological perspective to others on the board, will that cause tensions? Is it taking a risk to appoint a fairly recent Christian as a trustee, or someone who is not strong in their faith? Not necessarily:

I think there's something wholesome about having people who aren't necessarily strong in the Christian way but are part of you because they have another strength. You're not taking too great a risk by having someone who is committed to what you do, but is perhaps very young in faith – it's a developmental thing for them personally.

However, someone could be quite a mature Christian and yet not be suitable as a trustee because they are either not willing to consider taking risks or too eager to do so:

Someone who had an excessively conservative approach would not be a suitable trustee, but equally someone who is too enthusiastic, even using the language of faith and 'God's called me' would not be appropriate either. There is a tendency to be too safe, too cosy, perhaps because people are not well-fitted to the task you've asked them to do. But there may not be other people available or willing to take the role, so they're doing the best they can. Sometimes being risk-averse can be because people have got too narrow a vision of what they're called to do, or it could be that the chair or minister may be by personality a more risk-averse person and therefore is not taking a lead, not encouraging a more risky approach in others.

Even retaining the Christian dimension of a charity can be at risk if it is not carefully monitored:

It is a good idea every now and then to do an audit of your ethos and values and where you're at in it, and in terms of assessment of risk, have a discussion every now and then about whether you're still being true to your Christian calling and what are the dangers you might face to that being undermined.

Some kinds of ministry inevitably involve risk. That may be in the nature of the work undertaken or its location, or perhaps both:

A charity I was involved in was reaching out to prostitutes, looking at why they were on the street, looking at preventative measures, so dealing with their addictions, lack of family and lack of self-worth. The first steps of an organisation for the people trying to reach them are a very risky process – people go into dangerous parts of town, they're very, very vulnerable. In a conventional charity sense, you have to mitigate your risk and that would say, 'How would you protect your staff and volunteers?' But in that situation, by the very nature of the charity, you're never going to do anything unless you take a lot of risk, so trustees have to have a really good discussion about how you actively do take risk, not how you don't take risk. You have to have processes that are thought through, and people have to know how to behave in certain settings, but you take the risk that things might go wrong because that's why you exist.

For agencies working internationally, there may be potential risks to security. One of my fellow students when I was at missionary training college went to work in a dangerous area where she was actually kidnapped and held hostage for some weeks. Most mission agencies with workers in dangerous places have policies about how to minimise the danger as well as how to respond to situations like that. Mostly, they do not talk about them.

> *The security of our workers in some very vulnerable parts of the world means that we are very restricted in what we can say, even openly within the organisation, because if the security was breached it would drastically increase the risk for workers in vulnerable situations.*

Sometimes the only option for an organisation is a stark choice between taking a risk or closing down. In that scenario it is particularly important to know whether the proposed action is what God is asking you to do and not a desperate effort to continue when actually it would be more honourable to close down:

> *The app development for eBooks was a big financial risk because we were in competition with major retailers whose eBook systems were already up and running. We couldn't work with their systems so we had to create our own app. If we didn't take that risk, the work as a whole was just going to grind to a halt. Increasingly people were buying eBooks not printed books, and bookshops were shutting down all over the country. It was done thoughtfully and prayerfully, with a fair bit of research into what the options and alternatives were. We concluded that there was no viable alternative. If we hadn't taken the risk, we probably wouldn't have been able to keep going. Financially you can't keep going if you aren't able to sell your product.*

In some situations, the best way forward may be to merge with another organisation, though the Charity Commission requirements mean the two groups have to have similar Objects. A good match can be very positive in the long term, though there may well be costs in the short term:

You get to the stage sometimes with an organisation where, if they need to grow, they need a different framework within which to do that. For one organisation I know of there was opportunity to grow, but there wasn't the capacity either in staff or with finance to enable that to happen. There was an obvious fit with a larger network that they were already linked to, but there were implications for the staff and the CEO: the CEO would no longer be running his own organisation and while one member of staff went with him, the others had to leave. That was several years ago and the work of the organisation has not only continued but it has flourished by being part of something that had a bigger profile. It was the right thing to do.

On the other hand, growing can produce risks also, as this Baptist church found when it outgrew its building:

We deacons recognised that we needed to get God's leading in terms of what we were going to do, and we just felt God was saying that we needed to have continuous prayer 24/7 for forty days and forty nights. It transformed our prayer life and as a result God opened so many doors ... We'd made an approach to a church just down the road – it could take 600 – and they basically said, 'There's no way we're going to let you use this church.' But as we prayed, literally in ten or twelve days they came back to us and said, 'We've had a rethink. Not only are we going to allow you to use the church but we're going to paint and decorate it for you.'

That was a big risk as a group of deacons because we were committing to a course where we were planning for the church to grow and the risk was having enough resources and enough people who could lead different parts of the new work. Some people struggled to understand the changes, but we did what we did in good faith that God was leading us. In terms of managing risk, I think Christians can be a bit risk-averse. We need to be thoughtful and prayerful, but I think occasionally we need to be more confident in the way Christ is leading us.

What if ...?

This question needs to be asked repeatedly. It is especially important when a charity is first set up:

At a significant level in the church structure, or at a local level, it can be easy to get an idea, to have enthusiasm, and see something take off, but maybe there ought to be more thought at the beginning to the 'What if ...?' Things don't necessarily continue forever. Unfortunately, what happens if or when things go wrong is not always thought through in the way it should be. And sadly, people often get hurt.

It is also important to think about potential risks which, hopefully, may never happen. What if our CEO or minister went under the proverbial bus, who would take charge immediately? What if our building or church burned down or suffered from a major flood, do we have back-up copies of computer files; where would the work move to or the church meet in the short term? What if the treasurer or bookkeeper is taken seriously ill, does anyone know the password for the accountancy package on the computer? This is termed planning for disaster recovery and it is something that should be considered when assessing risk:

The risks I'm always in two minds about are those practical things like insurance – nobody likes paying insurance, but not every PCC that's decided to under-insure its building has fully thought through the consequences. If there are not many of you left, and this is a building which, if something catastrophic happened to it, wouldn't be replaced, you only need to insure it for demolition value. If you've got the custody of, say, a cathedral, you're not going to get away with demolishing it, or if you've got a church with 500 people, you're going to need a building and therefore taking the short cut of not insuring it properly and only having Public Liability Insurance ... it's those kind of areas where people don't always think through the consequences.

Managing risk

Risk is one of the areas in which trustees are most likely to be deemed negligent if they do not think things through carefully.

Risk-taking is a crucial area and risk needs to be managed conscientiously. It's important to establish good working practice, for example for safeguarding, and have thoughtful policies formally accepted and which everyone sticks to. Risks need to be managed, policies followed and agreed working practice adopted.

There are various ways to minimise risk, as well as having all the right policies in place and ensuring they are followed. There is much detailed advice available, but these are a few pointers which were proposed by the people I talked to.

Take good advice

For a Church of England church, advice will be available through the diocese, while other denominations would be wise to approach their regional leader or headquarters for help. A separate charity may find it is available from another local charity or a local agency set up to help charities. Sometimes it is necessary to pay for advice, say from a lawyer who knows charity law:

Trustees are personally liable for losses resulting from negligence – but not from reasonable mistakes. So take professional advice from a properly qualified professional – for which you may well have to pay a fee – avoid the good amateur, who claims experience from a different situation, which may not be applicable to your situation and could become dangerous advice. If properly advised, and things still go wrong, trustees have a good defence, and will not be liable, as long as they can demonstrate that they did not act negligently.

Have the right insurance policies

As well as the regular insurance policies, it is possible to buy Professional Indemnity Insurance, though only if your governing document allows you to:

This type of insurance only indemnifies trustees, and doesn't pay out for losses – in effect it is a means of providing money to protect your good name in court, if a claim is made against the organisation. It won't cover you if you have been negligent but it will if you made a misjudgement, having taken proper professional advice when appropriate.

Keep clear minutes

If you are ever challenged about an action you have taken, your minutes need to make clear that you assessed the risk and spell out why you went ahead.

Manage change

If the risk involves significant change, manage that change as well as you can:

We actually brought in somebody two days a week who was skilled in change management and we had quite a long consultation period. She went round interviewing members of staff individually, she came to board meetings, she obviously talked with me [as chair] and we had a small group that were core to it – not the whole board. She talked to everybody about ... their fears, what did they think about it, how did it square with what they saw. Then she came back with a paper to the board which said, 'These are the steps you need to take.' She set out the steps so we had a stage-by-stage implementation plan with a pretty basic timeframe for that.

We had some people who'd been there a long time and really couldn't grasp another way of doing things. Other people were thrilled and couldn't wait to get going. Some had issues of personal security or were concerned about the implications. Another issue was overwork for the staff executive team: their workload was huge because they were still trying to keep a programme going while taking on all this extra. Then we had to communicate what was happening to the wider Christian public: the idea you might be doing something so major for strategic reasons was quite hard to get across.

Above all, pray

Pray about what action to take, pray about how to take it, pray
with people affected, and do all you can to ensure the risk you
are about to take is a good risk taken in faith, not a bad risk that
will lead to huge problems:

> *In one village the PCC voted for closure of the church and the village
> came out in uproar. The first thing that has to happen if a PCC votes
> to close the church is that I have to hold a public meeting. I had no
> choice, that's the process, so I held a public meeting and sixty-two
> people came and shouted at me for the whole evening about how
> terrible I was to be closing their church — although it wasn't me that
> had voted to close it! I don't close churches, I don't think it's a good
> idea, and in our rural villages they're often the only public building
> left and you can understand why people are so angry: their pub's closed
> and their school's closed and their post office has closed and now you
> want to close the church. We're the last bastion for a lot of people.*
>
> *I was actually driving straight from that meeting to a retreat and
> I got there and thought, 'I have no idea what to do with this lot, I
> just don't know what to do.' I prayed a lot about it and I thought,
> the only way forward is to pray with these people. So I wrote to the
> churchwarden and the vicar and said, in two weeks' time I'm coming
> on the Saturday and you need to put out posters in the village. I said
> I'd be in the church for six hours and on the hour we'll pray and in
> between time people can come and talk to me. All we need is some
> hospitality, some drinks and biscuits, and welcome people to the
> church. It was in September and it was a lovely day and I just sat
> outside on a bench in the sun and over fifty people from the village
> came. I sat and talked with people and listened to them. Then we
> prayed every hour. At the end of it the report that I wrote said, 'No,
> we don't close this church', and I said that I thought we needed to put
> somebody in there to support ministry and nurture them a bit. We
> had a priest who was prepared to offer some time who was non-
> stipendiary so it didn't cost the diocese anything. The situation was
> quite transformed by the turnaround from what the village expected
> to happen to what did happen. Two people Christmas Day the year
> before, sixty-two people Christmas Day the year it happened. There's
> a big turnout about once a month now for a service and they do great*

weddings and funerals and baptisms and so on. So they are now a village church.

For me, prayer is always the answer, and it certainly is when you have no idea what else to do, but it's quite transforming because it's not what people expect and through that they hear things they don't expect.

It is often not easy to balance risk and faith, but our God is trustworthy and if we prayerfully seek His guidance and help, we can take steps of faith with confidence that He will be with us and help us.

Making our Christian faith a basis for all we do as a charity should provide a basis for wanting to govern well and have a clear vision of what part our church or charity is playing in God's kingdom, help us to demonstrate our faith in how we go about our ministry and enable us to get a good balance between faith and risk. Working on these aspects of our role as trustees will help us to leave godly tracks for others to see.

Questions

Is your church or charity more inclined to take risks or to be risk-averse? Why do you think this is?

What risk can you recall that has been taken in, say, the last five years? How did it turn out? Looking back, why was it a risk and do you think it was taken in faith? What part did prayer have in the decision to go ahead?

What is your experience of balancing risk and faith?

SECTION 2

PERSONAL TRACKS

5
Who? Me?
Gift and Calling

To these four young men God gave knowledge and understanding of all kinds of literature and learning. And Daniel could understand visions and dreams of all kinds.
(Daniel 1:17)

Getting the right people with the right skills who supported the ethos and values of the charity was a challenge.

Charities cannot exist without trustees; it is a requirement of registering as a charity. But who should those trustees be? Careful thought and prayer is needed, whether an organisation's founder is looking for the first trustees, an established board needs to appoint new members, or an individual is considering becoming a trustee:

I was never keen to be a trustee, and I'm still not eager to be a trustee, but without trustees it wouldn't be possible to establish these kinds of initiatives. For me the common theme through all these things has been about enabling the church to work together to serve the community – and to work together in a way which wouldn't be possible or even desirable for any one church to do on its own.

It is vital for any charity or church trustee board to find suitable people, especially as it may not always be thought of as an important way of serving God:

> *It's hard to find trustees generally. There are a lot of Christian charities in the area, all of whom are looking for trustees, and possibly only a small pool of people whom we know of who might be suitable. I would like to see churches encourage people to consider trusteeship so that there are more people who think, 'I could do this.'*

As trustees become more aware of the responsibilities the role entails, some people are frightened off. That can be true of any charity, but it's become a particular issue in England for churches in denominations which were previously exempt from registering as individual charities but now have to do so, or soon will. The churches with larger incomes had to register first but the requirement is gradually being rolled out to all:

> *People at the moment are scared of taking on the role of PCC. There are those who stand easily because they don't understand they're becoming charity trustees; they just want to be a part of what's going on and they see it as another church committee. Those who have some glimmer of what it is to be a trustee are increasingly scared of it. We're finding it really hard to attract treasurers, churchwardens, PCC secretaries, because they're the ones who perhaps recognise that they're operating a charity and therefore proper records have to be kept, and the responsibilities fulfilled. So we find quite a lot of places where people say, 'We can't expect anybody to stand because there are lots of responsibilities and liabilities.' One of the things we need to communicate to PCCs is that however little money they have, whether they're registered separately with the Charity Commission or not, they are a charity and they are trustees.*

It saddens me to hear Christians making that sort of response, as they seem to be asking the wrong question: instead of looking at reasons why they should not take on the role of trustee, I want to encourage people to consider whether this is something God wants them to do. Has he given them a passion for the charity's work or to see the church move forward, or do they have gifts or experience which would be useful to this group of trustees?

Daniel's experiences

In Daniel's life we can see three different instances of him taking on new responsibilities. In chapter 1 we find Daniel and his friends being trained in the language and learning of the Babylonians. At the end of that time they passed the king's assessment of them with flying colours and entered his service. The abilities they had and the skills which they had developed made them suitable for new responsibilities.

Chapter 2 gives us a different perspective: Daniel put himself forward for a big responsibility. King Nebuchadnezzar had had a dream and had summoned his wise men and demanded that they interpret it. They expected him to describe the dream so they could then tell him what it meant, but the king refused. The situation became more and more confrontational until the king ordered that all the wise men in the kingdom were to be executed. We aren't told why Daniel was not among the wise men the first time but nevertheless he and his friends were included in the round-up. However, we are told that Daniel used wisdom and tact to find out what it was all about, and then asked the king for time. The four friends pleaded with God to have mercy on them and God answered, revealing the dream to Daniel. There is a lovely song of praise by Daniel in which he clearly acknowledges that his wisdom and insight are God-given gifts. Subsequently his description and interpretation of the dream are accepted by the king and as a result all four of the friends are promoted.

Later in his life, in chapter 5, we find him with another big challenge, this time because someone else recommended him. When King Belshazzar saw the mysterious writing on the wall, he was desperate to know what it meant. Just as years before, the wise men could not tell him. But the Queen (or perhaps the Queen mother) remembered Daniel and described him in such glowing terms that the king was prepared to give Daniel an opportunity to interpret the writing – which he did, with God's help.

These three scenarios are similar to the main ways in which new trustees are found, and why they agree to join a board: because of the skills and abilities they could bring, because they offer themselves, or by someone else's recommendation. We can use these as springboards to consider how trustees are recruited and why they might respond positively.

Gifts and abilities

It is great if someone is willing to stand for election as a deacon or to a PCC, but that is not necessarily enough:

> *In local PCCs* [and similar groups which are elected, such as Baptist diaconate] *there's often a feeling that if anyone is prepared to do it then the church is happy to have them. It's important to be aware of people's enthusiasm and appreciative of that, but we do also need people who can engage to as much of a degree as possible with what it means to be responsible for the life of the church in that place and the way in which the church can exercise its proper role and governance and all the rest of those kind of issues which come into it for a PCC. You need people with different gifts on a PCC, you don't want everybody to be the same.*

If there is not a good spread of gifts and abilities, it can unfortunately lead to a board that does not function well. An experienced trustee who was asked to join a church board was dismayed at what they found:

> *It was a very much 'cobbled together' board, made up of people who said they would do it but lacking some expertise and professionalism.*

A board which functions well is helped to do so by having a good balance of gifts and abilities among its trustees. However, that rarely happens without some thought and planning by the board. It goes without question that a new trustee should at the very least be interested in the work of a charity or committed to a church, but what can they contribute which fills a gap in the board and strengthens it in a valuable way? These are important questions, but they are not always considered:

> *What governance basically needs to say is, 'We need a person with these sorts of skills.' But they themselves don't know, they haven't worked out what they are each doing, so they don't know where the gaps are. It's too often been, 'So-and-so is a nice person in my church, they seem to have some time, so let's get them on,' without thinking whether they have the right skills and would be a good fit with who they already have. There's also been a lot of one type of person, so instead of having a variety of different backgrounds there's been a lot of teachers or retired teachers* [as trustees of a charity doing schools work] *or a lot of ministers. Sometimes when a ministry is started, say from Churches Together, there's been a representative from every church and that's normally the minister or associate minister or church youth worker. In that case even though they're doing schools work, they've had no teaching or education background within the mix of trustees. Another Trust will have a lot of teachers, but no one with a finance background or some other experience they can bring. They end up with just one or two points of view and tend to do the same things over and over because they haven't got that breadth of experience to make better decisions.*

A charity board usually recruits their own trustees, whom they either appoint themselves or recommend to an AGM for appointment, so having a careful look at what skills they already have and what they need should not be too difficult:

> *We had a trustee recruitment subcommittee of the board who tried to keep track of the needs of the board. I developed a grid of roles, responsibilities, background, churchmanship, gender, experience of governance, experience relevant to ministry [of] current trustees. This is so useful because it shows where the gaps are.*

However, it is not quite so straightforward in a church situation:

One of the positive things about most charity boards is that they can choose their own trustees. The problem with most church trustees is that they are elected by the church members and so it can sometimes be more about popularity and people's willingness to stand, rather than about the needs of the church and what is missing.

At one time I was in a church where there were a lot of family connections among members of the congregation. One person in particular was looked up to as a kind of 'patriarch' of the family and that sometimes impinged on decisions in the church: if he approved of someone who had been nominated for election as a deacon they were much more likely to be voted in than if he did not. A vicar or minister might well feel their hands are tied and they have to accept who the AGM votes in, but there are ways in which the election process can be guided, though that does not automatically eliminate potential problems:

It is quite tricky for PCCs because you can't say, 'We only want people with a background in business', or 'We only want people with these and these skills', but there are ways and means of doing it. One of the challenges for PCCs is, to put it bluntly, an awful lot of prayer — that sometimes doesn't happen — that God will call forward people with the kind of skills they need, along with other people who may develop such skills either in their faith journey or in their journey of trusteeship as they learn quite gently what that might mean. If the PCC prayerfully considers before the AGM and then shares with the congregation, 'As you're thinking about whether you'll stand for PCC this year, we could really do with someone who could give us x, y or z.'

There's a tension there because the Church Representation Rules say anybody can stand and so you find churches with a PCC where the incumbent is tearing their hair out because no one will say anything in a meeting, or you've got a PCC with a lot of people who've decided this is how to get the church to be the way they want it to be, and all come and be activist about it and know everything there is to know about charity law and spend their whole time battling against mission priorities.

All this assumes that anyone who might be approached to join or be elected to a trustee board knows what gifts they have as well as what skills they can offer because of their life experience or their professional training. There is much teaching in the New Testament, particularly in Paul's letters, about God-given gifts and skills and it is a topic well worth studying both individually and corporately in a church setting. Paul makes it clear that God gives everyone gifts. Our life experiences, job training or work experiences also contribute to what we can bring to the leadership and running of a church or organisation. Anyone considering whether to become a trustee (or school governor or any similar public service role) would be wise to think and pray about what they would be able to offer to a board, perhaps write it down if that helps, and then talk and pray it through with a trusted friend, their minister, or someone who is already a trustee.

Sometimes another person can see what gifts an individual has by watching the way they live and therefore may be able to encourage them to consider becoming a trustee. A mature Christian couple moved into York and started coming to the church I attend. As I got to know them, I could see that they had plenty of experience which potentially could be valuable to Christian charities in the city. When an opportunity arose, I talked with them about the wide range of ministry going on through local charities and encouraged them to consider becoming trustees of one which particularly interested them. That did in fact happen within a few months, and one of them was elected to the PCC too. Using one's skills and experience in this way goes hand-in-hand with being excited by what a charity is doing or the direction a church is heading and is often why a potential trustee agrees to stand for election or to join a trustee board.

> *I agreed because I believed in the vision, that it was valuable and doing a good job and that I had interests and skills that would benefit the charity.*

Offering oneself as a trustee

This happens especially when a particular need has been made known and someone responds. They might feel God wants them to say yes; they may even want to put it in terms of God called them. I had that happen in a lovely way. I had been chair of YoYo (York Schools and Youth Trust) for a while. One of the staff was secretary to the board, but because she was not a trustee she couldn't play the full part that a trustee secretary can. One year we held a dinner for those who had supported the work for five years or more and among those invited was a couple. The husband was not as keen to come but the wife felt she should. After we had eaten, the team and I shared in more depth than is possible in a public newsletter, including the need for a secretary. Afterwards the wife waited to speak to me and told me how she had felt God wanted her to come to the dinner and she was willing to find out what would be involved in her becoming the secretary. She was, literally, a Godsend, taking on the role efficiently and effectively and taking some of the burden off me. A couple of years later I started looking for someone to succeed me as chair and met with various board members individually to find out if they would consider the possibility. The secretary's response was that God had called her to be the secretary so, no, she would not consider being chair as her gifts were better suited to the role she had and she knew the new chair would need her support.

Here's another example, which happened in a slightly different way:

> I had just been at a meeting of the trustees I was employed by, and in the context of that meeting it was said that it would be good if I could get involved in another local charity because the work they were doing and the resources they were developing had a lot to give to our work and to enabling us to serve the city. I was told, 'If you're able to offer yourself to them as a trustee we would encourage you to do that.' I went home and the first message I picked up on my answerphone was actually a message from a trustee of that organisation inviting me to

join their board. I thought, 'I don't have much choice about this, I'm going to have to do this!' There was a very clear sense of God's calling.

I did something similar myself. When I was living in London I was on several boards and councils. My parents, and my brother who had always lived with them, were 200 miles away in York and I could see that my mother was finding it more and more difficult to cope with everything and needed me alongside her. As the possibility of retirement came closer, I stood down from my trustee roles as I reached the end of a term of service. I was sometimes challenged to continue and I began to reply that I had no intention of travelling back to London for trustee meetings but if, when I reached York, I was asked to be a trustee of a charity which interested me, I would do so. At first it was simply a way of saying 'no' to any new such role in London, but over several months I realised that it had become a God-given desire.

I had heard about YoYo and, having always done youth work, I was definitely interested in their outreach into schools in the area. Within a few months of moving, a mutual friend who knew of my previous trustee roles suggested to the then chair of YoYo that he invite me to join the board. He and another trustee came to see me and at the end of our chat asked whether I would consider becoming a board member. I immediately replied positively. 'Wouldn't you like to pray about it?' was his reaction, but I was able to assure him that I didn't need to pray about it because I already knew the answer: it was what I had been telling people in London!

It is often the combination of gifts and skills, becoming aware that there is a particular need, and a sense that God wants you to be involved in meeting that need which leads to making an offer. It is much better to happen that way round than for someone to find themselves on a church or charity trustee board without any clear idea what it means:

A lot of people turn up having been volunteered by their friends and not really understanding what they've allowed themselves to get into.

I don't think they realise that they were voted there by the church membership in order to represent their interests — they are not delegated, but they are voted for as people who the members think will represent them in a good and helpful way to take forward the things that are important to them in the mission of the church.

In a church the decision-making group, whether that is deacons, elders, a PCC or whatever, are also trustees if the church or its denomination is registered as a charity. In the interviews I undertook in research for this book I found that it was quite common for people on such groups not to realise that they had become trustees:

I think PCC members or Church Council members often don't see themselves as charity trustees, and I think that's a problem. They are trustees of the charity of the church and if they don't recognise that, they could be not fulfilling the Charity Commission's requirements or missing out important things.

Several interviewees experienced that in one way or another:

My appointment as one of the pastoral staff was a long, drawn-out process of meetings, discussions, talking through issues, attending some meetings, making presentations, and then I was appointed as a community engagement pastor but also to the board as well. The focus was more on the role. It was a weakness that the trustee side wasn't highlighted.

When I became a deacon I was made aware that I would become a trustee, but there wasn't a lot made of it. Actually, it makes me think that we're just in the process of appointing two more deacons and I wonder whether they've been told that they will be trustees. I knew beforehand but I'm not sure that they've been told — they may not even be aware of that.

It was only when I became a minister and was presented with the rule book that I understood the link with the Charity Commission and realised that I had been a trustee before. The Charity Commission elements were hidden behind the rules and regulations of the church. It's become more apparent recently. As bigger churches have had to register with the Charity Commission in their own right and submit names and proof of identity and things like that, so in recent times it's become a lot more obvious.

Encouraging someone to become a trustee or be elected to a church's governing body is a responsibility in itself, and one that many church members don't understand as well as they perhaps ought to when they vote to elect these people:

I think to a certain extent people throw away their votes because they don't really understand how important it is, that they can affect the thinking of the church by the way they vote. Some people think, 'This is the way it's always been', or, 'This is what everybody wants to happen therefore I ought to vote for it.' We need to hear different voices and I think often in the life of the church we've had situations where people think they need to follow the crowd because these people have been here longer, or they've got more experience, or they're a better Christian, or whatever.

So, one way to find new trustees is to pray and make known the need for a particular skill set or experience, then trust that God will challenge someone who could fulfil that role so that they offer to stand for election or join a board.

Recommendation

In my experience this is the most common route to becoming a trustee of a charity, especially one where people need to have different backgrounds – perhaps from different churches in the same city, from different parts of the country, or even, with an international agency, from other parts of the world:

I was invited to go on the board – I was a department leader in the mission and had leadership skills so it was thought I might be able to contribute to the board.

I knew the organisation well because I'd done some training for them, I knew the CEO, I was on board with their values and what they were trying to do in terms of helping people find their vocation. It gelled with what I was, and linked in with what I do. With another trustee board where I'd also already done some training for them, it seemed a natural progression. They wanted someone who had international links, which I had, so I fitted that slot for them.

I was recruited because their primary role is actually housing destitute asylum seekers. It was part of the church, it's a church charity, but also I've got good third sector experience in supported housing.

The need to fill the gaps on a trustee board can easily lead, not only to people being asked to become trustees for the wrong reasons, but also to them accepting for the wrong reasons. When I was appointed leader of Radio Worldwide, as far as WEC International, the mission agency I belonged to, was concerned, I was a team leader or ministry leader. However, because our work was very different from that of our mission headquarters, the ministry had separate membership of organisations such as Global Connections (then the Evangelical Missionary Alliance). Therefore, outside WEC I was seen as an agency leader. I was a woman in my mid-thirties and there were then very few women or younger people leading mission agencies. I soon found myself being approached by a number of organisations asking me to join their board or council. I quickly learned to ask myself, and sometimes them, whether the invitation was because they were eager to have me as a 'token' woman or younger person, or whether the request was because of the nature of the work I was involved in or the particular gifts I could bring to their table. I am not the only one who has faced that!

One tends to get approached as the 'token' woman and I wasn't going to be the 'token' woman.

When someone is recommended, it is important for a board to look carefully at what that person would contribute, how they would fit in and whether they would fill a gap.

> *When I was chair, we brought somebody on as a trustee who just didn't fit; it wasn't just that he was not on the same page as the rest of the trustees, but he almost didn't listen to what other people were saying. He wasn't attending regularly – and regular attendance is important. He decided to resign but I was on the brink of going to talk to him about whether being a trustee was a good fit for him.*

When I was looking for a new chair to succeed me at YoYo, a recently retired teacher was recommended to me. From what I was told, she seemed just the sort of person we needed. But nevertheless, there was still a process to go through to make sure both parties understood what would be involved if she did join the board, and that needed to happen before we considered the possibility of her becoming the next chair.

Recruitment

How the invitation to join a board is arrived at varies quite a bit. It may be set out in the governing document, and there is general guidance in the Charity Commission's *The Essential Trustee*:

> When charities recruit new trustees, they should think about:
>
> - the skills and experience the current trustees have, and whether there are any gaps
>
> - ensuring new trustees are eligible to act
>
> - ensuring new trustees do not have serious conflicts of interest, or getting Commission consent and putting procedures in place to manage the conflicts
>
> - how to help new trustees to understand their responsibilities and the charity's work.[1]

An informal approach to looking for new trustees often works well in a local setting where there is a good network between churches. There may be a regular email circulated to church leaders and others and a request in that may elicit suggestions. Current board members, staff and volunteers may be able to make suggestions of potential trustees, who can then be contacted personally. Recruiting this way does depend on whether the charity can reasonably expect all its trustees to be practising Christians. It may not result in finding suitable people or addressing the skills gaps identified. One consultant to trustee boards concluded that for many of them the recruitment process is 'appalling':

> There is very little done in terms of advertising, of skills assessment of what is needed, and it tends to be a personal approach. People are normally asked because they are perceived to have some interest in that charity already, or in an associated one and they say, 'That sounds a good idea, yes.'

When considering an approach to a potential new trustee, it can be helpful to think about why men and women agree to take on roles, because they tend to do so for different reasons. I was interested in finding out what 'belonging' means in church, particularly because of Dr Grace Davie's widely publicised proposition that it is increasingly common for people to believe without belonging, and equally, people are now more likely to belong to church before they believe.[2] I therefore undertook a personal research project which looked at how church 'works', especially socially, for women in the congregation. The findings were published in *Eve's Glue*.[3] A smaller project subsequently looked at how the main findings about women were different for men. Personal experience suggests the factors about belonging which were uncovered then are still relevant, one of which is the reasons behind why men and women take on roles:

Women tend to ask:	Men tend to ask:
Who will I do it with?	Does the job need doing?
Who will I do it for?	Does it use my gifts?
Who asked me to do it?	What role will I have?

Outcome:	
Involvement builds community	A role provides identity

I have found this relevant when approaching new trustees, although as always with gender profiles there are exceptions. I have found it important to get to know a potential new trustee, if possible by at least one face-to-face meeting. A woman may well be interested in knowing who the other trustees are and a bit about them to find out what they might have in common. They may also want to know why I approached them and whether I can be trusted, so I have usually shared something of my background as well as my experience as a trustee. When that recently retired teacher was recommended as a possible future chair for YoYo, we met two or three times and talked at length before any official steps were taken.

On the other hand, a man may not be too bothered about meeting me (although I would always want to if possible), and may be quite happy to correspond by email. He will want to know what useful part he could play in the board if he were to join and what would be expected of him. One such situation was when two people who had been trustees for a while unexpectedly left the board and moved away at about the same time, and most of the remaining trustees had only joined within the previous couple of years. A man who had been our treasurer three years before had resigned when he went to train for ordination. He was now back in York as a curate and not wanting any extra roles in his first year. But we were in the midst of a major change in strategy and I urgently needed someone on the board who knew where we had come from. A conversation with his vicar and an email to him led, after time for the two of them to talk and pray about my request, to him agreeing to join the board as long as all that was expected was for him to attend board meetings without taking on any other role. He proved a very useful addition to the board as he also understood our finances, but finances are a matter for Chapter 11!

For larger or higher profile charities a more professional approach may be necessary, as one large charity found:

> They've only got five trustees at the moment because they've messed up their recruitment process. They have got four more just appointed by going externally. They took on a headhunter who has made a good job of bringing people forward – still too white and middle class in my view, but it's a big step forward and they have diversified from a bunch of friends.

For national or international agencies, it may be necessary to advertise more widely and perhaps even employ a recruitment company to find potential trustees. The board may need to include people from a similar background to those the agency serves:

> Getting people from non-Caucasian backgrounds is difficult. I think that's partly a cultural thing because in some cultures pushing paper around is not really seen as very important – there are better things to do with my time. Finding people from the secular world who have really good business experience and are prepared to use it on behalf of a charity is hard too.

In practice, personal recommendation still carries a lot of weight. But just because someone has been asked to become a trustee does not mean they have to say yes! A good recruitment procedure will allow time to find out what it will entail and whether what would be expected of them matches what they are willing and able to contribute. They will need to get to know the work and the people involved – trustees, staff and possibly also volunteers. That might be quite a simple process, especially for a smaller charity:

We had an approach from the person who was then leading the charity, asking me to be a trustee. We went away and prayed about it and I decided I would like to become a trustee. I sat in on about three meetings so that they could get an understanding of me as a person and I could get an understanding of them and the ministry. I think chemistry is important; how is this going to work? That gives you an opportunity of weighing what a charity is actually doing rather than what you thought it might be doing, and praying about whether this is something God wants you to do.

In a larger charity, or one with quite demanding expectations of trustees, a more specific approach may be helpful all round.

I have sometimes advocated that a 'buddy' be assigned to new members to check in with them from time to time during the first few months, just to manage their expectations or frustrations in relation to their board membership.

Trustees agree to stand for election in a church or are willing to join a trustee board for a variety of reasons, but once the recruitment process has run its course any new member needs to be helped to play a full part as soon as possible. What that part might be we will consider in the next chapter.

Recruiting well shows a board is taking its future seriously, another mark of trustworthiness.

Questions

What made you willing to become a trustee, or if you are not one yet, what would make you willing?

What gifts and skills do you have that are currently or potentially useful on a board?

Do you know anyone whom you could encourage to stand for election in your church, or who would have much to offer to a charity you know of? What steps can you take to help them move towards that?

Has your board ever made a bad appointment? What did you learn from that situation?

6
Playing Your Part
Roles and Responsibilities

*I put in charge of Jerusalem my brother Hanani,
along with Hananiah the commander of the citadel,
because he was a man of integrity and feared God
more than most people do.
(Nehemiah 7:2)*

*Trustees need to understand that it's more than just turning up three or
four times a year and voting on a few things; it's much more involved than
that but also much more fulfilling than that.*

So, you have been elected or appointed as a new trustee –
congratulations! Or the AGM or board has just elected or
appointed one or more new trustees – congratulations! Or
perhaps your new organisation has recently been granted
charitable status so that you are now a trustee – congratulations!
But what happens next?

*When we set up a new Local Mission Partnership I now sit down
with the new trustees and ask them if they understand the
responsibilities. So I make sure that at least the first trustees have a
real understanding of what they've let themselves in for, hoping that
they pass that on to the next trustees.*

That passing on of understanding ideally happens with a good induction. The Church of England's dioceses provide training for new PCC members but in most situations, whether churches of other denominations or none, or separate charities, that 'passing on' has to be done internally:

> Those involved at the very beginning will for the most part share a vision, understand that vision, and understand the story of how that vision came into being. That isn't the case for the second generation or subsequently, for whom it will be important if they are to become part of the ongoing story and develop and protect the vision.

Sometimes, though, the boot is on the other foot. The new trustee may be the one with experience who can help shape a board which has perhaps been struggling or too amateurish in its approach:

> On one board I was on, quite a few people had been trustees elsewhere and had previous experience. It was a highly skilled board, so a lot of people had experience of being on boards and had had charitable experience. There was a good understanding of roles and responsibilities but in my current church board I would say nobody really has an understanding of their roles, responsibilities, and liabilities.

Registering as a charity requires the appointment of trustees, so some people find they have become a trustee almost by accident!

> It became apparent we needed a body that had a distance from an individual church but could represent several. The school were putting up barriers to individual denominations, but by creating a separate body the school was open to us. In that instance we linked up with an umbrella body to give us a little bit more integrity in the eyes of the school. So it was a necessity – to be honest, if I could have avoided it I would have because it created a lot of paperwork and quite a lot of hassle.

In a situation like this, the group need to work together to examine their responsibilities and establish how they can act effectively:

> To move forward we realised we needed to get charitable status. There was a quorum of a few of us who were trying to push the vision forward. I was involved in the vision, trying to make it happen, but it needed to move to a charitable status so that it could properly fund-raise, receive funding etc. We're still in the process of getting a lot of things sorted out, like bank accounts, moving the person who's employed by a church onto the charity, job descriptions, pensions etc. So we're buried in that mundane stuff just now and haven't yet got as far as things like policies for recruiting trustees.

> Trustees of a new Trust now have to think through a lot more what the charity is about and what they have to do. That means the new Trusts are much better at understanding what's involved.

Induction – questions to answer

There are four questions that people ask, often unconsciously, when they first join any new group, and a good induction process will help new trustees to answer these.

Who am I?

This involves considering what you bring to this trustee body: are you the representative of a particular church or denomination, or here because of the gifts and skills you can offer, or perhaps because you are passionate about the ministry. 'Who am I?' also involves asking, who do I have to be to become accepted here? Do I have to offer to take on a responsibility or join a subcommittee, or will that be decided for me? What would ease me in to relationships here – offering to bring cake, being willing to pray publicly, or perhaps spending time individually with other trustees?

If the 'Who am I?' question is not answered, the new trustee may remain hesitant, be wary of contributing, and find it difficult to trust the others on the board.

Who are you?

Ask not only what are other trustees' names, though that is a good start, but where have they come from? What is their personal story? Why are they on this board? What do you, from your background, need to know about the others in order to trust them and to feel confident to join in discussion and put forward ideas? The corollary is, what do the others need to know about you to know you will make a worthwhile contribution?

If 'Who are you?' remains unanswered, it will be hard to make the level of commitment needed, or to join in wholeheartedly when joint action is considered.

What are we here for?

Is the vision and direction clear and does it excite you? What about the strategy? How is the vision achieved by this group? Ask not only what does being a trustee involve, but does it seem to you that this board is heading in the right direction to fulfil why it exists, and doing that in a relevant and appropriate way for the context in which it works?

If a group is not agreed on what they are there for, it can either become very competitive, with everyone battling to get their own ideas listened to, or apathetic as people opt out.

At a vision-building day, the initial question is often why a church or organisation exists; in other words, its purpose. At one such day with a mission agency, half those present said one thing and the other half strongly disagreed and replied quite differently. No wonder they could not agree on future vision and strategy – they were not starting out from the same point! Disagreement like that is rare, but vagueness and uncertainty are unfortunately fairly common. Chapter 2 considered vision and direction, but if this cannot be communicated easily and clearly to a new trustee, that should be a warning sign that the whole board probably needs to work together to rethink what they are here for.

How are we going to do it?

Or, what are the rules round here? Where are the boundaries between the trustee role and that of the staff, so it is clear who does what? How are decisions made and followed through? Who are the real decision makers (not always the chair!)? Do the ground rules work here, or could we consider changing them a bit? If so, how would we go about that?

We will look at these issues later, especially in Chapter 10, but if there are no ground rules, a 'free-for-all' can lead to power struggles as those with clear ideas try to get their own way.

Induction – learning the ropes

Understanding in more detail what a charity does, including some of its history, is important, as also is knowing whether you could work with this group of people. But there is more to it, and a well-planned induction process should provide an introduction to the commitment expected and what being a trustee for that charity will involve:

> There are all sorts of issues around legal and financial responsibilities and safeguarding, which someone wouldn't necessarily understand right from the beginning, as well as the responsibilities towards the Charity Commission. It's not something to take on lightly as there is a commitment and a responsibility.

> In a charity that's been going, say, twenty-five years, there can still be that old attitude of, 'Just come on the board and we'll let you know as you go along what's involved.' A big problem lies with charities that have been going a long time and they don't have proper plans and procedures in place.

A comprehensive induction would include: what the vision and strategy are to achieve what they exist for; the financial position and how funds are raised and spent; particular relevant issues, such as safeguarding if the work is with children or vulnerable adults; something of the history and key people who have been involved; how often the board meets and any other meetings which trustees are expected to attend etc. A good understanding of the Aims and Objects is vital too, although they are not always available or clearly set out for local churches.

> *I think to be honest, the trustees don't always understand the Objects and Aims – I've never seen the Objects and Aims of the Baptist church or a Trust document. I've been a deacon for a year and I've not yet seen anything like that.*

New trustees should be encouraged to read the Charity Commission's publication *The Essential Trustee*, which is available on its website.[1] The charity may have a paper which sets out the role, function and responsibilities of a board member. One board I was on had a three-page document which listed the responsibilities under five headings: spiritual, setting strategy, sharpening, stewardship and statutory. There are various publications written specifically for PCCs, such as *The PCC Member's Essential Guide*,[2] and some more general ones which will be of help to similar groups such as deacons or elders:

> *We need to understand the responsibilities we've got, connect with where discussions are, where direction is. We need to be alerted to where there might be problems, including some of the personality issues which may be around – so a confidential induction helps us to know where we fit, and enables a discussion which helps people to understand where they might have a distinctive contribution – which might be different from why people have encouraged them to join.*

A new trustee needs to know too what policies and procedures an organisation or church has in place. A handbook may exist which brings all this together, though this may be aimed at staff or volunteers rather than trustees. A separate trustee handbook is worth considering:

I haven't found a lot of charities with reasonable handbooks and it is quite surprising the number of charities who don't have anything.

In my current board of trustees I've started pulling together a trustees handbook so we can have clarity in our role.

A good induction or training should enable everyone to make a worthwhile contribution, even if they have never before been in a position with such responsibilities:

I've got considerable experience in the parishes where I've been parish priest, with people who in their wider life didn't hold any roles with particular responsibility in relation to organisations, who may not have come from a strong educational or academic background or have professional skills or experience. But they felt that they were called to the role of PCC, and they've made a great contribution. If people come without knowledge of what responsibility that brings with it, then it's up to us to help them to gain that knowledge and take up that position in an informed way. I always made sure that I met with people when they started on the PCC to help them understand what that meant in a gentle, informal way, but helping them to get hold of the responsibility and the power that comes with that.

An induction is a two-way thing, and needs to work well so a new trustee can play their part:

The way things have changed and regulations have tightened, nowadays I think it's essential that there is some induction.

Job or role descriptions

Some boards have job or role descriptions for their trustees, and dioceses usually make available sample ones for PCC members. Not everyone agrees what they should be called, but they do agree it is important to have something in writing:

I don't like the term 'Job Description' – people equate the term 'job' with remuneration and this is not a remunerated role. I prefer the term 'role' description — I think there's some value in differentiating that. We have a role and responsibility as trustees.

Trustees neither have a Job Description nor are they employees, but simply volunteers. Nevertheless, it is helpful for them to have written details about their appointment, terms of reference, responsibilities etc. These are necessary for them also should there be a breakdown in relationships. For example, my organisation requires all its trustees to confirm every three years that they still agree with our basis of faith, duties of trustees, value, vision and so on. If they don't do so, they are not re-elected as trustees, and we've actually had this happen to one person.

If a generic job or role description has been used, ideally it will have been adapted to the local situation:

I think it would be helpful for PCC members [and deacons, etc] to have an indication of what their role entails, ideally something written down, which would enable them to have an idea of the scope of the role, and the commitment you're asking of them, because that's different in different places. You have PCCs which meet every month and you're expected to attend a subcommittee in between, while there are others which meet four times a year and that's it. So having a clear view of what the expectations are may well take away some of that fear and uncertainty.

Older charities may not have needed to set out expectations for trustees, but it is becoming increasingly necessary:

With most of the charities I've been involved with, that's something which has developed over time, not only to protect and develop the vision but to meet legal requirements, to exercise good governance, to ensure new trustees understand the responsibilities they're taking on — which are not light or small.

If there is not a general Job Description, there may be ones specific to particular roles, especially those usually termed 'Officers': the chair, treasurer and secretary.

General responsibilities

In the 1970s there was a craze for posters with pictures, many of them with animals, and a caption. One I remember from what was a fairly difficult time personally was a picture of meerkats with the wording 'The harder I dig the deeper I get in the hole'. However, the one that came to mind as I planned this chapter was a laid-back gorilla with a bemused look on his face and the caption 'You've just told me more than I wanted to know'. For a new trustee who has just joined a board and had a comprehensive induction, that can be exactly how they feel! But if there has not been an induction for whatever reason, it can be difficult to grasp what is involved.

> *There can be a nice warm feeling: I like this vision, I like these people in this organisation, they're people who have the same values as me, this is something I'm happy to be attached to. But I think the weighty responsibilities that go with being a trustee are not well worked through.*

How to make sense of the role, what part each one can play and how, are all important considerations in moving forward after an induction. Some aspects are clearly defined by the Charity Commission, denominations and legal requirements, but there are other less tangible aspects that are vital as well.

There is a commitment involved – being a trustee is not like joining a club, and it is normally expected that trustees will turn up for meetings unless there is a good reason why they cannot attend. Before they come, they should have read any papers and carried out anything they agreed to do at the last meeting. Once at the meeting it is important to listen carefully, weigh what is said, and respond appropriately:

> *It's about human interaction and you can see lots of powers at play when they're making all their decisions and how they listen to one another.*

We should be able to expect of each other that we know where we are qualified to comment and do so with knowledge rather than opinion.

Confidentiality matters too and it should be made clear to new trustees what they can share and what must be kept within the group of trustees. That is an area where integrity is important:

I've learned about the nature of confidentiality and what would happen if [a particular issue] *got into the public domain – great damage could be done ... Those circumstances can be very difficult, and even some trustees may not know until a very late stage what has had to go on – so you have to be trusted.*

Spiritual responsibility

Paul tells the Christians at Colossae:

Whatever you do, work at it with all your heart, as working for the Lord, not for human masters.
(Colossians 3:23)

He spells out in Romans 12 what that means in relation to using our gifts, where he not only encourages the Christians in Rome to use the gifts God has given them, but in some cases describes how to do it well:

If your gift is prophesying, then prophesy in *accordance with your faith* ... if it is giving, then give *generously*; if it is to lead, do it *diligently*; if it is to show mercy, do it *cheerfully*.
(Romans 12:6-8, emphasis mine)

'In accordance with your faith ... generously ... diligently ... cheerfully ...' are all attitudes that will be needed at some point in a trustee meeting! Jesus wanted His disciples to love each other as He loved them. It wasn't a suggestion – He specifically said it was a command (John 15:12) – but sadly, we don't always behave that way, especially when we feel strongly about an issue.

In a couple of meetings I've told people they need to apologise — at one they didn't and walked out, at another they did.

There are sometimes crucial issues or crises which have to be dealt with at a board meeting, and trustees may have very different views about how to deal with them. Continuing to behave in a Christian manner towards one another while expressing differing opinions is the mark of a healthy respect for each other and, more importantly, a desire to see God's will done in the situation.

The board which had that three-page document on trustees' responsibilities, having put spiritual responsibility as the prime responsibility then listed how that would be worked out in practice:

- We are accountable to God for our stewardship

- We should be seeking the glory of Christ and the extension of his kingdom

- We affirm our commitment to Biblical values in determining our strategies, in relating to all external bodies, in running [the organisation] with integrity, and in establishing and maintaining interpersonal relationships within and without the organisation

- We regard prayer as a major responsibility and seek to be open to the Holy Spirit

- We strive to apply Christian thinking at all levels of our work.

Your board may want to word such a statement differently, but it could be a useful stimulus to think about what spiritual responsibility means in your context. It is particularly helpful in a church, where it is important to differentiate between the spiritual responsibility carried by the minister and that which lies with the trustees.

Joint responsibilities

On the Charity Commission's website there is a helpful summary of trustees' responsibilities, which lists six overall essential areas:

- Ensure your charity is carrying out its purposes for the public benefit

- Comply with your charity's governing document and the law

- Act in your charity's best interests

- Manage your charity's resources responsibly

- Act with reasonable care and skill

- Ensure your charity is accountable.[3]

We have, or will, look at each of these in other chapters, but the reason for repeating them here is to remind trustees that all of a trustee board is responsible corporately for all of these and everyone needs to understand how each of them is carried out in their context. Fulfilling these effectively is actually quite powerful, in that they affect how the ministry and mission of the church or charity are carried out.

People often don't really realise that they're in a position to affect the missional outreach work of the church by their contribution and their attitude, and that PCC isn't just a group of like-minded people getting together to have a discussion about their interests, there are legal responsibilities.

If recruitment or elections have been well planned and efforts made to fill the skills gaps, then each individual will bring something slightly different from the others. It will not necessarily be only one aspect. When we needed a new treasurer for YoYo, I was delighted not only to find one (that often isn't easy!), but to find one who had children in a school which YoYo visited regularly and who could therefore bring feedback from

a child's and a parent's perspective as well as taking on the financial role. People with skills and experience are increasingly important as more and more legislation applies to charities:

> *I watched the board change from being basically a group of missionaries or associated supporters, to having at least half the people being there because they brought specific skills that were relevant as the board transitioned to heavier legal requirements.*

Looking at that Charity Commission list of responsibilities carefully shows that there are some assumptions behind them. We considered in Chapter 3 the need to define how the public will benefit from what a charity or church does. It might not be easy to agree on what the 'charity's best interests' are. For example, in the schools work of YoYo, would it be in the best interests to be able to visit more schools occasionally, or to spend longer and more regular time in fewer? Those sorts of considerations are shaped by vision and strategy. 'Managing ... resources' is often thought of as financial, but what about resources of staff, volunteers, property, time, expertise etc? People from different backgrounds and with a variety of life experiences as well as gifts and skills will be able to contribute breadth to discussions about such issues.

It is not always easy to get the balance right in understanding the overall responsibilities and it is not uncommon to find a board which is so worried about making mistakes that little if any time is given to positive action for the future.

> *I would say quite a lot of trustees are scared about their liabilities. To me if you're running the charity well, I don't see what liabilities there are, but I'm a risk-taker! I think the misunderstandings have got worse as the amount of legislation has increased and the question of what trustees should do has got harder, so trustees are increasingly spending time on the detail which should either be dealt with by staff or by a subcommittee because it means they have less and less time to spend on strategic thinking. Part of the problem is that trustees are often spending too much of their meetings firefighting and far too much is reactive rather than proactive.*

Specific responsibilities

Not everyone on a board has a specific role, but some will have. There are three key positions that every board needs and which are usually termed the 'Officers': chair, treasurer and secretary. The chair is such a vital position that it will have a whole chapter to itself! These Officer roles can be difficult roles to fill because they carry significant responsibility.

> *Treasurer is always challenging, not I think because of the maths but because there are an awful lot of regulations and it requires computer skills and familiarity with the way the church wants it recorded. That's always difficult, particularly when you get to be a bigger charity and you have to do things like double-entry, it begins to go beyond what you can work out for yourself.*
>
> *I think Church Council secretary is also always tricky because I think it's a gift, a skill. The pool you're pulling from for those two roles always feels small, outside or inside a church.*

> *It's definitely harder to find people with financial skills. We have a post which has a financial role, but we recognised the need to back that up with a trustee role with financial knowledge. We've also had difficulty finding people with appropriate legal background — that's very, very hard to find because most lawyers have not worked in that sort of area, not even in corporate bodies outside the charity sector, let alone charitable bodies.*

Treasurer

A good treasurer is a great blessing but the larger the amount of money they are dealing with, the more demanding it becomes.

> *Because the turnover was increasingly going up, we got to the point where we needed someone who was a qualified accountant because of the skill and expertise they bring. The accountant we got comes from another church, but he's still in support of the ethos.*

It is sometimes better to pay for the services of a treasurer than to muddle along with no one really knowing what they are doing. In YoYo we decided to outsource our payroll work, and joined the local CVS (Community Volunteer Service) so we were able to benefit from the favourable rates they charged.

> *I know Trusts which don't have a treasurer. Sometimes they second out the treasurer's responsibility outside the board, which is OK, but then you have to have financial skills within the actual trustee body to understand what's happening.*

It may be especially difficult to find a treasurer in a small church, and it is a particular challenge when the Church of England combines several small parishes into a multi-parish benefice:

> *It may be that in six little churches you have six people who are willing to look after £20,000 pounds each because it's a few big bills: the insurance, the electricity bill and the freewill offering* [or Parish Share] *but the rest of it is fairly small. But they wouldn't be willing to look after £120,000 when the churches come together because it feels too big and scary.*

In one village I heard about a local person who didn't actually go to church regularly but had nevertheless taken on the role of treasurer for the Methodist chapel and the parish church because they wanted to contribute to the overall life of the village. Sometimes it is necessary to think outside the box!

Secretary

A reliable secretary can make a big difference to the smooth running of a trustee board. They may draw up or suggest items for the agenda, particularly by reference to previous minutes or an annual schedule. Gathering and circulating papers in advance enables trustees to understand issues beforehand and so can save a lot of time in a meeting. The secretary may be the person who prompts when a vote is needed and ensures it is taken correctly and recorded accurately. At the meeting they are the person who keeps a record of what goes on and from that creates the minutes.

Taking adequate notes is not the easiest thing: sometimes you get copious notes and think, 'Oh my word!' and other times you get too little and think, 'I don't know what happened at that meeting.' If something went wrong it would leave you quite vulnerable.

I was PCC secretary for several years and did all of these things, but always in consultation with the rector who chaired the meetings. He and I would sometimes meet in advance, not only to agree the agenda, but also to discuss which items should have papers circulated in advance and who should be asked to produce them. Much of our decision-making was by consensus, but some items required a vote in order to have legal weight, and we would agree which those should be. When I was chair of YoYo I liaised with our secretary to ensure all these matters were attended to well. At Christian Research I was secretary to the board, so attended board meetings where my responsibility was to take the minutes. I did not draw up the agenda but I was expected to circulate it, and to gather and circulate papers ahead of a meeting.

There are various other specific roles and responsibilities which a board may need, depending on their particular situation. Whether these are carried by a trustee or outsourced is well worth thinking about.

There is a perception that people need someone with a legal background and they find those difficult to get – there aren't enough Christian lawyers out there. But I would question whether they need someone with a legal background because you can buy in legal expertise, you don't necessarily need it on a trustee body, though some might.

The one people find particularly difficult is someone with marketing or fund-raising experience … they are constantly looking for someone with that background, and I think they probably do need it as that is often the area where a charity is weakest. They find it hard to get someone on the staff with these skills because of the salaries they pay, but you need someone on the trustee body who understands how marketing works, so that when strategic plans are presented there is someone who can critique it appropriately.

Safeguarding is an area where there is an increasing amount of legislation and it is vital for churches and also for charities working with children or vulnerable adults to have access to guidance and help in this important responsibility. Again, the person appointed does not have to be a trustee but should be officially appointed as a safeguarding officer. There are other aspects too where it is important to have someone who understands the responsibilities and liabilities:

> There was a lack of awareness of personal liabilities – for example, all the trustees are financially liable for everything so if everything goes pear-shaped, it is all the trustees' houses which are on the line. Trustees thought that they'd got insurance to protect their personal wealth from any comeback. It then transpired that the insurance was for the church in the case of bad decision-making by the trustees!
>
> There were no HR [human resources] or safeguarding policies and lack of awareness of health and safety issues. So, for example, I asked what the fire evacuation policy was and when did we last have a fire drill. We never had! So I said 'we need to' and was challenged as to why we would need that. I said, because we could be prevented from holding public meetings, which is fairly fundamental to what we do as a church! So we held a fire drill, which didn't go down well. Thankfully I wasn't there as I wouldn't have been able to wipe the smug smile off my face, because they realised that no one in the main auditorium could hear the fire alarm ringing! People were very embarrassed, but then appreciated that having a fire drill was an important thing to do. That's one of numerous examples.

Yes, there is a lot to learn about roles and responsibilities but it is also very rewarding being a trustee, and telling church members or supporters about the joys as well as the frustrations will hopefully encourage more people to consider becoming a trustee:

> I don't think that a lot of the people who support a Trust understand what trustees do. That needs to be written about in communications so supporters understand what trustees do, and not only about the job, but also about the joys of being a trustee. Then people see not only

that trustees are giving up their time, but that the reason they give up their time is that they believe in it and they're getting something back from it.

When all the trustees pull their weight and carry out their roles to the best of their ability, it reveals their trustworthiness in practical ways.

Questions

Is there a well-thought-out induction process for new trustees on your board?

What responsibilities of trustees do you think are the least understood on your board? What would be the best way to address this?

What do you personally 'get back' from being a trustee, and are you able to share that with supporters, other members of the congregation, or friends who might be potential trustees?

7
The Buck Stops Here
Role of the Chair

*It pleased Darius to appoint 120 satraps to rule
throughout the kingdom, with three chief ministers
over them, one of whom was Daniel.
(Daniel 6:1-2)*

*A good chair can help set the culture of meetings, in terms of establishing
or not establishing a healthy environment for debate and discussion. I've
seen both.*

It is fairly safe to say that at some point in your life you will have
come out of a committee-type meeting thinking or perhaps even
saying to someone, 'That was a complete waste of time!' It may
have been at work, church, or in your local community. Other
times you will have left such a meeting pleased with what has
been decided, clear on what action is going to happen and
knowing what you need to do before the next meeting. The
difference is most likely to be due to how the meeting was
conducted, and that is the responsibility of the person who
chaired it.

The chair is the person who holds everything together on a
board of trustees. It is arguably the most important role and
having a man or woman as chair of trustees who has the right

mix of vision, faith and leadership is key to good governance. (In passing, you may wonder why I use the word 'chair' throughout, rather than chairman or chairwoman, or even chairperson. One reason is that the Charity Commission uses the term 'chair', for example in *The Essential Trustee* and similar documents. While that is good guidance, I personally prefer it because the other roles – trustee, treasurer, secretary, as well as others such as vicar, minister, CEO – are all gender neutral. I have never been a card-carrying feminist, but I do much prefer to use the gender-neutral term rather than single out one of the roles on a board to be defined as male or female. If you disagree, please bear with me!)

There are many resources for leaders, Christian and secular, but there are very few which consider the role of chair of trustees. This chapter will therefore deal with the qualities of a good chair, how trustee boards choose a chair, and the differences in the role between a church and an independent charity, rather than looking at leadership *per se*. There is considerable overlap, but not all chairs are good leaders, and conversely not all leaders are good chairs.

The role of the chair

The Charity Commission offers the following summary of the important role of chair.

It may vary depending on the charity's circumstances. The chair usually:

- helps plan and run trustee meetings (and in a membership charity, members' meetings)

- takes the lead on ensuring that meetings are properly run and recorded

- takes the lead on ensuring that trustees comply with their duties and the charity is well governed

- might have a second or casting vote if a vote on a trustees' decision is tied, but only if this is specified in the charity's governing document

- may act as a spokesperson for the charity

- acts as a link between trustees and staff

- line manages the chief executive on behalf of the trustees.[1]

Qualities of a chair

The Charity Commission description is predominantly a businesslike approach with a focus on processes and procedures. While that is undoubtedly important, the people I interviewed when researching for this book were almost unanimous in wanting a relationship dimension as well. This is one of the more succinct responses about the desired approach of a good chair:

Someone who's very consensual, approachable, who is able to challenge and support at the same time, and has the confidence of all his or her peers. Also someone who knows where they are not skilled and ensures people with those skills are on the trustee body.

The two are both needed: a clear understanding of the necessary processes and procedures, married with relational skills which can enable the board to work well together. Combine these with a vision for and excitement about the ministry, and the whole board is motivated:

We had an excellent chair who had come from an administrative background and got people organised and kept people up to date on things. He came in with humility, ready to learn, bringing administrative skills and a background in business. In the first year he set about, at his own expense, travelling overseas with the international secretary, finding out what was going on first-hand. Then he brought back to the rest of us his excitement at what he'd been seeing as well as his knowledge of what we needed to know and act on so as to drive things forward.

Being a chair is quite demanding, so understanding the ministry and being excited about its vision is a significant motivating factor:

The first thing is someone who's really committed to the work and vision of the charity, because if they haven't got that they're not going to give the time and energy that the role is going to need. The chair needs to be somebody who has that and has sufficient time to give. If they haven't got the time for this as well as everything else they may have taken on, they're not going to be a good chair.

Here is a more comprehensive summary of what makes someone a good chair:

A good chair is somebody who has a good, fair mind. They have a good sense of all the governance issues and are a good leader of people. They build great, confidential relationships with the chief executive or the minister. They engage with their trustee board individually and basically shape the discussions – not load them, but shape them – so that they lead a team and are rigorous in testing 'Are we going in the direction we said?' They can delegate work and challenge people in a rewarding rather than a violent way. They do need to be fair and understand different personalities and temperaments and the stress in an organisation. I think they have a great role in counterbalancing the stresses people feel and intervening at times to lay the law down and say 'We mustn't do that until people are feeling better about this', or whatever. They need to keep a watch on the temperature of the organisation.

Nehemiah's qualities

Let's take some of those factors and consider how they were lived out by Nehemiah and can be applied in practice.

A good sense of the issues

Nehemiah knew that his task was not going to be easy, so right at the outset he requested official approval for his mission, as well as permission to obtain the resources he would need. He had realised where problems might arise and did what he could to forestall them.

> If it pleases the king, may I have letters to the governors of Trans-Euphrates, so that they will provide me safe-conduct until I arrive in Judah? And may I have a letter to Asaph, keeper of the royal park, so he will give me timber to make beams for the gates of the citadel by the temple and for the city wall and for the residence I will occupy?
> (Nehemiah 2:7-8)

The very first thing he did on arriving in Jerusalem was to go and inspect the size of the task before him. He did it before he did anything else because he needed to understand what would be involved.

> I went up the valley by night, examining the wall ... The officials did not know where I had gone or what I was doing, because as yet I had said nothing to ... [those] who would be doing the work.
> (Nehemiah 2:15-16)

As the wall grew, there was mounting opposition from those who had a vested interest in Jerusalem not being rebuilt by the Jews. Their opponents eventually resorted to the accusation that Nehemiah had appointed prophets to proclaim him as their king and threatened him with sending that news back to King Artaxerxes (Nehemiah 6:6-7). Nehemiah saw straight through them and sent them the reply:

> Nothing like what you are saying is happening; you are just making it up out of your head.
> (Nehemiah 6:8)

The issues for a church or charity are not always immediately obvious, and it may well require prayer to discern not only what they are but also how they will affect the work, something Nehemiah did repeatedly from the day he heard of the situation back in Jerusalem (Nehemiah 4:4-5,9; 5:19; 6:9,14).

Arriving at a trustee meeting without a clear idea of what the issues are that need to be discussed and without planning how to approach them in the meeting is fairly certain to lead to confusion and a lack of clear outcomes.

A good leader of people

We saw in Chapter 3 on values, image and reputation, that one of Nehemiah's values was an interest in people. He understood how to motivate and organise them. He kept their focus equally on the task of rebuilding and on God. And the response in Nehemiah chapter 3 was amazing: almost everyone set to and built a section of the wall. Later, when the opposition was seemingly getting the upper hand, he encouraged them:

> Don't be afraid of them. Remember the Lord, who is great and awesome, and fight for your families, your sons and your daughters, your wives and your homes.
> (Nehemiah 4:14)

Good relationships between trustees are important, as we will consider in the next chapter. It is fairly straightforward in a good trustee meeting, but sometimes the chair has to step in quite forcefully, especially where people are getting worked up about an issue where there are differing opinions.

> *One of the challenges is that Christian organisations can often begin a meeting with prayer and then behave terribly. I always find that really challenging. It's not to say that people shouldn't disagree about things, but it's the way we engage with the discussion. I've had to remind people about the nature of our being Christians gathering together – not very often, but I have had to do it. I've had to stop people who are being extremely offensive and say to them, 'This is not how we behave as Christians.' I've had to say, 'At the beginning of*

this meeting we are committing ourselves to listening to each other and that we'll respect each other even if we don't agree with each other.' And I've had to remind people about that during the meeting.

For a trustee to leave a meeting feeling they have made a worthwhile contribution, which was listened to, is as much about how the chair led the meeting as it is about the trustee's willingness to speak up.

They can delegate work

When the enemies threatened to attack, Nehemiah acted immediately. Some of the people were taken off wall-building to become sentries. Did they resent being asked to stop building in order to stand guard? It seems unlikely; Nehemiah was finding solutions to a tough problem by involving everyone in confronting the danger:

> I stationed some of the people behind the lowest points of the wall at the exposed places, posting them by families ... From that day on, half of my men did the work, while the other half were equipped with spears, shields, bows and armour.
> (Nehemiah 4:13,16)

A chair who tries to do everything will soon be overwhelmed by the amount of time and work involved, especially in a larger organisation or church. Certain things definitely ought to be delegated, which is where a good secretary and competent treasurer are, literally, a Godsend. Actively involving other trustees helps those individuals feel valued and strengthens their sense of responsibility. I have always considered my role as chair to be overseeing and coordinating the work of the board, which inevitably means delegation. When there is a strong sense of trusting one another and recognition of people's different gifts and contributions, it has often been true that another trustee could carry something through better than I could, though always with my support and encouragement.

Challenge people in a rewarding rather than a confrontational way

Once the wall had been completed there was a gathering to read the book of the Law of Moses (Nehemiah 8:1-3). As the people listened and had the Law explained to them, they realised how far they had fallen short of it. We read that all the people were weeping and Nehemiah could easily have condemned them. Instead he directed them to:

> Go and enjoy choice food and sweet drinks, and send some to those who have nothing prepared. This day is holy to our Lord. Do not grieve, for the joy of the LORD is your strength.
> (Nehemiah 8:10)

The end of that verse is often quoted but we rarely think about the context: it was challenging, but instead of judging the people because they had broken the Law, Nehemiah rewarded them. Trustee boards do sometimes go through challenging and difficult times, but acknowledging that with a positive gesture goes a long way in strengthening trust and relationships. A meal out, or even something as simple as bringing home-made cake to the next meeting, does wonders for trustees' willingness to press on.

Intervening at times to lay down the law

Nehemiah did this on more than one occasion when he found that the Law of Moses had been broken. The clearest examples are in chapter 13 where he discovered that the temple had been misused when Tobiah had moved into one of the rooms with Eliashib's permission. He 'threw all Tobiah's household goods out of the room' (v8) and returned it to its proper use. Later he dealt quite harshly with men who had married non-Jewish women. In our context it is vital that the chair knows what laws are relevant to the church or organisation and ensures what the Charity Commission terms 'compliance'. Going back to that description of Daniel, the chair should do everything possible to ensure the board is 'neither corrupt nor negligent'.

Responsibilities

The responsibilities of a chair are much wider than the actual two or three hours or so of a board meeting. They start well before with good planning and preparation and continue afterwards to ensure that agreed actions and decisions are carried through:

> I absolutely abhor it when you turn up for a meeting and the agenda is put in front of you, and no papers to go with it.

> I've been in a number of situations where we've had a weak chair. That's made board meetings difficult to prepare for and difficult in the action of them. We now get better agendas earlier and a good set of explanatory notes so that we know the issues that are going to be coming up. There is good preparation for meetings — in our case it is the chair who does that, makes sure that the agenda is put together and there are good explanatory notes. Though he might be getting some of that from others, he gathers it all together. At the meeting he would be making sure that everyone had a chance to speak, summarising, checking that everyone is happy with the decisions that are being made — and explicitly making sure that we have made a decision and that it has been minuted. In our case the chair would take responsibility to monitor the action of those responsibilities — so he's a very active chair.

The actual running of the meeting is up to the chair, often with support and guidance from the secretary. A well-run meeting is much more productive and even enjoyable than a badly run one:

> A group of trustees may be a place where there are fantastic ideas for all sorts of brilliant initiatives but at the next meeting they're still discussing the same things; nothing has actually moved on. You need a chair and a secretary who can keep the meeting on track, can focus on those things which are most important at that moment in time but

also refer back to previous action points to check progress. If you know you're going to another meeting and there on the record of the minutes of the last meeting it said you'll do something, even if you only do it at the eleventh hour, you're going to do it, rather than sit there at the meeting and say, 'Oh yes, I said I was going to do that but I haven't done anything about it.'

A good meeting has to have personality, not just be enslaved to the task; even the difficult meetings have to have a degree of fulfilment and enjoyment because you're taking a responsibility and there has to be a sense that different people with different gifting and skills are wanting to work together. That's not easy to get to but that would be a really successful meeting.

It takes skill to run a meeting well. Some chairs may bring those skills from their business life, but my experience is that they develop the more you do it!

I don't think chairs do that bad a job but they do need to know how to draw out the quiet person in a meeting, how to facilitate good conversation, how to make sure the creative voice speaks out, how to get a decision at the end of a meeting which everyone owns. How many chairs are there around who have those skills? – and many ministers don't have them either!

It is part of the chair's role to help other trustees understand their responsibilities and to play their part, so it may involve knowing how to handle people who can be awkward:

It can become unhelpful when people don't understand the responsibility because you may need to challenge them but actually they're such lovely people that you don't want to do it. Good chairmanship is a really crucial thing in this.

You want there to be a warm and relaxed environment in a church meeting, which will enable people to participate, but on the other hand people need to understand the responsibilities that they hold. As chair you need to enable everybody to engage in taking those responsibilities

on board. In any such group you will almost inevitably have 'stock'
characters who will behave in particular ways and will quite often try
to dominate meetings. But if you're asking people to take on trustee
responsibilities you have to enable everyone to engage with the issues
and step into their role as trustees. They need, first of all, knowledge
of what the responsibilities are and secondly to be able to accept the
role without other people riding over them – you can't ask people to
carry that responsibility without enabling them to do it.

A chair is a facilitator who can elicit helpful contributions from
all the trustees and guide them towards a consensus:

The success of a trustee meeting is very much down to the process of
the meeting, and the chair has responsibility for that process. I'm a
process person, a facilitative-type person. I want a clear agenda and
from that I would produce for myself a working agenda that would
guide me through the meeting, with specific questions that needed to
be raised, where I would try to put in a break, where I would try to
put in prayer. I would consider what the possible outcomes might be.
I'm interested in getting results, but I often don't mind what the results
are. I don't want to be driving to get the results that I want, I'm
looking for results to come from the consensus of the group – I'm
looking to build consensus all the time.

The goal is for decisions to be made collaboratively and that means
trying to get everybody to have their say, whether they agree or not.
The best meetings I chair are the ones where we go in with one idea
and come out with a completely different idea and there's been a
shaping. We haven't gone in with a fait accompli, we've gone in with
a problem, an idea, and we've resolved it in the meeting. That to me
is a sign of a good meeting, particularly if we can hear the negatives
and address them ... one of the hard things about being a chair is
hearing the minority view in the meeting rather than after the meeting.

There is an important point there – 'I don't want to be driving
to get the results that I want' – being chair does not mean
getting your own way! However, the chair is also a trustee and
so has the right to share their own opinion. Sometimes a board
needs to hear the chair's opinion, which may be based on a

wider understanding of the issue under discussion or previous experience of a similar situation.

A chair's responsibilities continue after a trustee meeting is over. In many situations the CEO is present at trustee meetings to observe and inform. That enables feedback to other staff or volunteers, but if the CEO is not in the meeting then it is the chair's role to be the go-between. In YoYo, even though the CEO did attend meetings, I also made a point of going to the next staff meeting to report on the trustees' meeting and hear any reaction or response. This was particularly important if we had made a difficult decision: one time we sadly had to make someone redundant, and explaining how that process would take place and giving staff an opportunity to speak out about it meant I could take the flak rather than the CEO. It is, though, very important that the chair does not undermine the CEO and that the boundaries of their responsibilities are clearly understood and maintained.

The chair often acts as the CEO's line manager as well, which is especially important in an independent charity. In a church which is part of a denomination, there are dioceses or region-wide structures in place, which means a minister has people to turn to. In an independent church or a separate charity the chair needs to provide at least some of that support:

> The relationship between the chair and the CEO is crucial, so I saw it as my job to support him in his role. Every month I either met with him or had a Skype call so that we didn't end up with big surprises. I did his appraisal and I held him to account too for his time off, especially when work was very heavy. I saw that as one of my principal roles, to support him in doing his job. Although you have to have a relationship with your CEO, you have to be able to be objective and dispassionate at times, and that's a tension which you have to hold. You have to do some pretty heavy stuff together and you have to be able, as a chair, to be objective about that relationship and sometimes stand back and ask hard questions.

In my view the relationship between the chair and the CEO is critical, so I met with the CEO every six weeks to keep informed, get an update on how things are going, see how he is doing because you have a responsibility for the pastoral well-being of the CEO – I was also his line manager. Being CEO can be a very lonely role and he or she needs someone to share some of the burdens with.

That relationship is particularly important if the charity hits a crisis. Then the chair and CEO may need to work together to resolve the situation if possible:

Both the chair and the CEO carry a huge responsibility so if it's serious enough I think they should both take the responsibility and see what needs to be changed.

They may not even be able to share what's happening with the rest of the staff or trustees in a case where confidentiality is paramount:

As long as the controversy is not about the chair, the chair of trustees has a crucially important role to be a friend to those bearing the heat of the situation, a wise judge and someone who can discern and discuss what the boundaries of confidentiality are. Those circumstances can be very difficult, and some trustees may not know until a very late stage what has had to go on – so you have to be trusted.

Differences between a church and a separate charity

There are several ways in which the role of a chair is different in a church than in a separate charity. Some of these are linked to the nature of the relationships among board members, which we'll consider in the next chapter, but some of the differences are about the actual role.

Minister chairs, CEO does not

In a charity, the role of CEO and chair are distinctly separate: the CEO is an employee, and is not usually a member of the board. Indeed, if they are a trustee that can cause difficulties:

Historically we had a titular chair but the meeting was actually led by the staff member who was doing the legal, financial and administrative work so there was no chair activity. In other situations, having the CEO on the board has been a bad situation because they tended to want to lead the trustees as they led the organisation – they weren't technically on the board but they were deferred to too much.

The key thing is the relationship between the chair and the CEO so that they could work well together, listen to one another, learn from one another. That relationship is critical for good governance – if that relationship is not working, if there's a breakdown in it, that's a danger signal.

In most churches the minister would expect, and usually be expected, to take the role of chair of meetings, including those which do trustee business, because they are the church leader. This can be a difficult balance. It is all too easy for some board members to defer to the minister because he or she is their spiritual leader and therefore must be right. This can be a real problem, especially in areas where the minister has little or no experience, such as a big building project. They do indeed carry the responsibility for overall leadership, but that does not mean they always need to chair meetings:

When I was a churchwarden, the vicar was a good chair, but when he wasn't there for any reason I often chaired the meetings. In my current church there is a lay chair of the PCC.

It is true that vicars are expected to be the chair of their PCC, but legally they don't have to be. In my charity we sometimes ask other trustees to chair meetings, especially as my hearing is poor. Different modus operandi and personality of a fresh chair for meetings can be stimulating.

There are pros and cons to the minister or vicar being chair of the church's trustees:

> *The pros are that they're usually the person who has the knowledge of the wider issues. That can sometimes be the experience of other people on the PCC but I think the vicar has a unique position in that respect. They know about almost everything that's going on in their area and what the needs of the community are. Sometimes that's difficult to handle because some of what they know is confidential. Generally, people, even if they work in the local community, are working in professions or roles where they see one aspect of the life of the community. Clergy are in a unique position of seeing life across the board in their community in a way that nobody else does. So there are real pros to that because the vicar brings all of that with them into the wider discussion, and that was certainly true in my parish experience.*
>
> *Cons: I've come across situations where there is deference to people in authority and there really can be in relation to the clergy, although I must say that my experience is more that people are quite feisty – and that's good, I like that! There doesn't seem to be a lot of kowtowing to the clergy; there's respect for them but people are prepared to challenge them, which I think is good. But it can be problematic if people give them too much respect.*

Leadership and collective responsibility

A board is collectively responsible for decisions, so no one trustee is free to act alone, whether making a decision without consulting others on the board, or changing a decision without approval. This is a particular temptation for the chair. It is much clearer to implement in a separate charity, but it also applies to a church board when its members are acting as trustees:

> *The chair of trustees and the senior pastor basically decided to change what was agreed and have a slightly different approach. I challenged that and said it should have been decided by trustees, seeing as the previous course of action had been approved by a full board of trustees.*

Overall leadership of a church is the responsibility of the minister, but that does not give them freedom to act independently when it comes to trustee responsibilities. This can at times cause confusion, and may be exacerbated by the theological position of the church, whatever its denomination:

One of the challenges is that at, if you like, the two extremes of the theological spectrum in different ways you have the sense that the minister is a very powerful individual. In the middle ground you quite often find a quite collegiate environment. If you go to the 'Father knows best' high Anglo-Catholic end, they're probably running their PCCs very well, meeting every month, but there's a danger of deference. At the other end of the spectrum where it is all about 'Here is our leader who has been called of God to lead us', you may have a two- or three-man leadership (and it usually is men) who may or may not be part of the PCC, but they're actually running the church. So sometimes in more evangelical churches the division of responsibilities between the legal PCC charity and the leadership becomes quite blurred. You can get tensions then, where the PCC says, 'But aren't we supposed to have a part in those decisions?' and the leader says the PCC are being really difficult and trying to block his every move.

There have been times when things haven't gone quite to plan and I've been concerned as to whether I do have any backing behind me, but that's probably more a ministry thing than a trustee thing. As a trustee you have the confidence of making decisions together but in ministry you're more on your own. Some trustees know the rules and they play by the book and those people, when you're on their side, will back you, but if you cross them, they'll use it against you.

This becomes more of an issue when a minister chairs an independent charity because unless they are careful to think about the difference in the role, they are likely to try to lead in the same way as they do in their church:

Some chairs are in danger if they're not careful of becoming the effective CEO and they do need to understand that they are not a top CEO over the staff member CEO. They only represent the whole trustee body; they can only act on behalf of and after consultation with the whole trustee body.

Appointing/choosing a chair

We have already noted that in a church situation the obvious choice for chair of trustees is the minister, though it is possible – and often wise – to appoint someone else to take the role. However, in a charity there is no such seemingly obvious choice and it is up to the board themselves to appoint one of their members to be chair or to find someone new to join them as chair. One of the dangers is someone who wants to be chair for the wrong reason.

It is important that the chair is not someone who wants the job out of vanity.

Sometimes there's someone who, perhaps because of their ego, wants to lead, 'I'll do a great job, this is for me', and they get into leadership but then they just bully everybody else into doing what they want. They come across as, 'This is how I think the Trust should be run', and nobody else gets a say and there's no proper debate.

Finding a new chair can be really difficult for some charities:

My experience is that the trustees will nominate someone who is already a trustee and ask them to be chair. Perhaps that person has a bit of a guilt trip and agrees to do it. Very few think about it ahead of time and ask questions like, 'Who is going to be the next chair?' and 'Why do we think they'll make a good chair?' A lot of Trusts find the person who's done the most amount of work or been a trustee the longest and ask them to be the next chair. So unfortunately the person who's the most committed usually becomes the next chair. While they are committed, they've been seen to give time and perhaps they're very good at what they are doing, they may not be a leader, they may not be good at managing people. Part of being chair is managing the rest of the trustees, making sure everyone has their say and does what they've said they'll do. Very often people who are good at doing the work are not good at the leadership side of things. Sadly, that person, because they're committed, tries to do everything and can get burnt out in a year or two.

A decision made in that way, almost by default, can lead to someone taking on a role they don't understand:

As a chair I felt I just got thrown into it. I'd observed what the previous chair did and I've chaired other things so I had a bit of experience I could bring to bear on the role, but I soon realised that a chair has a significant role which I think is perhaps not fully understood. The person who leads the staff, everyone understands that role, but I think perhaps the chair's role – not everyone understands that.

Reflecting on how a good chair of trustees leaves those tracks of trustworthiness made me think of Good King Wenceslas!

Mark my footsteps, good my page,
Tread thou in them boldly[2]

Being chair of a board of trustees is demanding, time-consuming and carries quite a lot of responsibility. But it can be hugely rewarding. Enabling a church or charity to move forward, to be more effective in its ministry, and see the kingdom of God growing as a result, is a real joy.

Questions

If you are already chair:
What do you find most rewarding about the role?
What do you find most difficult?
What steps could you take to help you carry out your responsibilities more effectively?

If you are considering becoming a chair:
What gifts or experience would you bring to the role?
Where would you need training, or support from other trustees, to be effective?

If your board is looking for a new chair:
What skills are missing from the present board?
Have you considered looking outside your current group of trustees to find the right person?

8
Bricks or a Building
Relationships and Boundaries

*In humility value others above yourselves, not looking
to your own interests but each of you to the interests
of the others.*
(Philippians 2:3-4)

*Relationships within the trustee board and between the trustees, the CEO
and the staff, are important.*

Our house developed a nasty crack in a side wall. It could have
been caused by the so-called Boxing Day floods in York at the
end of 2015, but the insurance company was not convinced, so
we had to organise – and pay for! – getting it repaired. A
member of my church had the right skills to take it on and he
made a superb job of it, but what delighted me most was that
he matched the replacement bricks with the originals so well
that it is now impossible to see where the crack was.

The book of Nehemiah is about building, though I am not
the first one to notice that! When I googled 'books on
Nehemiah' I was presented with more than twenty titles.
Charles Swindoll's *Hand Me Another Brick*[1] takes Nehemiah and
his wall-building as 'a timeless example of leadership', while

Alan Redpath's Christian classic, *Victorious Christian Service*,[2] draws out elements of building a 'structurally sound spiritual walk'. Building a wall is hard work, but a pile of bricks is no use unless each one is built into its place. In the same way, a collection of trustees achieve little unless they learn to work together, each one contributing their particular gifts and skills to fill a gap in the wall. Ideally, they will fit together so well that there are no cracks! And their wall will dovetail into an adjoining wall, which is the staff and volunteers of a charity or the congregation in a church.

The relationship among trustees is an area where Charity Commission guidelines are not much help:

> *My problem with the Charity Commission is that it is all about the fiduciary side – it does very little about the strategic and visionary work of trustees or about relationships. It's only interested in the regulatory issues, so it misses out how teams work, it misses out the team responsibility – it does talk a bit about the corporate need to make decisions jointly but it does very little about the strategic role of trustees or about understanding the environment the charity is operating in. It's backward-looking all the time.*

> *If you look at the Charity Commission website, there's nothing about taking time out, having retreat together, going away together. I'm fortunate in that I'm invited by a trustee body to its retreat because they're either thinking about their charity's future or about its governance and they can't do that within normal formal meetings. So I often end up with them in nice retreat centres – and all of them say it's the best meeting of the year! But I don't think there's enough of that.*

> *The informal is much more difficult when you are scattered across the country, therefore you have to put in place formal mechanisms to create the informal opportunities. The biggest issue for trustees is the time implications, and that is very difficult in the business world in which most men and women now operate: it's very hard for them to get time off on a regular basis, so trustee meetings are getting squeezed into evenings and Saturdays if you want people who are working*

rather than retired. That makes it even more difficult to do the
informal because it's even difficult to find time for the formal meetings.

Relationships between trustees matter because they affect how
the board carries out its work: do they trust each other, does
everyone pull their weight, can they disagree in a helpful way?

> *The relational dynamics of the board were very, very important,*
> *because we all were actively involved in decision-making – we didn't*
> *always agree but there was no animosity in decision-making. There*
> *was a genuine freedom to disagree and have a contradictory opinion*
> *to someone else without any animosity. In the board I have just joined,*
> *people are starting to become aware that the relational dynamics of*
> *the board are important to be able to have good decision-making.*

Different kinds of relationships

There is a fundamental difference in the relationships trustees
of a church have with each other compared to those in most
charities. In a church the trustees live in the same area, know
each other before they are elected and may have worked
together in one of the church's activities. A charity usually draws
trustees from a wider area, perhaps nationally or even
internationally, and it is quite likely that they have never met
before they join the board. Both scenarios have pluses and
minuses:

> *In a church people are thrown together much more intimately and you*
> *overlap with them in all sorts of different ways; there's not just one*
> *singular relationship with the charity. You're involved in a diverse*
> *range of ministries in that church, with a wide range of people and*
> *diverse pastoral situations. All sorts of family relationships can come*
> *into play in churches, which is much less likely to happen in charities.*
> *I think governance in church life is far from easy because of those*
> *situations – people have longer histories which come to bear on*
> *decisions; sometimes it's the glue and that's good, but sometimes it's*
> *a real problem.*

Such close relationships may also exist in a small, local charity. They are particularly likely in one which has grown out of one church or was created to support one individual and so the first trustees are all friends or family of that person:

> That's good in that they understand one another but it can be a con in terms of process. They might have a conversation outside a trustee meeting and then think a decision has been made, or people may not say something because they don't want to disagree with a friend and upset them. The danger is that instead of doing the best for the charity, people can think about not upsetting someone who is a friend, so the question is what comes first, 'I don't want to upset my friend' or 'This is not in the best interests of the Trust so I'll speak up'?

When board members do not know each other before they become a trustee, then relationships between them have to start from scratch. That is particularly true when people come from various locations or different Christian backgrounds:

> Like all relationships the more time you spend together the deeper it goes, so any opportunities trustees have to get together casually, or go away for a weekend are important. That happens more easily in a church situation where you're functioning quite closely together on a number of different levels both in ministry and socially, so that builds relationships. When you've got board members scattered around the country that's more difficult: sometimes having two or three days together that are a mixture of business and relationship-building, having time to get to know what's going on in individuals' lives, how to pray for one another — when people are wrestling with big decisions it's important to know what's on one another's hearts. Sometimes that's hard because some of the people who are on boards are very busy and these extra times can be hard for them to find time to take part in, but when it's possible it's a great blessing.

I have experienced these differences on boards. Locally most of us did not know one another before we joined the YoYo board but it was easy to, say, have coffee together; on a PCC I was already working alongside others in the youth work or had been in the same home group; while on the various boards I have been on whose trustees were drawn from across the country I had only met one or two previously.

Developing relationships between trustees

I can certainly attest to the value of creating time to get to know other trustees, especially on a more scattered board:

> *I do think there needs to be a sense of connection, so once a year we had a twenty-four-hour board meeting where we stayed overnight. That evening we went out and had a meal together and chatted so we had time and space that wasn't business. It was more efficient in terms of business, actually, because you only made the one journey but you had a long half-day each side.*

Something like that can be helpful even for a locally based board:

> *One of the things I found really helpful was the amount we did together outside of trustee meetings – various things including whole weekends away to focus on the vision, to pray together, to eat together, to have fun together, to build a bond between a group of people who otherwise wouldn't know each other that well. Where that has been the case, it has really benefited the work of a charity – but it hasn't been the case with every charity I've been involved with. Building relationships outside of the meeting can be really helpful.*

> *We meet up outside trustee meetings, we socialise, we chat, we talk about life – more than just the charity, so we can pray together and pray for each other. I suppose we're trying to build up a sense of family as a group. Because it's quite a small charity there is a sense that we're all one family but with different roles.*

Building strong relationships is not only so trustees feel comfortable with one another, it can also make for more productive working:

Trustees should be quite demanding of each other: there's a mutual accountability and I think the chair should encourage the building of various relationships, not to create divisive sub-groups but to get people sharing ideas and working together in creative groups. There needs to be time for them to talk together, to share something of life together and, if they're disposed to, to pray together. Then it's good to have specific times when a board and leadership meet together without an agenda to, as it were, take the temperature together of where the organisation is at.

Trustee and staff relationships

Trustees not only need to get on well with one another, they need good relationships with the people who do the day-to-day work of the charity or maintain the life and ministry of a church. Those people may be employed or volunteers of a charity or members of the congregation in a church. Without those good relationships, the work of trustees – and of the leadership – is more difficult, partly because they do not trust each other, but also because they may not understand what each contributes to the organisation or church:

Some of the challenges in the current board are the legacy issues where the church leadership and board of trustees didn't get on at all and had a mutual distrust.

We needed to hear from the senior staff. The difficulty was that the CEO thought the trustees were interfering. This had become an issue before I became chair – trustees had been discouraged from going to the headquarters. I know the previous chair regularly popped in, but trustees were seen as people who were 'out there', who had no idea what the ministry was doing, who just interfered. The secret is in the word, 'trustees' – trustees need to be trusted not only by the staff but also by the supporters.

Those kinds of situations are not at all helpful because neither the trustees nor the staff are able to support and enable each other in a way that furthers the ministry. There are various ways of trying to engender good relationships:

> I personally think that you have to do a range of things that are relationship-based and are not about hierarchy. I am all for very, very 'flat' structures, where people recognise different levels of responsibility but equal status and the vital importance of each person, whether trustee or staff, to the enterprise as a whole. You can only do that by having time together, by listening to each other, doing something social together, and sharing some of the tough issues of the organisation together. Trustees need to be available, to be good listeners and wise responders to criticism. In churches people make all sorts of criticisms, get all sorts of ideas, which are not solidly based on facts or what is really being attempted, and sometimes a fear of change comes out in really odd ways. So I think leaders and trustees need to spend quite a bit of time just engaging with people.

A church context varies: if there is only one minister and no other staff, then that person will almost certainly also be a trustee. It is different in a larger church, especially in a denomination, such as the Church of England, which has rules about whether church staff can or cannot be trustees:

> Some of the rules that have been passed recently can be helpful for some churches and unhelpful for others. It is now far easier for those who are employed to be members of PCCs. It was never completely impossible, but generally the rule was that if you were already employed you could be elected to the PCC but not the other way round, and now some of those restrictions have been lifted. But if you have a large staff then you could see all those people being appointed to the PCC and it could become a bit unwieldy.

Including senior staff, or perhaps all the staff if it is a small team, in the informal events and away days can be tremendously helpful. One of the first boards I was on spent a whole day in the organisation's offices once a year. Part of the day was a time for individuals to get to know each other, part a gathering of everyone to eat lunch as well as to share and pray together, and part a separate trustee meeting when staff members who did not normally attend a board meeting could tell us about issues affecting their aspect of the work:

> *In charities the board can seem way 'out there' and not really close to the staff or close to the issues. It's important for people to know the function of the board, why we have it, and for the board members too to value the staff as people, not just for the work they do.*

> *Multi-day meetings have been a great improvement for us. We have one a year when the executive team and the trustees use the same venue and have meetings, eating together and then meeting, either together or separately. That's been very useful.*

These relationships between trustees and staff are helpful in understanding and motivating people, both ways round. But there is a limit to how far they can go:

> *There's a level of intimacy that you can't get to, you're not able to be the 'buddy', because there are times when you need to make a hard decision – perhaps you have to make some redundancies and so this or that person will have to go. The level of relationship needs to be that I am interested in you, I value you as a person, I'm thankful for you, I value what you do, I'll pray for you, but I can't be your 'best buddy' because of the kind of role that I play.*

There are situations from time to time where confidentiality within the board is vital, for example, if there is the need to consider whether to make redundancies, or even to close down the charity. Letting the cat out of the bag on such an issue before there is a clear decision on what to do and how to do it creates uncertainty and distrust and usually ends up being very counterproductive:

> *There's nothing worse than gossip, which can cause enormous damage in communities, especially small ones.*

Paul's perspective

In Philippians 2:5-11 Paul writes one of his most humbling and poetic passages about how God became a human being in the person of Jesus Christ. Paul challenges his readers to have the same attitude as Christ, and he precedes and follows the sublime poem with a challenge to have good relationships. In the early verses he pleads with the Philippian church to make his

> ... joy complete by being like-minded, having the same love, being one in spirit and of one mind. Do nothing out of selfish ambition or vain conceit. Rather, in humility value others above yourselves.
> (Philippians 2:2-3)

He follows the poem with a plea for obedience to God and to work at our salvation, and then asks that they:

> Do everything without grumbling or arguing.
> (Philippians 2:14)

This is such a high standard, and yet Paul is convinced that the people in that young church could demonstrate the love of Christ by their attitude to one another. I wonder what our churches would be like if every one of us made the effort to live in this Christ-like way? However, it is not only a challenge to whole churches but also for any community of God's people, however small or large. Some of what he asks for is actually exactly what is expected of trustees: they are required to act in the best interests of the charity and not in their own interests, to come to decisions by debate and discussion rather than destructive arguing with each other, and to always act for the benefit of those whom the charity serves and therefore not out of personal ambition. Christian trustees perhaps have an even greater responsibility to act in this way, because they have the two reasons for doing it: charity requirements plus Paul's encouragement.

There is an old Jewish joke that says if you've got two rabbis you've probably got three opinions, and often the church seems like that as well. Not only are there big theological differences, smouldering resentments from historical events long ago, and radical variations in styles of worship. There are also personality cults, clashes over leadership style, arguments on issues of moral behaviour, cultural politics, and so on.[3]

Those problems are more common than we like to think and are often deep-rooted. Locally there are two villages which to someone driving through seem like one, but there is deep distrust between them because one village was Saxon in origin and the other was Viking. There is one vicar for both parish churches – potentially difficult! When trustees come from different theological backgrounds it can be hard work to build good, trusting relationships, and difficulties can arise over things such as whether people are used to formal or informal prayer, or comfortable to share communion together without a priest present. Then there are issues like what you do about the expectation for diversity, especially if you have differing opinions on LGBTQ+ matters. People may or may not be comfortable with applying for funding from the Lottery. There are so many ways in which our different backgrounds can lead to disagreement which, if not confronted, festers into distrust. I have found it is best to openly discuss such differences, not only with individual trustees but with the whole board so that you all understand where others are coming from. It is wise to minute such discussion or decisions in case you are challenged on the matter so that you can at least prove it has been discussed.

Conflicts of interest and of loyalty

While it is great to have good relationships within a board, it is important to remember that we all have a wide variety of other relationships in our lives and sometimes this can lead to what is termed conflict of interest, or conflict of loyalty. There have to be boundaries, and understanding where those lie is not always straightforward:

> *You're wearing a slightly different hat wherever you go and some people find it difficult to know what the boundaries are between those different roles, to remind them to think about their various roles and declare when they have a conflict of interest. We need to remember what other things we bring with us into a situation. I'm not sure there's enough emphasis yet on the confidentiality of information so that it's not carried from one place to another. For clergy it should be second nature, though it isn't always, and for other people if it isn't within their professional experience where they are practising that all the time, they need to learn to do it. They need, too, to be aware of the implications of a decision for other people.*

Conflicts of interest or loyalty arise in all sorts of ways:

> *All our churches and organisations are absolutely riddled with conflicts of interest. Conflicts of interest can be about financial gain, but the ones that get missed are what are technically called conflicts of loyalty. So if you're a trustee, say, of two closely related charities, and you're in the meeting of charity A, you have to take your decisions for the benefit and furtherance of that charity, ignoring the effect it may have on charity B where you also have an interest in seeing it do well. You must use the resources of charity A for the benefit of charity A and it must not be for the benefit of charity B even if it's a good idea. Very, very woolly thinking takes place in Christian areas where that sort of situation occurs. So a fund of money could be there and people think 'there's need over here, so let's do this' and it could be quite illegal to do that but the good-naturedness of it all overrides recognising that.*

> *For example, you need some work done and Jim, the local joiner, is married to the flower arranger so you just give the work to Jim and don't consider that there are possible trustee benefits. Giving the work to Jim is just part of being a church family. But actually, in Trust law, PCCs are not exempt from the need to make sure that that individual wasn't part of the decision, it was duly weighed and so on.*

> *It's all do-able, but people need to understand how to do it in such as way that they stay beyond reproach.*

These conflicts occur for the best of reasons, but almost always where the potential difficulties have not been thought through:

> *It can be a particular issue in small local charities where they are set up to support one person and so the original trustees are very likely to be family and friends and you may have a relative of a beneficiary on the board. It's important to have a conflict of interest policy so that when there is a conflict of interest, they declare it. I actually hold a register of conflicts of interest. Another issue is members of the same family serving on a board: at my previous church there was an unwritten rule that husband and wife could not both be PCC members, nor could spouses of church staff, so that there was not that conflict of interest built in from the start.*

> *The smaller Trusts will have policies about finance so that so-and-so's brother-in-law doesn't get the job just because so-and-so knows he could do it, but they have that policy because of finance, not because of conflicts of loyalty. I have seen situations where the spouse of a worker may be on the board – we can't make it mandatory but we do strongly encourage that they don't do that – but if they want to do it they should have a policy in place to set out what it means to have that conflict of interest situation. They need to understand what it means when they are discussing salaries, work and other things because it's totally inappropriate for the spouse to be in those conversations.*

It can be particularly difficult for church leaders to grapple with a wide range of potential conflicts of interest, often affecting their own position:

> *The very nature of the Church Council is a conflict of interest, because I am an employee and as chair I could shape things to give myself an easy life if I wanted to. In a church there are so many intertwining conflicts that it's quite hard to unpick them. They would be raised by those who are familiar with business, but other people wouldn't be aware to raise them. At one of my churches we're looking to make an*

appointment and one of the people applying is a member at another
of my churches, so I've said that I can't be on the appointment panel
because that would put me in an awkward situation.

My wife refuses to be on the Church Council because she feels she
would be in a position to have undue influence, but that's her personal
preference because at another church locally the minister's wife is chief
steward so she would automatically be on the Church Council. I'm
wary of that because it is a conflict. In a charity what is said in a
meeting stays in a meeting unless it is explicitly stated otherwise, but
in a church there is a blurring because the church leader is a member
of the family so it works more like a family than like an employer–
employee situation.

Particularly in small churches there may be little or no choice
about who becomes a trustee, and that needs careful thought:

We come across this with situations such as both husband and wife
being on PCC or both being churchwardens, or the vicar's husband
or wife being on the PCC. This happens all the time in churches. It's
not necessarily a bad thing as long as there's clarity about it, but it
does need to be managed well. People cope well when there's clarity,
but if it's all too matey and those things aren't spelled out – and you
can spell them out in a perfectly good way without upsetting the
meeting but you do need to say it – then it's difficult for people to
behave appropriately and not cause mayhem.

Having partners on a trustee board may be unavoidable in some
situations, but it is wise to avoid it if possible. It is extremely
difficult for a husband or wife to be objective about a situation
or decision which affects their partner. Having a conflict of
interest policy is a wise step but it then needs to be applied; the
best way for that being that trustees should make a conflict of
interest declaration at the start of a meeting. This can be helped
by also having a conflicts of interest register in which each
trustee has to declare what could be potential conflicts, for
example, other trustee roles they hold or whether they are
related to a member of staff:

> *We openly discuss if there are potential conflicts — we have a conflicts of interest policy which sets out that someone can't contribute to a discussion or be involved in a vote if there's a conflict of interest and the matter will be discussed by others. So we're always trying to guard against undue influence and against conflict.*

Taking conflicts seriously is important because if a complaint about an apparent or actual conflict is made to the Charity Commission they are likely to investigate:

> *I know of a charity where a complaint has been made to the Charity Commission about bullying. The Charity Commission has written to the chair of trustees, who is taking it very seriously, but the person who is the subject of the complaint is the founder, who also raises all the money, and the founder's spouse is one of the trustees, so of course there is a conflict of interest issue there which complicates the whole thing.*

It is worth noting that the Charity Commission is now more concerned than it used to be about these kinds of issues:

> *There is now better documentation of conflicts of interest but less understanding and guidance on conflicts of loyalty. I don't think enough is being done in charities about a conflict of interest or conflict of loyalty register. I am just filling in the paperwork for a charity where I've been the independent examiner and it's the first time I've been asked the question about whether any contracts have been awarded to a relative or related party of a senior staff member. I haven't been asked that question before. I think the declaration of a conflict is quite well done, but the implementation of that is not so well done; for example, a person may be allowed to remain in the room while an item in which they've declared a conflict of interest or conflict of loyalty is discussed.*

Clear thinking about these issues is mainly the responsibility of the chair, but it is also up to each trustee to act with integrity by not only declaring any conflict but taking appropriate action, such as withdrawing from a meeting while the relevant item is discussed.

Boundaries

Conflicts of interest and loyalty arise within boards surprisingly often, but similar issues occur beyond that, particularly between trustees and staff, and sometimes also volunteers or congregation members:

I really believe in boundaries, but it's not easy to set them because different people will relate to the ministries they're involved with entirely differently. People have to know what the role of trustee is, and they need to be able to respect that person in that role. A person who's in the position of making decisions needs to be trusted to make that decision even if people outside the decision-making process don't agree with the decision. For the process to be successful there has to be a recognition that somebody's made a different decision to what I would have made. How you establish that boundary can be by practice, by making it clear in meetings what the responsibility is and what it isn't, and by drawing people in to a level that's appropriate so that they don't feel things are being forced on them.

Relationships can be more complex in a church or small charity, even though the actual governance work may be simpler:

Local charities tend to be quite small and therefore there aren't so many fiduciary issues as there are for national charities, [which makes] governance simpler. It's much more personable and friendly but there is a tendency in those local charities for trustees to get too involved operationally and there is not enough differentiation between what an individual does as a trustee and what he or she might do as a volunteer in the same charity. That happens quite a lot in small local charities, because when a trustee is volunteering they should be accountable to the CEO or a senior staff member, but because they are also a trustee there can be a feeling of, 'You shouldn't be telling me what to do.'

Whatever size you are you need due diligence towards charity law, but actually in a smaller charity it's highly likely that there will be complex and significant relationships between the board and all of the people involved in the charity. Therefore it's much harder to actually separate governance. Quite often in a smaller charity or local church the board will be working for or with the charity or be related to people who are. In a larger charity it's easier for the board to have a right sense of distance, but the downside of that is that they can lose touch with the coalface. Scale is a potential problem and a potential benefit.

The most obvious area where boundaries are necessary is to do with employment. Trustees are the employers in charities as well as in some church contexts:

There are different contexts for boundaries: I think it's important for trustees to have good relationships with each other, but as an employer with an employee, I don't think it's appropriate if you're managing people to be having teas and coffees with everybody on your staff team outside work. I would see that as a boundary.

Some boundaries relate to complying with legislation. As trustees we are employers, so I think in a Christian charity context it's extremely difficult. In one charity that was easier because we were employing people of all faiths and none, so there was a distance there which was very helpful. It enabled us to make objective decisions as an employer without having personalities and relationships thrown in.

But in church, boundaries are hugely blurred because employees are members of the church, so often they're friends. That has made it extremely difficult when we've had to make HR [human resources] decisions. In a recent HR decision I declared a conflict of loyalty because my husband and I were the primary pastoral and friendship support for the couple concerned.

Lines can easily get blurred about who is responsible for employment issues, particularly with pastoral matters: it is all too easy for trustees' pastoral concern to conflict with their role as the employer:

Within Christian ministries and charities there is confusion about managing somebody within the employment. I think there's pastoral employment management and pastoral care of an individual, and you need to separate those two out. If there is a problem within the employment, you need to address that according to proper processes. There may be disciplinary issues involved and they need somebody independent of that to engage with them on the spiritual pastoral side.

Earlier in the chapter I quoted a situation where 'the CEO thought the trustees were interfering'. Sometimes they are!

I'm not talking specifically about the ones I've been involved with, but just listening to what other people have said, there are often blurred boundaries with trustees intervening or interfering in things which are really not their business.

When you have other staff that are doing other things, you need to know who is responsible for doing what, and not stepping on each other's toes. There shouldn't be any 'dirty delegating', a trustee giving someone a job and then doing it themselves.

To avoid that as much as possible, it is really helpful to set out some principles about who does what, who needs to know what, what is in the trustees' remit and what is the staff's responsibility.

These matters of conflict of interest and conflict of loyalty, and the boundaries necessary for good governance, can seem daunting and constraining, but they need not be:

There have to be boundaries, but it depends so much on the organisation: how it works in one will be very different to another but there has to be opportunity for trustees to have confidential discussion about aspects of the work. But that's a very different thing from owning and sharing the vision, which has to happen right across the work.

Working well together without giving any cause for concern to people who observe you leaves good tracks, as outsiders recognise that you are doing as good a job as you can while maintaining and furthering the charity or church's vision.

Questions

Questions for trustees
Are you clear about the areas where you personally might have a conflict of interest or conflict of loyalty?

Questions for the chair
Is there a conflicts of interest register? If yes, how do you ensure you take appropriate action based on it? If no, when have you been aware of these kinds of issues and taken action anyway?

How would you rate the relationships on your board: poor, could do better, muddling along, pretty good or very good? What would help to maintain good relationships or improve less good ones?

SECTION 3

ORGANISATIONAL

TRACKS

9
Finding the Right Shape
Structure and Strategy

It pleased Darius to appoint 120 satraps to rule throughout the kingdom, with three chief ministers over them.
(Daniel 6:1-2)

He found great visionaries, but they were not so robust in how things worked out in practice ... translating the vision into strategy could improve.

There are two ways in which structure is important and both affect strategy: the type of registration a charity has or the way a denomination regulates its trustee bodies is what one might call its external structure, while the charity's internal structure is often closely linked to what it aims to achieve. These both impact how a charity functions and are becoming more important as the amount of legislation affecting charities increases, sometimes with unintended consequences:

One of the problems is that systems and laws aren't designed for tiny charities. Things on the financial side, like software the tax people require, you struggle to find things like that which are designed for small, low cost, not-for-profit operations. You might be looking at

thousands of pounds to get what you're supposed to have and your
total income might be not much more than that. Advice, by and large,
is similar, it comes at a cost. In the youth trust I was involved in
setting up, we were tiny, starting with one worker, and it was quite
an onerous amount of money to just fulfil the letter of the law, with
lots of red tape, much of which was irrelevant to us. I found it very
burdensome and distracting from the actual work that we were set up
to do. I could see the reason for it, but it needed about four trustees to
manage the legal bits and one person doing the mission — and that
seems the wrong way round; what you really want is four people doing
the mission and one person making sure all the boxes are ticked. For
me, scale is an issue.

External structure

This has an impact on independent charities and on churches
which belong to one of the major denominations. When I
moved to York and started to worship at the local church, I
soon realised that the Anglican structure it had then was having
a negative impact on its strategy. There were two churches in
the parish which were linked in a team ministry, but in practice
were fairly independent of each other. Each had a District
Church Council (DCC) and representatives from these formed
the Parochial Church Council (PCC). When I was elected to the
DCC and the PCC I discovered there was considerable
duplication, with many issues being dealt with twice or even
three times as one group reported to the other. PCC meetings
were often very long and could not always complete the
business. Time was being spent on detail and there was little
opportunity to consider the bigger picture.

About that time we were required by the diocese to go
through the complicated process of ceasing to be a team
ministry. At the end of the process, which took a couple of
years, we became one church with two buildings and the change
of external structure also gave us the opportunity to rethink the
internal structure. We set up working groups, which freed up

time to look beyond the day-to-day nitty-gritty and look at the bigger picture.

This kind of external complication of structure occurs in various denominational situations, such as Anglican multi-parish benefices and Methodist circuits. How it works in practice is often not easy to simplify while keeping in line with denominational principles, which can also be complicated by a lack of clarity about the role of trustees because that is hidden within the rules and regulations:

> *I think it would be quite hard to piece it together because it's in this big rule book called* Constitutional Practice and Discipline, *which is a tome of about 800 pages. There is a section under the local Church Council which is the trustee body, but it's more about how you are an Officer in the church than it is the charitable status – I think you'd have to read between the lines to find that.*

For independent charities, the type of charity they choose to be happens at registration, which may be in the early days of its existence or at some later time:

> *One charity where I was a trustee had been established for a number of years before it became a charitable Trust, so it sort of morphed from what had been a planning group to a body of trustees, whereas with a number of other charities it was a shorter route between being part of a working group to facilitate something happening and then becoming a trustee to see it moving on from an idea to a reality.*

There are pros and cons to what structure is chosen and sometimes that raises significant issues:

> *Some forms make life more complicated. I was in a charitable company limited by guarantee and you finish up having two meetings at the same time for different reasons to fulfil legal protocol. It also depends on the membership structure of that company and in the example I can think of, a lot of the supporters were members of the company so therefore you needed an AGM with the members. It*

ended up, I felt, being a bit of a waste of time – it fulfilled the legal requirements but for no obvious gain.

Having said that, I've also seen a pure Trust in a situation where they shouldn't be a pure Trust, they ought to be something else. In a mission agency I know none of the staff have a legal relationship with the Trust, the legal entity. They are most definitely not employed by it but neither are they in any sense members of it because it's a Trust, which doesn't have members. So it's a very ambiguous situation and one which has had to be addressed. I believe a lot of older charities are pure Trusts, which in the present legal situation is inappropriate, but then you've got the old charitable companies which seem to me to be hidebound by the way they have to work because they are a mix of charity and company. The only thing I've not worked in is a CIO so I don't know how that works.

Trustees may be unaware of what type of structure their organisation is, even though it may affect how they function:

People think fuzzily around these issues. If you are part of a discussion to say what sort of model should we adopt or what should we change to, and you're being professionally advised about that, then the issues are live for you. But generally speaking, you inherit one form and you're not necessarily aware of the characteristics of other forms. But trustees need to understand what they are and aren't allowed to do, what structure they need, and what the tax consequences are. There's help on the Charity Commission website on that, but people need to go into that wisely.

In a situation where the charity has a linked trading company, the type of structure is really important and can significantly affect strategy. Here's an example, where the trading company had to close but the Trust continued:

When the whole thing was set up in the eighties there were not that number of different models and options. If there had been, I don't think the charity would have been set up in the way that it was. But having said that, separating the trading company and the Trust probably meant that it's been easier for us to close the trading company while maintaining the work of the Trust. If we had been a CIO and it had been one organisation, the Trust side of what we do probably wouldn't be looking at a viable future now.

International structures

Life is also complicated for charities which are part of an international organisation:

The majority of those who work internationally are part of a network, so things that would traditionally be decided by the trustee body here have to be decided somewhere else. That doesn't quite fit with UK law so they have some issues around that. I don't think there are enough clear agreements in place about how that works in these international bodies. For example, you have much less control of your strategy because it has to fit into the strategy that's been decided at the international level.

In most such cases, each local entity will have its own board, which is set up and operated under the charity law of that country. It can be hard to work out ways to balance the freedom to make relevant local decisions, with the expectation that the various boards will work to internationally agreed vision, policies and goals:

In an international charity there are local boards in each country functioning as a charity there, but because of the partnership agreement they have, there is a board of governors above that that they need to work with. There is no legal requirement that they have to, but they are willing to. So there is more complexity, more things to think through; there are cultural issues too – about how people view boards and how they function and work in different cultures and jurisdictions.

Trustees of international charities have become more aware of the implications of their complicated structures, particularly as their workforce has become more multicultural:

We needed to become more global and less Western – all of our policies and procedures had a very strong Western feel, they fitted our world view. I felt we needed to begin to change, to recognise that God's Spirit is at work all over the world and these churches all over the world have a passion for mission and want to be involved in mission – and we are an organisation that does that. That passion that they have needs to refresh old organisations. Old organisations can easily become stale and it happens oh so often.

I came across a book by Gerard Arbuckle[1] and his thesis was that religious orders started with great passion and great work. It was hard, sacrificial work, but what happened very easily was that the organisation began to turn within itself, to look after and care for one another. That is important in the life of an organisation, but that inward-looking and caring became the focus of the organisation and the vision was lost. His focus was that religious orders needed regularly, maybe every fifteen years or so, to go through a process to refind their founding values and recommit to them so that their vision and focus stayed on that. We tried to do that, but it was difficult because of different cultures.

Our governance structure was very Western as well and we needed to open that up too. We actually reconfigured our whole governance structure, which meant that our governance structure is more complicated now. We didn't change our Constitution and we all agreed the wider vision, so each of the local charities around the world signed a mission agreement to work in partnership together for the mission vision. We all signed this partnership agreement and then each local body applied it within the laws and regulations of their own context.

Past decisions can also add complications to the structure and therefore governance of an international organisation:

There were significant challenges where legal issues in other jurisdictions were complicated. In my time we had two legal issues under Indian law and one under Italian law. In all of them it became very difficult because there was a relationship with a British charity and British workers in a foreign jurisdiction, not only in the present but also in the past. That was a significant problem because we were dealing with legacy issues of unwise decisions made sometimes generations back. You would say they were not part of the UK Trust, but actually they were because the foreign territory had titled the property in the name of the UK Trust. There have been a couple of situations like that which have taken up a lot of UK board time.

It is clear from some of these contributions that the kind of structure a board is working within can have a major impact on strategy because it can constrain how much freedom a board has to develop and implement its own plans and goals.

Daniel and structure

Daniel had to work within the structure devised by King Darius, in which he was one of three administrators that appear to have been somewhat similar to the top rank of the Civil Service. The structure was specifically designed

> … so that the king might not suffer loss.
> (Daniel 6:2)

In other words, Daniel and the other two administrators carried the can if anything went wrong. Earlier in his administrative life he was in the service of King Nebuchadnezzar, whose administration had a plethora of people in different roles. When Nebuchadnezzar set up the image of gold, there is a list of those who were required to worship it:

> Satraps, prefects, governors, advisors, treasurers, judges, magistrates and all the other provincial officials.
> (Daniel 3:2)

Daniel had no choice about the structure and where he fitted into it, and quite often that is the situation trustees find themselves in. They did not choose the structure of their church or charity and are unlikely to be able to change it – and if they do decide to change it, it involves a lot of often detailed legal work. The attitude of trustees to their structure usually needs to be to make the most of the opportunities it gives and seek to find creative ways to work within the restrictions.

Internal structure and strategy

Situations like those above are a potent reminder that decisions about structure should give careful consideration to the future implications as well as current expediency. And that is as true about internal structure as it is about external:

> *About two years into my time as chair of the board, we did a review of the whole governance process. We formed a subcommittee for governance which looked at good procedure and we drew up a governance handbook. That was important because you bear quite a big responsibility as governors – you're really, as I see it, the stewards of the vision. You're not there to micromanage, you've got staff to do that, but you are there to steward the vision, steward the financial resources, ask the questions. As part of this whole governance thing, we drew up job descriptions and terms of service. We wrote it as a living document because we realised this was not set in stone forever, but as law changes, we need to change with the law.*

Although external and internal structure may be linked, a board of trustees has more control over the internal structure, about how the church or organisation functions. When I joined the board of YoYo, the staff were doing excellent work in schools across the city. They worked in two teams, one in primary schools and the other in secondary schools. There was occasional overlap to support one another in big projects, but mostly the two teams' programmes were quite separate. In many ways that structure worked well, with staff developing tremendous expertise in communicating with their age group of children or young people. However, there was a major drawback: there was no continuity between the primary and secondary school work. Children moving up to Year 7 (aged eleven) often remembered YoYo from primary school, but they didn't know these people who came along and said they were from YoYo too. There were also practical issues: the two staff in the primary team had fifty-six primary schools to cover, while the secondary team of three people had twelve secondary schools and a sixth-form college. It was therefore logistically easier for the secondary team to visit any one school more regularly than it was for the primary staff. YoYo's vision was (and still is): 'Enabling every young person during their school years in York to see and hear the Christian faith being communicated in creative and understandable ways.' We weren't fulfilling that as effectively as we wanted to, so could a change in structure enable us to have a new strategy?

Over a period of about eighteen months, first the board on its own, and then trustees alongside staff, thought about our vision, reviewed what had already been achieved, looked at what more could be done, talked through ideas and possibilities and considered their implications. At the end of the process we reaffirmed our vision, but agreed to move to three teams working in geographical areas of the city and doing both primary and secondary work. The new structure enhanced the vision, brought it up to date, and provided impetus to fulfil it even more effectively than previously.

The change in structure and a new strategy were inextricably linked, which is why strategy is in this chapter with structure rather than being part of the chapter on vision. The change in YoYo's structure had considerable implications for trustees and staff. The schools' workers needed new job descriptions and therefore also new contracts of employment. Trustees agreed it was also an appropriate time to review salaries, which had been based on the expectation that most schools' workers would only stay on the team for a year or two. We therefore paid too little for staff to be able to afford to live long-term in York, one of the most expensive cities in the north of England. Those changes needed detailed, time-consuming work, and required careful negotiation with staff as part of the change management involved. But it was worth it: one secondary school invited YoYo staff to visit the new Year 7 classes and as they walked into the room a shout went up, 'It's YoYo!' The work has flourished, with more schools visited regularly and better continuity.

The importance of strategy

Strategy is a key part of fulfilling vision:

> *I am struggling with a mission at the moment who have a clear vision and a strategy but I don't think that strategy will help fulfil their vision; there's a disconnect between the two but they can't see it.*

At Christian Research we were asked to help a fairly large church understand why their vision was not being fulfilled. There were several staff members, some of them constituting an eldership team while others worked in various roles for the church within a clear structure. Having talked to the minister, we decided to do an analysis of the eldership team's strengths. We found that the leadership was almost awash with creativity and visionary ideas, but they did not know how to turn them into reality and therefore had no strategies to make their ideas happen. We suggested they appoint an administrator with the relevant skills, and give that person the freedom to develop strategies. They did so, and within a few months there were plans in place which set out the steps needed to implement the more significant visions.

Strategy spells out what needs to happen to achieve a vision, and it also considers the longer-term implications of that vision. It has similarities with project management, which sees the big picture of the project but breaks down the implementation of it into manageable chunks. The vision helps shape the strategy so that anything which does not contribute to fulfilling the vision is ruled out. Unfortunately, not everyone sees the value or necessity of strategy:

> *A lot of our Trusts think they're too small to need a strategy! 'We only work in one school', or 'We're only a few people', so 'we just do things as they come along'. They're reactive and don't think they've got time to think strategically. Perhaps someone's had a bright idea*

or there's an opportunity in a school, or they have a new worker with a particular set of skills, and they think short term about these things. If, for example, they have a new worker with musical skills they think, 'Oh great, let's do something musical', but when that person moves on, that stops. Strategically, what's that going to do for you? Is it going to be useful to you to have a long-term strategy to do music in schools?

So many of the trustees, if you mention the word 'strategy', see themselves as volunteers who want to help and that they haven't got time to go through things like strategy. We try to help them to think more long-term, about what it is they want to do; to think about when their current workers move on so the next person isn't going to want to change everything, and that what you're doing now doesn't stop because it's focused on the individual rather than on the work of the Trust. That's where we're trying to push the people who just don't like the word 'strategy'.

Asking the right questions to develop a strategy is important, and so is implementing it carefully. Who is responsible for working it out? Who needs to agree the detail? Who is going to check progress? When should it be revised or renewed? How will you know when it is completed? These kinds of questions need to be on the regular agenda for board meetings so strategy is not left to drift along or run out of steam.

It can be essential to change the strategy in order to survive as an organisation, or to grow as a church:

At [quite a large charity] *the trustee body was helped to understand that the whole public sector funding environment was changing. As a result, they actually changed almost overnight how they funded projects. They did it quite quickly – perhaps a bit too quickly – because probably half the staff had to be made redundant and new staff ... brought in with different skills. but they now have a secure future which they wouldn't have had. They'd have closed if they hadn't changed. The trustees took the risks and made the decisions to make those changes.*

Changing strategy very often involves managing change. Change management is a whole subject of its own, with a plethora of resources. It is important to be aware of the implications of a change of structure and to plan for how that will happen:

> *It was very important that all the members were on board with the decision so the trustees not only had to be involved in the decision to change but also had to be involved in managing that change – well, not managing it, but ensuring that the management of the change was adequate so that the process ran as well as it could ... We were well served by those who managed that project, they did it well.*

Nehemiah's strategy

Part of the success of Nehemiah's strategy was that he had an effective overview of the whole project. He carefully researched what needed to be done, how big the task was and thought about what would be involved (Nehemiah 2:11-15). He considered what human resources he had available, and soon decided that everyone would need to be involved, including the priests, nobles and officials, whom he immediately approached to explain his ideas (Nehemiah 2:16-17). He also quickly became aware of where the opposition would come from (Nehemiah 2:19). Bearing all this in mind, he forged a strategy which gave everyone responsibility for rebuilding a section of the wall or one of the city's gates (Nehemiah 3). It motivated them so that

> ... we rebuilt the wall till all of it reached half its height,
> for the people worked with all their heart.
> (Nehemiah 4:6)

However, when the opposition intensified he adapted the strategy to respond to the new conditions, with half the builders becoming guards, ready to fight if there was an attack. When the opposition became personal, he refused to be side-tracked, sending the message:

I am carrying on a great project and cannot go down. Why should the work stop while I leave it and go down to you? (Nehemiah 6:3)

Another great biblical example of strategy which required a new structure comes from the life of Joseph. After Joseph had been in prison for several years, Pharaoh had a dream in which God warned him that there would be seven years of plenty before a famine which would last for seven years. Joseph was released from prison and put in charge of the whole land of Egypt and given responsibility to prepare for the famine:

> During the seven years of abundance the land produced plentifully. Joseph collected all the food produced in those seven years of abundance ... and stored it in the cities. In each city he put the food grown in the fields surrounding it. Joseph stored up huge quantities of grain, like the sand of the sea; it was so much that he stopped keeping records because it was beyond measure ... When the famine had spread over the whole country, Joseph opened all the storehouses and sold grain to the Egyptians ... And all the world came to Egypt to buy grain from Joseph.
> (Genesis 41:47-49,56-57)

The strategy was to store the abundant grain during the years of plenty so there would be enough food during the years of famine. To enable that to happen, Joseph developed an infrastructure of storehouses 'in the cities' (v48), keeping the grain locally rather than gathering it centrally. It was a very effective strategy, and in God's plan was what moved Jacob's family to Egypt.

Governance structure

Some boards do not really think about any structure for their governance, but there are various models which can be applied to how a board functions. There is a summary of these models and several others in Appendix 3.[2] It can be really helpful to choose one which seems most appropriate and seek to implement it. The two I have come across most often are the Carver Model and the Nolan Principles.

I am more familiar with the Carver Model, which 'is an integrated set of concepts and principles that describes the job of any governing board. It outlines the manner in which boards can be successful in their servant-leadership role, as well as in their all-important relationship with management. Unlike most solutions to the challenge of board leadership, its approach to the design of the governance role is neither structural nor piecemeal, but is comprehensively theory based.' However, as with any model, it has its pros and cons:

> *I don't particularly like Carver Governance because I think it's too tight, but it's got some fantastic principles and one of those is what it calls moral ownership. I don't think enough charities have enough moral ownership.*

The Nolan Principles were published by the government in 1995 as The Seven Principles of Public Life and are described as 'the basis of the ethical standards expected of public office holders'.

> *The Nolan Principles of Public Life are something which have been brought home to me from what I might call professional charity trustees who've been part of our journey over the last few years. I talk to PCCs about what's expected of PCC members, and when you look at the summaries of those seven principles, they're entirely compatible with gospel and New Testament values, and therefore what you hope those who are Christ-like would be doing, in terms of transparency and honesty and those kind of values.*
>
> *I think there is something to be said for finding a way to articulate those, perhaps in a more spiritual way, to help bridge some of that apparent gap between the secular principles and PCCs. For example, we should be open and transparent about our money, and there's something about how we do that in living our Christian life. So if we're giving some of the funds of the PCC to other organisations, we should be sharing that with the wider congregation and not just*

deciding that the vicar's favourite pet project is this and therefore we're going to spend some of the money on it. That kind of openness should exist in our churches, so there is something in those Nolan values that perhaps as churches we could do more with. That would help remove some of the concern in the wider charity world that churches are treated as special cases, or in some way are not being open because we think you can trust us because we wouldn't do anything immoral or illegal because we're Christians. Sadly, there are Christian charities which find themselves doing both from time to time.

Another possibility for helping to develop strategy – and some other aspects of trustees' responsibilities – is a project management tool:

Something that I have encouraged in the training that I do is to use a project management tool known as RACI. It basically says, if you're running a project, who is Responsible for what, who is Accountable for what, who do you need to Consult about what, and who needs Information about what – that's what the RACI stands for. Something I encourage trustee bodies to do, at least between them and their staff and their wider membership, is to say, 'What is the trustee body accountable for, who is responsible for doing it, who needs to be consulted about it?' Too often they would ask the question, 'Is this proposal correct, can we approve it?' rather than 'Who have you talked to about this, where have you taken advice from, who have you given this information to? If it's something that's going to affect somebody, has that person been informed that this is going to happen to them?' Trustee bodies are not asking those sorts of questions.

Thinking through together about which model to choose and how to apply it can lead to some fresh understanding and clarity about strategy. It is a useful way to spend at least part of a trustee away day, especially if a board is unclear about the way ahead. It is all too easy for a board to muddle along, reacting to situations rather than being proactive. That can slip into negligence without meaning to, which may have a negative impact on the reputation, ministry and activities of the charity.

Giving thought to how to work best within your structure and developing and implementing appropriate strategies is a positive, forward-looking approach which helps to make your church or charity effective for the kingdom of God.

Questions

Do you know what your board's external structure is? How does it affect what you can and cannot do?

Have you a clear strategy which works towards fulfilling your vision? How often is it reviewed? Is it supported by your internal structure?

If you are not already using one of the models of governance in your board, can you plan a time to consider the various ones and discuss together how to apply the one you choose?

10
Let's Get Organised
Successful Meetings, Decision-making and Policies

Everything should be done in a fitting and orderly way.
(1 Corinthians 14:40)

Trustees need to understand that not only do they have authority and decision-making power, but also that carries with it the responsibility to do it well.

It was 'shambolic' and we're now trying to make it more professional, formalising things, developing policies and so on.

Having a clear vision and a strategy to fulfil it is very important in enabling a church or charity to move forward, but it is not the whole story of what trustees are responsible for. There is a lot of run-of-the-mill detail which needs to be done well, including financial matters and accountability, which we will consider in the other two chapters in this section on organisation.

Understanding the responsibilities

There is much more to being a trustee than turning up to meetings, but that is a good start! I am a member of a camera club and I very much enjoy the meetings, but it is a hobby, so I only go when I don't have another commitment. Being a trustee is not a hobby because of the expectations and requirements, so it has to be taken seriously:

> *Their particular responsibilities as trustees often come as a shock to people; they have no idea that being a member of the PCC includes that responsibility. Times when I've seen that dawn on people have usually been around financial decisions or property issues. I make it clear to people that as someone from the central support of the diocese I can't enforce particular things. It really is their decision, whether it's something to do with the transfer of a property, or to do with land or the finances of the church. It starts to dawn on people that they do have a say in this, but equally they need to understand that not only do they have that authority and decision-making power, but also that carries with it the responsibility to do it well and the fact that they could be personally financially liable if it goes wrong. That's when people start to wake up – and sometimes step away – from those responsibilities.*

It can be particularly hard to find trustees who understand that responsibility, let alone are willing to take it on if, say, a church is mainly made up of people who don't carry much responsibility elsewhere:

> *You want trustees to have skills and experience, but if you've got a very grassroots-based church, you're then trying to make up a board of trustees out of nice people who've offered to help but don't necessarily have the experience and skills you need to run a charity well.*

Nevertheless, if being involved proves quickly to be worthwhile for someone, they are likely to make the effort to do their best. Trustees give significant time to the role and their willingness to do that should not be taken for granted. It is much more rewarding to be part of a group where you know what is expected of you and so do all the others, so you really work together for the good of the charity or church, and therefore for the good of the kingdom of God.

A successful meeting is one that results in a number of clear action points, clarity around who is taking those actions, within what time scale, so everybody leaves knowing what it is they've signed up to.

Successful meetings

The role of the chair is a key factor in making a trustee meeting (or any meeting!) successful. But there are practical things that contribute as well.

Good preparation

We have already considered the role of the chair and secretary in creating an agenda and it is important to circulate that well ahead of time. The governing document will set out any rules which may have to be followed, such as how much notice must be given for a meeting, especially an AGM. My approach is that there should be no surprises at a meeting, nothing – certainly nothing major – thrown in without warning. Accompanying notes are sometimes helpful to point out what decisions will need to be made and whether or not there is a paper on a particular item. It may also be necessary to seek expert external help or advice and preparing the agenda well ahead allows time for that to happen:

Being sent timely agendas and notes and stuff before a board meeting so you don't get things sprung on you twenty-four hours before you've got to discuss them, that's really important. You can't make decisions if you don't have the right information, so that's crucial to me. I think it's important to consult outside the board for expertise if something is beyond your usual remit.

A board meeting flows much better if everyone attending it has prepared. Papers are circulated so that they can be read in advance, as it is a waste of time to have to summarise or even read them during the meeting:

> *Preparation is very important; that often doesn't happen. In the church situation that was one of my frustrations – you had open-ended discussions before any serious groundwork had been done. That groundwork might include a sub-group of people coming to a meeting having thought through a particular issue, perhaps produced an A4-size summary setting out the background and what they see as the way to go.*
>
> *There should be a good mixture of agenda items, some new things – blue-sky discussion that stimulates board members' discussion and relates to the vision – as well as the detailed things they have to deal with. Board meetings do not need to go on for hours and hours if they're well prepared for. Especially in a church, they can go on too long, endlessly into the night!*

A sub-group may meet only once or twice to deal with a particular issue, but groups which are set up on a longer-term basis can be very helpful. In the Church of England, the Standing Committee is an official sub-group of the PCC and has particular responsibilities, but that need not be the only subcommittee. When my church was required to change its structure (from two churches in a team ministry to one church uniting both, see previous chapter) it gave us the opportunity to develop governance which worked *for* us rather than against us. The working groups which were set up have a mix of PCC members and others who are involved in that area of the church's life. They cover aspects such as pastoral care, youth and children, mission and outreach, and staff management. These groups do the groundwork on issues and present ideas and proposals to the PCC with the pros and cons, ready for them to discuss and decide. The result has been that PCC meetings move more quickly and easily to decisions. More people have a say about the activities they are involved in, and when they first began, they also helped to draw the two churches closer to each other because there were people from both of them on the various groups:

> *I think it's very important that people are not just there for a meeting, that there are subcommittees that are looking at particular areas and you're looking for people willing to do work in the background so that board meetings are efficient and use the time well. Subcommittees can present ideas, what's important in the decision and the pros and cons.*

The planning needed for a successful board meeting is similar to the advance planning for any activity: think it all through carefully and try to anticipate all the possibilities. Nehemiah must have done that kind of preparation for the dedication of the wall of Jerusalem. In chapter 12 he sets out the details of the event: the Levites and musicians were brought in from their home villages; first the priests and Levites purified themselves and then they ceremonially 'purified the people, the gates and the wall' (v30); two choirs led processions in opposite directions along the top of the wall, each followed by half the leaders, who are all named, and their precise route is described; at the end of it they offered 'great sacrifices' (v43) and everyone, including women and children, 'rejoiced'. There must have been meticulous planning to enable all that to happen smoothly but the outcome was a very memorable day!

Time
The purpose of an agenda is to guide the discussion so it deals with matters in a helpful way:

> *It's focused, it doesn't wander too much off the agenda, the business you set out to do is done in the time – you don't spend hours and hours on it and get exhausted and get nowhere. There's a right balance between business that simply needs communicating and what needs a proper chewing over and discussing. Some items need swiftly whizzing through, others need good consultation, so getting the balance of reports to the meeting and items for discussion is part of what you do as a chair in shaping the agenda and making it a useful meeting. I think people hate meetings where they just sit there nodding, they want*

meetings where they contribute and have opportunity to express their thoughts.

When there is a really big decision to be made, then it may take time to reach agreement. I have sometimes opened up a topic for preliminary discussion, but made it clear from the start that any decision would be taken at a future meeting. That gives people time to think about it, mull it over, discuss it with friends or family if appropriate and pray about it. I have also made it a practice to allocate rough timings to different items on the agenda, which helps to make sure you cover everything.

Involving everyone

Trustees give up valuable time to attend board meetings. If they have prepared well beforehand, they will have ideas, comments and suggestions to contribute to discussions. It is part of the chair's responsibility to enable those to be heard:

> *There has to be a time when you cut off discussion, you don't let people talk for the sake of it, you don't let just one person talk and you make sure you include the person who doesn't necessarily speak up very easily but who often has the best thing to say.*

Good minutes circulated quickly

I was once on a board where the minutes only arrived with the agenda a couple of days before the next meeting. By then it was too late to act on anything I had agreed to do between meetings. As chair I have always wanted to see draft minutes within a day or two, and when I was PCC secretary I usually produced them within twenty-four hours. Although minutes are not official until they are ratified at the next meeting, they do prompt people to take action they had offered or agreed to do. They also remind people to pray about the various issues as sometimes the importance or enormity of a decision only really hits when you read it in stark black and white and have time to think about it.

The Quakers use a method of agreeing minutes which also checks that everyone understands what has been agreed. After a discussion the minute is written, read out and agreed before proceeding to the next item. I can think of various situations where that would have been very helpful and avoided repeating the discussion at the next meeting because people had gone away with different opinions about what had been agreed the first time!

When I first joined, decisions tended to be almost unstated, too much so, there wasn't enough minuting or of the chair checking that we were making a decision. As we've had to transition into a more modern structure, we've benefited from good chairs who've been summarising, checking that everyone's on board and ensuring decisions are minuted accurately. That's been a big improvement.

Minutes should be reasonably detailed, especially when recording major decisions. Something about the discussion should be stated, what led up to the decision, and quoting any independent specialist advice on the point. If the decision is ever questioned, especially by the Charity Commission, then having the narrative of how and why the decision was made will be of great importance.

Prayer

Hopefully, as Christians, trustees will have prayed over the agenda, taking the opportunity to consider what their response could be to the various items. Prayer during a meeting can be significant too. When asked what role prayer has in decision-making, these were two of the responses:

We would like to argue 'a whole lot' and that when we arrive at a meeting there has been prayerful thought about what happens. I do strongly feel the Spirit moves in meetings and things get shared, but the amount of time we might break for prayer and wait on the Lord in a meeting or explicitly make space for that undermines the idea that it is as important as we might like to say! If a meeting is contentious, we may pause and say, 'This needs some prayerful thought,' and encourage everyone to do that, but by-and-large we just 'go for it'.

When I first joined, there was no prayer but since we've now got a new chair and some new trustees, we do now start the meetings with prayer and asking the Holy Spirit to give us wisdom in meetings and decision-making.

Planning prayer into an agenda is also not a bad idea!

When I was putting together an agenda, even for a three-hour meeting, I was looking at points where we could interject a time of prayer. The prayer wasn't the bread either side of the sandwich!

We would have prayer, not just at the beginning, but in the course of a board meeting. If we come to something and we need to, we'll just stop and pray about it. We're prepared to put an item on one side and come back to it giving time for prayer. We might have a Skype meeting after a board meeting just to pray, or we might have a time of prayer and fasting when we commit on our own to pray and fast. You're not doing it together but you're doing it at the same time.

Developing a pattern of prayer in and for trustee meetings is one of the things that helps to keep an organisation distinctively Christian. It was Daniel's determination to stick to his pattern of prayer which resulted in him ending up in the lions' den. When his opponents could find no fault in Daniel's conduct of government affairs, they persuaded King Darius to issue a decree that no one should pray to anyone but the king for thirty days. They knew they could catch Daniel praying and that is exactly what happened:

Now when Daniel learned that the decree had been published, he went home to his upstairs room where the windows opened towards Jerusalem. Three times a day he got down on his knees and prayed, giving thanks to his God, just as he had done before.
(Daniel 6:10)

How can you tell when a meeting has been successful? One way is to evaluate each meeting:

One of the things that Carver⁴ requires you to do is evaluation. I think it's a building block that the Charity Commission is missing. I would like to see all boards do both a meeting evaluation – how did we do in this meeting, did we fulfil our responsibilities, did we make clear decisions? – and then a wider evaluation every two or three years of whether the board is helping the charity fulfil its objectives.

Decision-making

There is very little about group decision-making in the Bible; I can only think of two examples. One is a bad example, when Joseph's brothers conspired together to kill him. It sounds as though Reuben was not part of the original decision and so looked for a way to soften his brothers' decision (Genesis 37). Sometimes charity boards do make a bad decision, or are in danger of doing so, and it's important to listen to a dissenting voice, as they may have a more appropriate suggestion.

The other situation which came to mind was the Council of Jerusalem. Paul and Barnabas had toured Asia Minor, planting a number of churches among non-Jews, but when they returned to Antioch they found 'certain people ... from Judea' who were teaching that those who wanted to become believers must be 'circumcised, according to the custom taught by Moses'. Paul and Barnabas strongly disagreed and were appointed by the church in Antioch 'to go up to Jerusalem to see the apostles and elders about this question' (Acts 15:1-2). What happened?

> The apostles and elders met to consider this question. After much discussion, Peter got up and addressed them. (Acts 15:6-7)

When the 'whole assembly' (v12) had listened to Paul and Barnabas, and both Peter and James had addressed them, a decision about the way ahead was made by 'the apostles and elders, with the whole church' (v22). The decision made then became the basis for all future outreach to non-Jews so it was important that everyone at the home church in Jerusalem agreed about it. It is a good example of how clear presentation of the issue, discussion among those in a position to make a decision, and then a proposal by a leader led to widespread agreement.

Churches and charities make decisions in various ways. Some charitable structures provide for the organisation to have members in a legal sense who are separate from trustees and have the right to vote on matters, particularly at an AGM. In some church and mission structures, the final decision-making body is a meeting of all the people who are members because they are committed to the church or mission, but they are not members in the legal sense. This can complicate matters because those non-legal members have a say in decisions, but they are not trustees and may not always be as well informed or as aware of wider issues as the trustees:

> *I think most of the people who turn up to a church meeting probably cast their eye over the agenda about five minutes before they come, have their own 'beans' that they want to share, and that's about it.*

One of the reasons church meetings sometimes go on a long time is because everyone wants their say on a particular issue, even if what they contribute does not add anything to the discussion. For charities and churches with a member-led structure, there is a real danger of confusion about who is able to make what decisions:

> *The mission agency I am part of has always been a member-led organisation and decisions have been member-led, therefore to introduce a board with governance and decision-making responsibility means it's been quite hard to negotiate the way that sits within the organisation's ideas about how it works. I sense the same in a Baptist context: Baptist churches have a similar structure and similar idea about how they govern themselves. When you bring in a board who have a governance responsibility it is a difficult interface between what is governance and has to be dealt with by the board and what is actually a decision that can be made by a member body.*
>
> *With the changes in charity law, the government has imposed a set of ways of working which to some extent cut across some Christian*

organisations' ideas about how they can make decisions. So 'body' decision-making, which is very much a Christian value deep in some Christian charities, is very difficult to interface with a board who actually take responsibility for governance. There's a great danger that either the board becomes a rubber-stamping activity or the reverse happens with the member body rubber-stamping the board's decision.

Some boards vote about most, if not all, decisions, while others seek to reach consensus and only vote when it is legally necessary:

We try prayerfully to get universal agreement, though very occasionally that isn't possible. So it's extremely rare that we would need to go to a vote, which would contrast with what I've been involved in at a church, where in a Baptist church decisions are made by the members and you do vote on things and you may have dissenting voices.

Consensus and unanimity are not necessarily the same thing. There is a difference between 'everybody for' a particular decision, which is unanimity, and 'nobody against', which is consensus. Reaching consensus may mean that some people are willing to go along with what is being proposed even though they may not be 100% happy about it. Making decisions in this way is a process and can take much longer than someone at the front speaking about a proposal and then moving a vote on it. The process involves

… hearing, listening to whatever is required, listening to one another, discussing, and seeking to come to an agreement. We would be looking for some measure of consensus, though not necessarily unanimity.

This kind of consensus helps everyone to feel ownership of the final decision. However, not all consensus is positive. I've been in situations where a board member started their comments with 'The Lord told me …' That can make others feel they can't question what's said, possibly leading to immense frustration and a poor decision-making process. Other times, consensus can be because nobody dares to disagree with the chair:

> *Unfortunately, you can have a bully chair and people just don't want to voice their concern or bring up something different because they think that if the chairperson wants to do this there's no point raising something different.*

Alternatively, there may be apparent consensus but actually it is because the board lacks people from a variety of backgrounds and with different skills who see issues from a different perspective:

> *Where you have most of the people from similar backgrounds they tend to say, 'Yes, that's what I think too, let's just do that,' and so you can get the same decisions – perhaps mistaken decisions – made over and over again with very little change where perhaps there needs to be change. The more variety and skills you have among the board, the better decisions that get made.*

A key factor is knowing who should make which decisions: is it the trustees, the church leader, the CEO, or the members – of either kind? It's particularly important in a church where there are many decisions that the minister makes as part of their regular duties and responsibilities, but they do need to be aware of what decisions they should not make on their own. If the boundaries are not clear then it is horribly easy for mistrust or disagreement to arise:

> *In the past the dynamic between the leadership of the church and the trustees was appalling and the trustees were called the 'No' men. They held the purse strings and they made decisions that the leaders of the church didn't agree with. Now that the board is becoming more skills-based and experienced, the approach and the relationships are changing between the leadership of the church and the trustees and thankfully it's improving.*

From time to time boards need to discuss matters which are not appropriate for everyone to be involved in. That may be because of a conflict of interest or conflict of loyalty, such as was considered in Chapter 8, but it isn't always the case. There are times when a board needs freedom to discuss a matter without having to be careful what they say, perhaps because a staff member is present. In those situations, it is wise to have an *in-camera* session, that is, a part of the meeting which is only attended by trustees. I have used that from time to time, but some chairs find it helpful or wise to make it a regular practice:

> Our board was set up such that the CEO was an *ex officio* trustee. That's very unusual; usually your CEO sits in on board meetings but is not a trustee. That created issues and I quite strongly wanted to change it, but the trouble is if you want to change that sort of thing you have to go through the Charity Commission and everybody thought that was too much hassle. We solved it so it didn't look like having a time without the CEO just when a problem occurred. At each board meeting we had half an hour when the CEO was not there and we could be free to raise issues. There are just times when you need to talk about how the person is doing or what's going on and it's just not helpful to have them there.

Policies and procedures

A clear and appropriate set of policies helps to run a charity well, and can sometimes make a decision straightforward: 'our policy says we do this, so we must'. They also provide some protection: if someone does make an accusation or, God forbid!, you end up in court, being able to produce a relevant policy, and minutes from your meetings showing how you applied it, is vitally important in your defence. Policies make sure there is proper:

- Compliance with laws and regulations
- Transparency and accountability
- Clarity about how things should be done and what is expected.

Some policies are legal necessities, for example when GDPR (General Data Protection Regulations) came into law in 2018 every organisation which held a database of contact details had to have a Data Protection Policy to comply with the legislation. Churches are expected to comply with safeguarding legislation and have a Child Protection Policy, even if there are no children attending regularly, and a Vulnerable Adults Protection Policy. Any organisation which is responsible for a building should have a Health and Safety Policy:

> *We do a lot to protect our reputation and we're very careful about that, the quality of decisions we make or the quality of courses we provide, but we also have policies in relation to safeguarding and everybody has been through Child Protection training and we have DBS clearance. There have been one or two instances where we've had to act on that and they've been well handled because people have had appropriate training.*

The important thing is to decide which policies your church or charity needs, based on what you are doing. Lists of possible policies and templates for them are available, perhaps from a diocese or denominational headquarters, from other similar charities, or by searching online:

> *The legislation that keeps us safe also leaves those of us running an organisation feeling constantly vulnerable. GDPR is a great example – being part of the Methodist Church is good because there's one data protection officer and we do what they tell us, whereas even for the Anglicans it's one per church. The instinct is to rush into inventing several thousand approaches to getting it right and wasting an awful lot of resources and manpower. In a small business or charity there's the feeling that we can't wait, we've got to do something even if it's wrong and you tend to overdo it. I feel increasingly it's burdensome and people don't want to be burdened with all this stuff, they just want to get on and do what the charity was set up to do, or in a church get on with ministry.*

Writing or adapting policies which are appropriate for your church or organisation can be time-consuming, and sometimes feels very demanding. But they are an important safeguard:

I know of a charity that provides counselling, so they're working with quite vulnerable people and I asked them if they have a Vulnerable Adults Protection Policy. One of the trustees said, 'Oh, I'm fed up with policies, I'm not having any of that sort of nonsense.' My response was to feel that I understood where he was coming from but that in their circumstances I wouldn't want to be a trustee without a Vulnerable Adults Protection Policy. They don't need a money-laundering policy – they don't even charge fees for their counselling, so they don't need that policy – but I think some of them don't think through what policies they do need.

Procedures go hand in hand with policies because they describe who does what, what they need to do and guidance on how to go about it. So, for example, my church has a Child Protection Policy which is based on one from the diocese and also takes into account the guidance from thirtyone:eight.[2] The policy is accompanied by a procedure which describes who needs to have a DBS check, who does that check and when etc:

I think quite a lot of charities are quite good at putting the policies in place but aren't very good at asking the questions and monitoring the implementation of them. They might not properly understand them, so they worry about, for example, GDPR or Child Protection, but most of them are reasonably good at putting policies in place.

The big decisions you may have to make

Most of the business of a board meeting is fairly routine so it may be helpful to have an annual schedule, for example to make sure each policy is reviewed annually, but not all at the same meeting. However, there are times when a really big decision with long-term implications has to be made.

Significant appointments

On two occasions I have been chair of a charity for only a few months when the CEO announced they were moving on, one to retire and the other to lead another related organisation.

Employment is the responsibility of trustees and over the years on various boards I have seen or overseen many new staff appointments. However, choosing the right person as leader can affect the future of a charity and you don't always get it right:

> We had two changes of management and what accompanied them were changes in philosophy and changes in location. The trustees had made the appointments but retrospectively would say they had not made the best decision. Those changes meant that a lot more work had to be done on the marketing side because of concern about the reputation of the charity – which was done and I'm happy to say that I think the net result was good.

Managing scarce resources

There are times in most charities and churches when resources dry up. While fund-raising and/or prayerful faith are usually our first resorts to tackle the situation, there are times and situations when thinking outside the box could lead to a different solution, not only for your own organisation:

> One of the challenges is that there are so many other initiatives and it's too easy to find one is 'competing' with other equally good, equally important and vital organisations. It often strikes me we would do well to see if we could cooperate a little more. One way we could do that, for example, is that we all find it awfully hard to find a good treasurer – good treasurers are worth their weight in gold! But maybe ten or a dozen charities could between them employ a treasurer who would work across all those charities.
>
> Similarly, maybe a fund-raiser so that the fund-raising supported a breadth of work rather than all of us fishing in the same pool when already church members are being invited to support a whole range of great things but can only really identify with a small number.
>
> I think that churches have very often got space which isn't used to the maximum – there's spare capacity in church premises, and rather than organisations having to rent space or people working out of their own homes, which is not necessarily easy to do, I think it would be great if we could identify more opportunities for this sort of support.

Redundancies

Nobody likes making staff redundant, but sadly sometimes it is the only way to enable an organisation to survive. There are proper procedures to follow in making redundancies, and if an organisation finds itself needing to cut back on staff numbers, then they need to do so correctly. It can take courage to make the decision but it is the trustees who have to bite the bullet:

In a Christian organisation – this was when I was finance director, not a trustee – we struggled to balance the books for a couple of years. I remember bringing to the trustees some proposals and saying these are not effective enough, but in everybody's discussions there'd been an implicit assumption of making posts redundant. So I had to ask them the question, 'Do you want me to go away and produce something where posts are made redundant?' A very good discussion came from that, but it was a really important question to raise with the trustees. It was a difficult thing to do, but it had surprisingly good consequences. In that situation the trustees had to formalise it, but the detail and most of the thinking about it was done by the senior executive. There's a process, but the ultimate decision must belong to the trustees in those sorts of situations.

Closure

Sometimes an organisation has to close. It may have accomplished what it set out to do, or that work may have been taken over by another organisation. Those are situations when the trustees can probably feel they have done a good job. There are times when an organisation closes because the vision has not been passed on so no one is willing to continue it. There are also situations which mount up until there is no way of continuing:

The model was established thirty years ago and has worked well for many years, but it's not working now. The model was setting up a trading company, which never had a great deal of reserves or money sitting in the bank, but has been able to pay its way in paying employed staff, its creditors and the overheads. It has always been a concern that those reserves were so thin that any unexpected event or adverse trading conditions would cause problems. What we've had most recently is a combination of factors which were insurmountable. The trustees had to make the decision to close the trading company, which is extremely unfortunate, but it isn't because there's no vision within the trustees. It wasn't an easy decision to go to the professional advisors and put the company into liquidation.

However the routine work of the board is managed, and whatever crises come your way, understanding the issues and getting good advice is important. That is why I conclude this chapter by again recommending Paul Martin's book *Faith, Hope & Charity*. It is also tremendously helpful to sign up for regular information – and to read it when it arrives!

I subscribe to the updates from the Charity Commissioners, and for a long time I have subscribed to a monthly email briefing by Daryl Martin. I find that a helpful digest of issues for charities and it alerts me to new stuff which is coming up.[3]

The Charity Commission newsletter is now sent out to everybody's inbox but I still don't know if it's read.

Why does all this detail matter? It is partly because trustees are more committed and involved if a board meeting feels worthwhile. But in the bigger picture, if we do the behind-the-scenes things well, the whole church or organisation is more likely to be well run, and so be able to thrive, demonstrate kingdom values and prove itself to be trustworthy.

Questions

How smoothly do your board meetings run? If there are regularly problems, why do you think this is?

How do you make decisions: consensus, voting, or a mixture? Could an alternative approach help you, at least sometimes?

Are there any aspects of your work which ought to have a written policy and do not at the moment? Could you take responsibility for finding out about and then proposing such a policy?

11
Every Penny Counts
Raising, Managing and Spending Money

May I have a letter to Asaph, keeper of the royal park,
so he will give me timber?
(Nehemiah 2:8)

I met one chap who's doing a sterling job but who keeps the accounts of
the church in a tiny notebook in his pocket!

The board meeting had discussed the likelihood of having to make staff redundant, though there was barely enough in reserves to pay redundancy money. Trustees had been asked whether any of them were willing to make an interest-free loan so salaries could be paid that month, with no guarantee they would get it paid back. It was crunch time: close now or pray and trust God for one more month?

A few days later the CEO was speaking at a church and at the end someone came up and engaged him in conversation for some time. Sensing there was something deeper going on, the CEO continued the conversation rather than speaking to others from the congregation. Eventually the question came, 'Do you need any money?' A positive reply brought a further question,

'How much?' Wisely the CEO answered that it was up to the person and God. A five-figure sum was named and the CEO tried not to shout and dance with joy, but to graciously thank the person for their generosity. Within a few days even more than had been mentioned was transferred to the charity's bank account. God had amazingly provided right at the last minute. Salaries were paid, loans were repaid, reserves were reinstated and no one was made redundant.

Many of us have probably heard stories like that, maybe even experienced them personally, but we also know they are the exception rather than the rule. For many churches and charities, having enough money to meet their commitments is a constant concern and matter for prayer:

> *In Christian charities and churches to some extent we are always setting faith budgets: we know where we think the money is going to come from, but we trust in God that he will get those people to give!*

Income for charities and churches comes from a variety of sources. The main one is giving: to churches by individuals and to charities by individuals or churches. While individuals are alive they often give regularly, and they may then leave a legacy in their will for their church or chosen charity. Churches may have a Gift Day or a stewardship campaign, either annually or a one-off for a particular project or financial need. Some charities and churches are able to supplement their income by charging for services or the use of their facilities. External funding may be sought from a range of sources including grant-making bodies, Lottery money, local council and government funding. Fund-raising is common, from cake stalls to major events, while sponsorship is asked for from friends far and wide for everything from a sponsored silence to running a marathon or climbing Mount Kilimanjaro.

Issues around giving

Discipleship

One of the big challenges for churches and charities is encouraging new givers. It is closely linked with discipleship: at what stage of a Christian's journey does giving become part of both their responsibility and their commitment?

The model of the early Church was that the giving to God was through the community of believers, and that's the model most churches apply. While churches do see new people coming in, the people who have often been the committed givers pass away. The challenge for churches is always one of stewardship, and stewardship is always about discipleship.

How early do you start those conversations about money and what do you say? Do you say that it costs us £1,500 a week to run this church, or that we want to help you to understand what it is to be a disciple of Christ and that part of being a disciple of Christ is how we use our resources? My sense is that it has always been the case that people go on a giving journey, which is around that discipleship message, one aspect of which is coming to understand that the call is on their wallets as well as their hearts.

One of the dilemmas is that you want to make the gospel about grace and it should be free, so it's embarrassing then to talk about money, or you talk about the nuts and bolts of running a church rather than about grace and that we should respond in the way we feel God has blessed us.

In a church there are, at least potentially, regular opportunities for teaching on discipleship or challenging members to give, while taking up an offering is part of almost every service, but that does not mean it is easy to meet commitments.

Capacity to give

We can fall into the trap of thinking that only those who are in good jobs and well-off can afford to give, so it is salutary to remember that the widow whose gift was tiny was commended by Jesus because he said she

> ... has put in more than all the others. All these people gave their gifts out of their wealth; but she out of her poverty put in all she had to live on.
> (Luke 21:3-4)

Across the whole population there is a widespread willingness to give. The Charities Aid Foundation regularly surveys charitable giving in the UK. In 2017 88% of the population participated in a charitable or social action, while almost two-thirds (65%) had done so in the month before the survey. Donating to charity peaks in the run-up to Christmas, while sponsorship peaks over the summer months when there are many sporting sponsorship opportunities. Only 5% of people said they never give to charity. However, trust in charities has been an issue following the various scandals in recent years, resulting in only 50% agreeing that charities are trustworthy, more women than men. Of all charitable giving, 19% was to religious causes of every sort. I believe it is highly likely that the majority of the giving to religious causes will have been to churches or Christian charities.[1]

Poorer people are not 'let off' giving. In Nehemiah, after the Book of the Law had first been read to the people (chapter 8), they gathered again to hear more, which led to the Levites confessing the sins of the nation throughout its history (chapter 9). The response was that the leaders, Levites and priests made a binding agreement to

> ... obey carefully all the commands, regulations and decrees of the LORD our Lord.
> (Nehemiah 10:29)

All the people agreed, even though it included a responsibility to give as God had set out in the Law. They therefore were agreeing to give money for the service of the house of the Lord

(10:32) and to tithe their crops to provide for those who served in the temple (10:37-38). Those people were almost certainly poor, whether they had returned from exile or were descendants of the poorest people left behind to work the land when most of the people were taken into captivity (2 Kings 25:12). Hanani tells his brother, Nehemiah:

> Those who survived the exile and are back in the province are in great trouble and disgrace.
> (Nehemiah 1:3)

It was therefore out of their poverty that they promised to give money and tithes. And that can still be true today. Those of us who have had the privilege of visiting churches in poorer countries of the world have often been overwhelmed by the generosity of believers, but it is also true in the UK:

> *The less people have, the more they are willing to give – that has been my experience all the way through life and ministry. I come from very poor communities and the church never had a problem with money! For some people it was the difference between whether they put the heating on or not: they gave their money to the church first, so it was a response of faith. The people who had more – and there were professionals in our churches as well who had good incomes – were challenged by the witness and giving of people in terms of their own giving.*
>
> *Giving to the church was something we thought and prayed about every year, and we had a stewardship officer who was shameless in encouraging people: week two in the church and you were on her list! She had a beautiful way of engaging people about money that was very natural. Prayer and teaching and a sense of gratitude are so important, rather than giving being seen as necessary to pay the bills – which is how quite a lot of people in the church see it.*

Meeting running costs
For both churches and charities, meeting the regular expenses and running costs is the most demanding financially. One difficulty is that in churches it can be hard to separate clearly

what are running costs and what is mission. For example, which does the minister's salary count as?

> *When it comes to doing something big and exciting and missional and you can articulate a vision, I don't actually find it difficult. With clarity of vision, people will often give over and above their regular giving for something they can perceive and see is in line with the charitable objectives, whereas for the day-to-day expenses it's much harder to convince them. Money is given for mission, but when you look at what we use our money for, if you rule out your own role* [as a minister]*, such a small percentage goes on actual mission. I think it's much clearer when it's a separate charity because all your overheads and running costs are clear and there's much more onus to communicate what you're spending your money on and why.*

Much of the money given in offerings to the church does go directly or indirectly to pay the minister and that can lead to them feeling uncomfortable or embarrassed to talk about giving:

> *I don't understand the thinking that I'm asking them to pay my wages; it doesn't even occur to me. But that is a real handicap for some ministers; it's in the forefront of their mind so they are embarrassed about discussing giving within the church. There's a particular challenge for ministers who are directly employed by the church, as they are in nonconformist denominations. I can understand that would be very difficult. It can also be difficult if Anglican clergy feel they are being asked to raise their own stipend when they're talking about freewill offering or Parish Share.*
>
> *I don't understand that mindset, it's not one I've ever had myself. I look at it that we're asking people to give in response to God's generosity and to support the life and mission of the church, which covers all sorts of different things, only one of which is meeting the cost of the clergy.*

Covering the background costs is an issue for charities also, especially missions, which have seen a significant change to more support directed towards individuals and projects rather than the day-to-day work needed to keep a charity running:

> *Getting core funding is very difficult: no one wants to fund that, they want to fund the exciting projects, they want to fund people, not structures. Just look at the foodbanks, they're a fantastic group of people, but it's much easier to raise interest in, donations to, and money for the foodbanks than it is to launch a campaign against the causes of many people going to foodbanks.*

Churches' giving to charities

Quite a lot of churches give away some of what they receive. My own parish gives regularly to four UK charities and four international ones and also tithes what is given on our annual Gift Day. In churches with that sort of policy, one of the questions for their individual members is whether to give directly to charities as well as through their church, and if they decide to give separately what proportion of their giving goes in each direction. For those in a church which doesn't give gifts to charities, the question for individuals is whether they should do so privately:

> *I did a private survey in one church asking individuals how much they gave to church and charities. Their question was, should the charity giving be done through the church or independently of the church, should they send money directly to the charity concerned? Some folk could handle both quite happily.*

Deciding what to give to and how are important decisions for individuals, and both churches and charities are wise to support people in making those decisions. Personally, I would love to see every church member supporting one charity beyond their church: if everyone was taught to find a charity whose work they can identify with, it would make it much easier for charities to find new supporters.

Who benefits?

Church members, whether they realise it or not, are giving to something they benefit from: the minister who takes their services (paid directly or indirectly), keeping the building they meet in in good repair and providing for the mission and ministry that many of the givers are themselves involved in. Money given to charities can seem to go to something more remote; the benefits go to other people, perhaps in faraway places or with staff they have never met. Part of the answer goes back to discipleship and helping people to understand why they should give:

> *While it is true that most givers do not receive any personal benefit from their liberality, it is usually true that they feel they have given as the Lord required of them.*

Difficulties sourcing finance

A pressure for charities and for special projects for churches is that there has been much less money available from grant-making trusts since the financial crash of 2008, though things were changing before that. Trusts rarely give away their capital, rather they invest it and make grants from the return on those investments. After years of low interest rates, the amount available has shrunk, with a corresponding reduction in the number of grants made and more specific criteria for applicants. Fewer will consider applications from religious charities, others may limit their grants to particular geographical locations, and most only want to fund new projects. Even then, there's no guarantee:

> *You're always in a bit of a chicken and egg situation around funding – it's a risk when you take on members of staff and start up new projects when you've only got short-term funding ... So you take decisions, believing that with x, y and z in place you should get the funding but you don't have it as a guarantee at that point.*

The kind of work a charity is doing can also make fund-raising or grant applications less likely to be successful:

> *The challenges were the nature of the charity. It was a hard-to-fund area, because it was looking for support for people who, as far as the media are concerned, do not have a legitimate right to any kind of support. So it was a matter of finding the right kind of philanthropic pot that you could go to. Above and beyond that it was looking at ways to generate our own income.*

Acceptable sources of funding

The constant need for money can lead to a lack of care or discernment in what sources are appropriate:

> *There is risk as to who you take money from. You need to research people who are offering you significant amounts of money. In this world where money laundering is around, you need to be quite clear that the money being offered has not come from a money-laundered source.*

There are particular issues around what is considered a suitable source of funding, especially ones which directly or indirectly involve some level of gambling. The most obvious of these is National Lottery money, but there are others that worry some people, such as raising money through raffles or prize draws. Individual trustees need to be aware that others on their board may have a different opinion on such matters:

> *There's a discussion to be had around whether you take Lottery money. I'm comfortable myself about that in some settings, and uncomfortable in others. It's a difficult area because the reputation around taking Lottery money is affected by the views of people looking in, whose perspective on whether it's a good or a bad thing may be different to yours, and you don't really have a chance to debate that with them. So trustees need to make clear decisions: if outsiders object to it, but at the same time it's a major source of funding and it's not judged as inappropriate by the trustees, they should have the courage to do it.*

I wouldn't touch Lottery money for anything to do with developing the church's ministry in evangelism, discipleship or anything like that, but in the area of social engagement it is a government source of money, and personally at the point of receiving it I think you are not directly responsible for encouraging people to gamble and you may be denying a really helpful source of money to enable your engagement with very needy people. Trustees need to judge their church's or organisation's position, and what is appropriate.

Communicating the need

Charities face important questions in looking for people who will pray for and give to them: do they publicise their needs and if so, do they do that in general or specific terms; how important are marketing and publicity materials compared with good communication with those who already support them; how much do they say about the sources of income or grants, such as the Lottery? The right balance on such issues varies from one organisation to another:

One organisation I was involved with raised funds from their supporters and used publicity materials and relationships with churches to establish ongoing financial support. With another, there was a principle of dislike of active fund-raising, so the finances were not linked to marketing activity. Finances come largely from people and churches who have heard about and know about the organisation. The strong connections are usually with individuals and churches that have, or have had, relationship with the mission's activity around the world. As times have changed the places money has come from have much more swung towards the contacts of individual workers, meeting their needs and their projects' needs.

Communication with supporters, long-standing and potential new ones, is an important part of the picture. Whether or not specific financial needs are publicised, it is vital to tell supporters clearly and regularly what is being done and how people are benefiting from the work:

Communicating the vision so people think it's worth giving – I think that's a challenge for all charities.

If they haven't told supporting churches enough about what is going on, the people who've always given will go on giving but getting new support is difficult because people don't know what they're giving to. When existing supporters move away or pass away, charities find that as the years go by, the funding reduces because they haven't gained new supporters. So it's important for Trusts to ask themselves how they are making themselves known to new churches or to new people coming into churches. They need to think about new ways of getting the word out there about what they're doing and how much money they need to do the work.

Fund-raising strategy

There are times when it is necessary or helpful to look at the way funds are being raised, and perhaps consider a different approach to either replace or supplement what is currently being done:

Most charities are financially driven, rather than seeing where things are shaping up. We did a very brave thing and totally reshaped the financial structure. The reason for that was not to be driven by finances but to set a strategy that would help us develop and to do that by changing the whole financial model. There was a very clear new financial strategy which, if you looked at it in the short term, could have been harmful financially, but was very clear about diversifying where the finances came from. So many wait for the crisis and by then they're too late to make those major changes.

Managing the money

Budgets

A key part of managing the available or anticipated money is setting a budget. That is sometimes done by a small group: perhaps the minister or CEO, the treasurer and the chair. It is an important document, not only because it puts into black and white what income will be needed to meet the commitments in the coming year, but also because it is a vital management tool throughout the year:

> *The budget was set by the CEO in association with the senior staff, which should have been linked to the strategic plan – though I don't think it always was – and the budget was approved by the board. The finance director and the CEO would meet with the treasurer, who was a trustee, and the treasurer was always quite deeply involved in budget discussions.*

Because the income cannot be budgeted in the same way that it can in a business, it is not uncommon to set a deficit budget, believing in faith that God will supply, though it is wise to have plans as to how to meet the deficit or what to do if it is not met:

> *We have done that once or twice recently because we have some legacy money, which has enabled us to do specific projects. There is no reserve policy for the church, so legacy money therefore is effectively available. Before that legacy money was available, we would have had a Gift Day and members would be encouraged to consider their giving and make a fresh statement of what they are able and willing to give – and as a result we have seen the budget met.*

> *With faith organisations, people don't set a deficit budget because they say, 'In faith, this is what we're going to do this year, so the money will come in.' To make that faith reality, in general it's lots and lots of letters to Trusts, going back to supporters, reviewing every couple of months whether you're getting in the needed money, making special appeals and so on. You also have to monitor what you're spending your money on; for example, there are a lot of Christian conferences where you can go and advertise, but you have to pay to go, so you have to ask the question, 'Is it worth having a stall at this conference, is it going to actually increase our footprint or whatever?'*

It is sometimes amazing to see how God supplies!

> *We are reliant on grants or donations. We don't have a very large turnover so some grant funds we can't access because we're not big*

enough. Every year we look at our reserves and our balance at the end of the year and think, 'How can that possibly be?'

I've never set out with a deficit budget and not been able to balance the books at the end of the day. It goes back to risk management and I think there are times when, with the knowledge you have of your supporters or your congregation, and the sense of straining forward for the growth of the kingdom, there are times when people should be challenged about their giving. But if time after time you set a deficit budget and don't balance the books, you have a different challenge, which trustees must honestly face.

Understanding the finances

Many trustees don't feel they understand accounts and budgets. When I first became chair of a board, I had to work very hard to come to grips with the pages of numbers which the treasurer produced. A helpful way to lift that burden from the board as a whole is to delegate the detailed work to the people who do understand the financial detail:

We had a finance subcommittee that dealt with the accounts and they met separately, so when finance came to the board, which it did pretty much every meeting, we were presented with a statement of facts which other members of the board had OK'd. We didn't need to know the finer details, so we didn't have to spend an hour going through the detail of the accounts, which some of us would have struggled to do. On the finance subcommittee they had someone who wasn't a governor and wasn't a member of staff but had expertise in that area.

We'd have budget spreadsheets at every trustees meeting so we could see budgeted spend, predicted spend, actual spend, see clearly what was coming in. We also had an accountant on the board and other people who had a very keen eye for the figures. So budget decisions were made by consensus but very much led by people with a considerable amount of experience and expertise.

Good practice around finance is to ensure you have those other people on the board who understand accounts and budgeting and can interpret the figures presented to them. If all the financial decisions are made by one person without proper oversight by the board, that can lead to negligence; for example, when no one is aware that funds are drying up or have slipped into an unplanned overdraft.

In small churches it is unlikely there will be enough people with the right expertise to form a subcommittee; indeed, even finding a treasurer can be extremely difficult, partly because of the increasing demands made on them:

> *Some of the things that I encounter were never regarded as particularly excellent practice – I met one chap who's doing a sterling job but who keeps the accounts of the church in a tiny notebook in his pocket! It's basically the in and the out and you could call that double-entry booking but it's not really! Helping people to see how they can enable others to help them with that is important: you don't have to be a church member to be the treasurer, so we have treasurers in various villages who belong to other denominations and who do the treasurer's work for the local church because they belong to the village.*

Financial trustworthiness

Looking at the accounts regularly and carefully and giving prayerful consideration to the finances is important for several reasons.

Monitoring income

Trustees should monitor how much money is coming in, and whether steps need to be taken to encourage more giving or seek alternative sources of income:

> *Money can be a very provocative area of life. I think trustees should set out to manage their funding arrangements in a very thorough way. Firstly, if they are doing something that people should be interested in supporting, they ought to give them every opportunity to give personal monies, and as much as possible give it in a sustainable and unrestricted way.*
>
> *People need to think through where is faith in raising money, and the sources they look to for that money in relation to the end product*

of what that money is supposed to do. I think the larger and more successful a ministry gets, the greater the peril of having to compromise from where you seek to get money. Trying to sustain what you do through changing economic circumstances is a really difficult thing to do.

Monitoring expenditure

It is vital to keep a watch on what the money is being spent on and important to do so in the light of your vision and strategy:

Stand back and look at what are the priorities and ask if the money is going towards those priorities or is it going in other directions? Trying to make sure that money was going to the key things they had decided were the key things to pursue.

The peril of fund-raising from grant-making Trusts, a local council and the like is that they provide money for their purposes, not the organisation's purposes, and for a limited period of time. Charities and ministries can therefore sometimes adapt to make their organisation fit to get that money, but that may not be precisely where they want their organisation to be. That can be dangerous in the long term.

It is wise, too, to think carefully about accepting gifts or grants which come with conditions attached. That may be perfectly acceptable if, say, the money is given to support a particular worker or project. When it causes problems is if the conditions include starting something new which is not in line with the current vision, or does not fit in the Objects of the charity. Fulfilling the donor's conditions may lead trustees to drift away from the core focus of the church or charity:

Unrestricted funding is a hugely liberating form of funding and needs to be massively encouraged, and I don't think it's understood well enough. Money without strings attached is crucially important.

Staying legal

It is too easy to assume that if money is being spent on why the charity exists, then it is being spent legally correctly:

In one of the charities of which I was chair, I resigned when I discovered a clear illegal irregularity in the accounts, which other trustees felt was justified. When I told a friend who was a solicitor about it, he told me to go and write down what I had done and why, giving the evidence for my action, so that if the irregularity came to light and I was questioned about my action, I would have the notes by which I could defend myself.

You must look after your own charity and the resources that have been given for that. If in a business you were paying somebody off, you would make an ex-gratia payment. But you can't do that in a charity without Charity Commission permission because any payment is not being made to directly benefit the Objects of the charity. Even though it's good personal practice, you are not free to do it without permission and that gets missed time and time again. Nor are you free to give money to another charity – there are ways round it but you must do it knowingly.

Money coming from or going to overseas is increasingly controlled as banks and HMRC (Her Majesty's Revenue and Customs) look for ways to reduce money laundering. HMRC has requirements for charities sending monies overseas and they also look at charity accounts to ensure monies are all spent for charitable purposes. Some churches have run into difficulties in these matters and found themselves facing a large tax demand, while international charities have had to develop new procedures and practices to enable them to fund overseas workers and projects.

Accountability

Charities have to lodge their accounts with the Charity Commission, and they must be compliant with the Commission's SORP (Statement of Recommended Practice).

This applies to churches too, though it may only be when a church has to register individually that the trustees become aware of the requirements:

> *They suddenly realise that the report and accounts that they've been producing haven't been SORP compliant for a long time. They've got away with it because the diocese will just take a set of accounts, but the reality now is that they have to do a properly compliant set of accounts.*

Difficult decisions

Finance is most often behind the need to make a difficult decision, such as making a member of staff redundant or even closing the organisation. It is one thing to close a charity because it has completed what it was set up to do or perhaps has handed it on, but it's another thing to be forced into closure because the finance is not properly monitored or managed:

> *Things went so badly wrong, because the model worked while there was funding in place, but was never really properly owned by the church. The Trust was set up with funding from big employers in the city and in time a longer list of organisations contributed. The funding was enough at one time to employ five people. But with the financial crisis of 2008 and following, almost all of that funding disappeared over a relatively short time. The charity faced the situation of diminishing funding and one by one those who were employed by the Trust were made redundant – I was the last one, and the Trust closed.*

Financial liability

Trustees can become very concerned about their financial responsibilities and liabilities. It is important to remember that trustees are personally liable for losses which result from negligence. That is why it is vital for a board to take professional advice when necessary and document why they took particular decisions – they are not liable if they have made a reasonable mistake, but they must be able to demonstrate that.

When we considered risk in Chapter 4, the matter of Professional Indemnity Insurance was covered and a board may want to consider that. Insurers who specialise in insuring churches and charities may include it with Public Liability Insurance, so it is a question worth asking when renewing or changing insurance. Keeping alert to what is happening in a charity should, hopefully, avoid any possibility of negligence. But remembering that Daniel was considered trustworthy 'because he was neither corrupt nor negligent' is a call to be aware of any possibility of corruption. Sadly, it is not unknown for churches and charities, including Christian ones, to find that some of their funds have been stolen or embezzled by someone they thought they could trust. Any suspicion about accounts always has to be investigated thoroughly.

As Christians it is too easy to go to one extreme or the other about money, either to become blasé or be overly concerned about it. Handling it well is another aspect in which trustworthiness is demonstrated, but money should not be allowed to control the vision or limit the mission of the church or charity.

Every penny does indeed count, but God knows how many of them we need!

Questions

Which takes priority in your decision-making: finance or vision? And where does faith come into the decisions about setting the budget?

Do you have difficulties getting trustees who understand finance, or finding a treasurer? If so, could you share a treasurer with another church or charity, or have a finance subcommittee which includes some non-trustees?

What positive stories about God's provision can you recall, which would encourage not only you but also the trustees you work with?

12
Who Cares?
Accountability

It pleased the king to send me; so I set a time ...
while all this was going on, I was not in Jerusalem, for
in the thirty-second year of Artaxerxes king of
Babylon I had returned to the king.
(Nehemiah 2:6; 13:6)

We are accountable to God in Christ for what we do, we're accountable to
one another as Christians, we are accountable to the wider church – but
it's a challenge to hold all these things together.

'Who would miss you if you closed?' is a question we used to ask as part of Vision Building days by Christian Research for churches or charities. The variety of answers varied enormously: some participants were very clear and had obviously thought about it, while others were stumped for answers! The question was aimed at helping them think who their stakeholders were, but it is the same people and groups to whom charities need to be accountable. In the interviews I did for this book I found a similar mixture of responses: most interviewees had a clear understanding, but not all:

I suppose ultimately we feel we're accountable to God for the decisions that we make; we're guardians of resources that people have given to us on a charitable basis. And the Charity Commission, of course – but beyond that, I don't know.

What is accountability?

Looking at dictionary definitions of 'accountable' it is clear that there are two aspects to it: first, being answerable about the actions taken and who needs to know about them, and second, the process of explaining them. Some forms of accountability are very clearly defined, especially those to do with finance, including HMRC or where the Charity Commission is concerned. But accountability is much wider than that:

Trustees are accountable in several directions: to each other within the trustees, to the beneficiaries of the Trust, the people who are employed by the Trust and the volunteers, to supporters and funders, to the wider Church – because if a Trust is operating in the name of the Church there has to be accountability to that wider Church, and there are ways in which any charity is accountable to the Charity Commissioners. If it's operating as a faith-based operation, all of that comes under accountability to God.

Accountable to others

This is where the 'Who would miss you if you closed?' question comes in, because the people and groups who would most miss a charity or church are those who either support it or benefit from what it does:

In a human sense, the board collectively, through the chair, need to be accountable both to their 'customers' (their client group), their staff and volunteers, and to their supporters.

Financial accountability is what most trustees tend to think of first, whether that is to supporters of a charity or congregation members who give to a church:

For any charity, there is accountability to those who support it, and that underlies what the Charity Commission is trying to do with its frameworks. They are saying, 'You are in receipt of money from the wider community and you therefore have responsibilities there, and we're reminding you of those, towards the people who have given. They have given with the intention that you will use the money for the purpose for which the charity exists.'

While accountability definitely includes finance, it is much wider than that.

The Charity Commission

All charities have a legal responsibility to fulfil charity law. This is 'policed' by the Charity Commission, and charities which fall foul of the requirements are investigated (or ought to be!), sometimes with the sort of devastating results we considered when thinking about risk:

We're accountable legally to the Charity Commission – we should be accountable to those who are funding us and supporting us. In a charity that's clear, why we are here, what we are doing and who is supporting us, but in a church there is a sense that we are trying to honour God, and sometimes the Charity Commission – and even the church – is an annoyance! In a charity the roles of everybody who's employed are much more clearly defined, there's much more care taken. The trustees of a charity potentially are stronger because they feel more clearly the responsibility of how the money is spent, whereas in a church, trustees tend to feel they're there to help the leadership.

HMRC

The Charity Commission is not the only body which may look carefully at a charity's accounts; so may HMRC. They can challenge expenditure which has not been spent on charitable purposes and issue a tax demand on what they consider uncharitable expenditure. For example, this has happened with churches which have paid their senior staff what HMRC considers as unreasonable expenses. If those expense claims cannot be justified as part of the public benefit required of charities, then a tax claim has been sent to the church. It is one of the responsibilities of trustees, particularly treasurers, to make sure the accounts and declarations for tax purposes do not hide anything like that.

Public benefit – the 'clients'

Charities exist for the public benefit and that implies an ability to demonstrate that the public are in fact benefiting:

> *We knew we were accountable to the law of the land and the Charity Commission, but there was also a huge sense of moral accountability to the people we were helping because they were destitute – by definition they had nothing. So to take away the little that we offered them was absolutely life-transforming in the most negative way. If we were negligent in decision-making, that had an impact on them.*

A denomination or network

Many charities and churches are part of a network or denomination, which will have terms and conditions that they expect the members of the network to adhere to. For Anglican churches this is set out in ecclesiastical law, but any group with such wider affiliations implicitly accepts accountability to that network:

> *By choosing to be on a PCC, by choosing to be part of the Church of England, you are in a sense accepting accountability to that body. In the wider Christian charities sense I would say that if you affiliate to a wider network, that is part of your accountability as trustees, as well as to your local body and the legal responsibilities to the Charity Commission. If you sign up to be part of a network and gain benefit from that network, whether that be the Evangelical Alliance or a particular network of independent churches or whatever, you have some accountability to them.*
>
> *Increasingly the public and the statutory authorities expect that. 'We've said we're part of them' therefore we will expect the wider world on occasion to view us through their lens. So, part of the responsibility trustees have is to consider whether they are challenging other people that they're working with to be open and accountable. If*

they're uncomfortable about what they are affiliating with, it will impact back on them as a body.

This wider accountability can be a difficult thing, especially when it cuts across local concerns. In the Church of England it is seen particularly in multi-parish benefices where there is pressure to act for the common good of all the parishes rather than for the specific interests of one. I suspect it could be true also in a Methodist Circuit, though I do not know of a specific example for that, whereas I was told about such a situation in a diocese:

> *There are seven parishes in one deanery, where over eighteen months, six have decided to become a united parish and the seventh is not joining in. They are sitting on a fortune that they are not contributing to the diocese, not even paying for their incumbent's costs when they've got huge amounts of money. We can't sell a vacant rectory because we can't until they've made a decision, so financially they're costing the diocese a lot of money while they're arguing about the detail. Their incumbent is really challenging them about what it says about them as Christians. So now the six parishes are in agreement and we've got this one parish, as it were, over here, and how we police that ... we don't really want them to kill each other! But it does get very intense at times between people in a situation like that.*

There can also be tensions when a church's income is over the threshold which requires them to register as a separate charity. Charity law requires charities to use their resources to the best benefit of the charity, which means putting your own work and ministry first, but that can conflict with the needs and requirements of the wider denomination or network:

> *People will say, 'We're not answerable to you because we're registered independently.' That is a tension for any denominational body: how much do we look after the interests of this church and how much do we look out to the wider body and look after its interests? We see this particularly with the ones who've registered and perhaps have more professional trustees or those with a legal background. They'll say,*

'The responsibility of trustees is to look after the interests of "our" charity and we don't believe it's in the interests of "our" charity to give you [the diocese] money.' We have to remind them that although it's a freewill offering this is what is paying for their incumbent and if they choose to only give us, say, £10,000, that's out of balance considering they have a big enough turnover that they've had to register as a separate charity. That is a balance for them, what is in the best interests of their charity, but part of what PCCs exist for is to help the Church of England flourish everywhere, not just in their own place.

When it comes to issues such as employment or safeguarding, there may be accountability within a denomination, although as some have sought to decentralise, it can leave churches and trustees feeling vulnerable. Having guidelines in place doesn't guarantee that they either can or will be followed:

Increasingly the Methodist Church has pushed things which used to be dealt with at circuit or district level down to the local church level, so now the buck stops with me. There are people I can talk to but if it's not right in the church it's my problem — so in that sort of situation I don't have trustee backing, even though they may have made the decision. The responsibility is on my shoulders and that's nerve-wracking. For example, it used to be that people who were employed were employed by the Circuit, but now individual churches have to do their own employment stuff, if we don't contract it out, so we're always wondering whether we're adhering to the regulations correctly. The trouble is that much of it is being done by volunteers whom I have to trust to be doing the right thing, and I don't have the time to check everything. I am aware of some of these issues that have taken place in big charities and I think, 'Well, of course trustees wouldn't have known that', because who has the time to go into the detail of what everybody's doing rather than manage the big picture? When you've got five churches, as I have, you have to trust that people are doing the right thing. There are systems that should hopefully show up things that are going wrong, but I think something could go on an awfully long time before that happened.

Members, supporters and donors

How accountability works out in practice is slightly different for churches and separate charities:

> *Personally as a trustee I feel accountable to God for what I'm doing and the calling that is there, and then obviously feel very accountable to the Charity Commission because they've given us permission to function and we need to fulfil their legal requirements and not do anything in any way that would undermine that. Accountability to our donors as well, providing good annual reports which show where their money has gone, how it's been spent, what's been achieved. In the church there's also a strong sense of accountability to God but maybe not so much to the Charity Commission. There's strong accountability to the congregation who are giving on a weekly or monthly basis, to help them understand what's happening with these resources and where they're being spent — and they're able to question that.*

Accountability to donors includes being answerable for how grants or other such financial provisions have been used. When YoYo was receiving grants to support staff, the recipient was required to write an annual report on their activities, focusing on how the money that Trust had given had benefited the work. A small local example is that our local Parish Council gave a grant to the church to install lighting on the footpath leading from a country lane up to one of the buildings. I was asked to take some before and after photos so the councillors could see the resulting improvement.

An international network or association

Mission agencies and relief and development organisations have accountability beyond the UK. In some ways this is very similar to a UK or local network, but it has some distinctive demands.

> The accountability we have within the Association counters some of the autonomy that offices enjoy — it's not unfettered. There are checks and balances as the Association, so there's that confidence which comes from

someone else keeping an eye on things, which I think is positive ... It has real potential to enable us to achieve more through being joined up than a very fragmented group of individual offices.[1]

As we have considered earlier in relation to international structures, this kind of international network carries with it cultural and legal considerations which have to be worked through carefully.

Accountability to one another

Trustees are not only accountable externally, they are also accountable to one another:

> If I'm on the board of something, I should be investing in it, and often for me, because we didn't have a lot of money it wasn't investment of money but it was investment of time, such as teaching for free. Accountability to my family – if you're spending a lot of time serving an organisation, you shouldn't be doing it without the support of your family. Accountable to each other as trustees, I'm quite in favour of board appraisals although we never quite got round to doing it. Two of us always appraised the CEO and that gave the CEO the opportunity to feed back a bit about his appraisal of the board, but in my experience there's not much goes on in terms of appraising individual board members.

Appraising trustees is where a job or role description for them can be very helpful, especially as trustees are volunteers and it is horribly easy to be vague about what is expected of volunteers:

> I think it's become increasingly important to have something set out. It gives some clarity – setting up a volunteer's job description makes both parties – the appointing party and the appointee – think about what might be involved and what should be involved and enables a discussion about how realistic it is. If people feel they can't fulfil it, it isn't fatal to the appointment, but it strengthens people's understanding of what's being demanded of them and helps them

think about it. It also creates a structure from which some accountability can be held.

It is often part of the chair's role to hold other trustees accountable. I have only once had to ask a trustee to stand down. The organisation's trustee job description contained the following statements: 'Willing to devote time and effort to the duties of trustee, including attendance at meetings' and 'Absence without permission from all meetings within a period of six months may lead to trustees resolving that a trustee has vacated office, and has thereby terminated the appointment'. The person concerned had only turned up once or twice a year during their three-year term and their contribution to the board was minimal. When I challenged that trustee, the person acknowledged that they hadn't pulled their weight, and agreed not to stand for re-election for a further term. To be honest, even if they had stood I don't think they would have been appointed!

While the chair is in a position to appraise other trustees and hold them accountable, who does that for him or her? This applies not only to chairs of separate charities but also to ministers. In most denominations there is an accountability structure, though it doesn't always function well:

My job description is to be and to follow my calling; plenty of expectation but it's rarely measured by anybody.

Ministers in other churches, especially but not exclusively independent ones, have no one officially to appraise them or to whom they are meant to be accountable. In that case it is up to trustees to consider what they can suggest, or actively put in place, to support the minister. Something similar can also be very helpful and supportive for chairs who are not a minister:

At one church I was at they asked me to be line manager of the minister. He and I had a monthly meeting, so he had a chance to offload things, I had a chance to offer hopefully an objective view of what I saw, and there was a friendship in that. A minister probably needs someone like that; if it can be done acceptably within the church and that's alright with everybody, OK. If not, he or she needs to be accountable to somebody in another church or a fellow minister, and that can be a profound friendship.

As in decision-making, there can be misunderstanding, sadly sometimes open conflict about accountability, particularly when the chair or minister is a strong leader who believes they have the right to make decisions without reference to anyone. Once those decisions have been made, that sort of person can be very defensive if they are challenged, which is actually rejecting accountability. One church I knew about had such a minister, who believed it was his God-given right to make decisions about how the church was run, what activities it undertook and how those were carried out, and how the money was spent. He had a group of elders, but he saw them only as providing spiritual support and would not even allow them to see the accounts. Sadly, over a year or two, a number of the key people left the church, leaving him with fewer and fewer people to undertake the mission activities or give the finance needed.

What accountability involves

Accountability doesn't happen by chance! There are legal requirements which should be part of the annual cycle of work for a board, particularly the Annual Report and accounts:

You have to publish accounts, to provide an Annual Report to the Charity Commissioners, and those things are public documents. Very often there will be some kind of annual meeting, but depending on the nature of the charity those things can be ... closed shops rather than being genuinely open to stakeholders.

In terms of honesty, openness and trustworthiness, those legal requirements matter. In the current climate accountability means having in place policies and procedures and ensuring they are adhered to, as well as following best practice in employment, governance and other such responsibilities. Lack of accountability is often behind the issues which cause charities to get into trouble.

However, accountability is just as much about good communication: who needs to know what, how best can they be told, what will strengthen links with supporters or keep the congregation well informed, and so on:

> *It makes sense to communicate to supporters because without them the organisation wouldn't be able to do x, y and z. Written communications have become more and more expensive but electronic communication and social media are increasingly important.*

> *You need to have regular reports internally, so the staff should report regularly to the trustees and the trustees to the staff. The trustees need at least once a year to report publicly to the supporters and you obviously have to report to the Charity Commission and if you're a Company Limited by Guarantee as well, to Companies House. So there are the formal reporting lines of accountability that the State demands of us, and that needs to be done in a timely way. It's awful to go to the Charity Commission register and to see Christian charity after Christian charity that hasn't submitted their accounts on time: it's dishonouring and it undermines confidence. It isn't so difficult, if somebody has their finger on the button, to keep to those deadlines. Then in the reports you have a great opportunity to tell the public what you are doing – reports are read by all sorts of people, so giving time to that accountability and finding the right people to do the crafting of the words is a really good and helpful thing.*

Accountability in a church or charity is significantly different to accountability in a business, and that can be difficult when a church or charity is also running a business. Even though it should be legally separate, church members or the charity's supporters often apply the same thinking, which can make it very hard for the business to thrive:

> *The church runs a café and we see it as mission, so we're always working in deficit. Some people say, 'Come on, we need to balance our books here, why can't we do this?' I've come to the conclusion that*

churches and Christian organisations are not good at running businesses and you'd be far better giving it to a Christian businessman and charging him rent and letting him get on with it. In a business environment you've got to be pretty hard-nosed, you've got to be able to make courageous decisions and sometimes decisions that people don't like. And that's very hard for charities to do in a setting where the people involved are very strong stakeholders – they're raising funds and some of those funds go to administration rather than the frontline ministry and that's where it becomes hard and we perhaps become more pastorally inclined than businesslike.

Financial accountability is hugely important, but it can have some negative effects. One is that it can become too important:

PCCs are accountable to the wider Church and they are also accountable to the congregation, in terms of how they are stewarding the resources of the church, whatever those resources are. They have accountability to live out the gospel, but sometimes they get weighed down by the money and the buildings so that they feel strangled and not able to engage with the bigger issues.

Another danger is that accountability can be allowed to control vision, and even divert a charity from its primary focus:

Most trustees feel themselves accountable to the, say, two or three churches which regularly give them big donations, even though other churches may support them financially or prayerfully or with volunteers. The danger with that is they can forget what they were set up to do and can be guided by their major supporting churches about what they should do, rather than being guided by their Governing Document. 'If we do this kind of work in this place, this church will continue to give us money,' rather than saying to the churches, 'This is what we were set up to do and we would be grateful if you would still support us, but we need to do what we were set up to do.' Trustees need to have that balance between what they were set up to do and what their supporting churches want them to do.

Keeping the balance is important so that accountability is clear but internally it is not allowed to control culture or vision in negative ways. Externally, the high-profile issues of recent years mean there are increasing demands for accountability by donors, current and potential supporters and the general public as well as the legal requirements.

Accountable to God

When Nehemiah asked the king for permission to go and rebuild the walls of Jerusalem, the king granted him permission but asked him to set a time when he would return. Twelve years later, Nehemiah did return to the king, although after some time he asked to make a return visit and was allowed to do so (13:6-7). However, Nehemiah clearly knew himself to be accountable to God as well as to the king. Twice he describes his situation in Jerusalem as due to

> ... the gracious hand of my God ... on me.
> (Nehemiah 2:8,18)

He repeatedly reminded the people that the rebuilding of the wall was primarily God's responsibility, not only theirs:

> The God of heaven will give us success.
> (Nehemiah 2:20)

> Hear us, our God, for we are despised.
> (Nehemiah 4:4)

> Don't be afraid of them. Remember the Lord, who is great and awesome.
> (Nehemiah 4:14)

> Our God will fight for us!
> (Nehemiah 4:20)

> This work had been done with the help of our God.
> (Nehemiah 6:16)

They offered great sacrifices, rejoicing because God had given them great joy.
(Nehemiah 12:43)

Towards the end of the book he three times asks God to remember him for what he has done, showing that he knew he was answerable primarily to God for anything he had achieved (Nehemiah 13:14,22,31).

Our accountability to God is the added dimension of accountability that trustees of churches and Christian charities should be constantly aware of:

They should be both individually and collectively accountable to the Lord. There has to be a sense of that being maintained.

This covers many of the things we have already considered in this book, for example:

- Seeking a God-given vision which contributes to the growth of His kingdom

- Getting a good balance between faith and risk

- Appointing trustees who are willing to take on the role as part of their service for God rather than because of pride or friendships

- Praying together if that is appropriate

- Running the church or charity well so that what outsiders see honours God

- Being aware in all decision-making and actions that what is done is for the benefit of others, not personal benefit.

Maintaining our Christian values and ethos in a challenging and changing world is a vital part of our accountability to God – and our trustworthiness.

Questions

Who is your trustee board accountable to, and how is that carried out in practice?

Are there any groups that perhaps you should be accountable to, but you currently are not? What could you do about it?

In what ways are you accountable to one another, and how is that worked out for your minister or chair?

SECTION 4

FUTURE TRACKS

13
Where Do We Go From Here? Succession Planning, Possible Future Trends

I heard, but I did not understand. So I asked, 'My lord, what will the outcome of all this be?'
(Daniel 12:8)

It's unlikely to get any simpler: legislation just seems to keep coming from different directions.

Daniel's question to the angel about the meaning of his last vision is how many of us sometimes feel about the situation of our church or charity. We see things going on around us, perhaps other charities in the area closing, or the church declining, and we do not know what the outcome will be. Maybe there are political or financial changes locally, nationally or internationally, or insecurity because of other factors. A board is wise to seek to understand what the implications might be. This is not the same as vision for the future although vision might be refreshed, redirected or grow out of such considerations.

This penultimate chapter focuses on two aspects of looking to the future in relation to governance: how an individual charity or church can prepare for the years ahead, and some suggestions of possible challenges and opportunities for Christian charities and churches as British society changes. It is impossible to completely future-proof our organisations, but there are some steps we can take that will help.

The local future

Succession planning – the leader

A significant part of preparing for the future in a church or charity is succession planning, not only for trustees but also for the key staff who actually carry out the ministry. This is particularly important if a founder leader of a charity believes the work should continue beyond his or her involvement. When I was editing the *UK Christian Handbook* we noticed how many organisations closed around twenty or thirty years after they were founded:

> *Many were run by one person, at least initially, and closed because the leader had not been able to find someone with the same vision to take over. So finding successors is an ongoing duty. Not everyone has a successor – Elijah had Elisha as his successor, but Elisha had no individual successor, though there were many prophets in the various schools of prophets that he looked after.*

In a charity, employment is the trustees' responsibility, so it should be part of their work to consider how and when a successor may be needed and to have contingency plans for if that has to happen sooner than expected:

> *The newer the charity is and the more entrepreneurial the charity is, the more likely it is for the vision to come from the founder leader. That can lead to a major problem when the founder leader moves on and the next person comes in who may have a slightly different vision, or is perceived by others to have a slightly different vision. I think of one very small charity which was established by a very dynamic leader who then moved on. The next person who came in had a very different*

vision, which I actually think was a more rounded and therefore better vision, but he was undermined by the founder. With a very strong leader there is founder syndrome, which can harm people and harm the work. What can easily happen is that you have a second leader who might have the same vision but their interpretation of it is nuanced differently and the strategy is different and sometimes the founder then undermines them.

I can empathise with that situation. When I became leader of a department of the mission I belonged to, the founder leader was still part of the ministry although working in a different location. Perhaps partly because I was a woman and much younger than him, he felt he could control what decisions were made and it was a battle of wills and tactics when I believed it was right to take a slightly different path. Some of the house church streams which developed in the 1970s and 1980s had a similar struggle to pass on leadership from the original leader, who was often very charismatic – in both senses of the word!

Succession planning in a church can be difficult, depending on the denomination, but it is not impossible. Here in York there is an example: St Michael le Belfry is a large Anglican church next to York Minster. A previous vicar appointed an associate, and when the vicar moved on two years later, the associate replaced him as vicar. Similar succession has happened in other Anglican churches. It is easier to do in a large church and is also not unknown in other denominations.

In most situations it is the role of the trustees to appoint a new leader so it is essential that thought, care and prayer is given to how that process takes place. It can be very problematic if the trustees and a new leader are in serious disagreement about the vision and future direction of a church or charity.

Succession planning – trustees
We have previously considered the wisdom of appointing trustees to fill a skills gap, which is an excellent way to work but often happens on a one-by-one basis or at annual elections. Particularly in churches or charities whose trustees serve for a

specific time, usually three years, planning further ahead is a wise move. I used to keep a list of when each trustee was appointed and therefore when they would need to be re-elected or stand down. When you can see two or three years ahead what gaps there will be, it gives time to find the right people without either party feeling pressurised into making a quick decision. Trustees are always needed, and not always easy to find, especially to fill specific roles such as secretary or treasurer, so the further ahead replacements are thought about, the better.

Succession planning – chair

What is true for trustees in general is even more important for the role of chair, especially in charities. A year into serving my final three-year term, I advised the YoYo trustees that I wanted to hand over as chair a year later so there could be a good handover period before my final three years came to an end. It did not work out that way, because although we had identified a potential new chair within that year, the person was not yet even a trustee! We appointed her as a trustee and left the discussion about becoming chair for some months, until it was clear she was potentially the right person and she was open to considering it. Prayer was a significant part of that, and it was a confirmation to both of us when she prayed that if it was right I would propose it soon, and in my prayers I knew it was the right time to approach her. It was some months before the AGM at which the appointment of chair would be confirmed and I would have to step down, so the trustees made a decision to appoint her as chair-designate, meaning there was time for a good handover. Choosing the right chair was considered in Chapter 7, but it is unwise to leave any discussion or action on the matter until after a chair has left. Not facing the issue in advance could even be considered negligent if the chair's departure was known about well ahead of time.

Passing on the values

When new trustees join a board, it can be a steep learning curve. The culture of an organisation includes 'how we do things round here' and even an experienced trustee may find there are significant differences in operation between boards. One of those differences which is not always passed on adequately is an understanding of the principles which underlie the procedures. While the values or principles may be set out in a document, new trustees need to understand and experience how they work in practice:

> *Our principles document very much affects the ways in which decisions are made, particularly on finance. We have principles on finance which are about the way in which we raise finance – we're careful not to be seen as an organisation that's always asking for money, and we're also very nervous about any link between money and influence. It's a heartfelt principle, not one that needs to be expressed a great deal, but it's understood implicitly a lot. As we've brought new trustees in, we've had to induct them in those principles so that they understand how we operate.*

Passing on the vision

I have seen two different scenarios develop when a new generation of trustees (or staff) do not take the vision into their hearts. One danger is that new people coming in, whatever role they take up, can interpret the vision in a different way, which may not be helpful. They may seem to have fresh ideas but if those are not in line with why the charity exists there can be problems. The other danger, particularly in older charities and organisations, is that there can be an implicit assumption that we know what we're here for, so let's just get on with the job. Gradually any passion or excitement about the work drains away and it can all become very mechanical and routine. Trustees need to be alert to this and challenge it when necessary, although they are sometimes the ones who create the problem:

In the early 1990s there was enthusiasm for the idea, and significant funding from a large local company. But then you got change of personnel, somebody retired and somebody new came, and then it was somebody else's idea and somebody else's baby and the enthusiasm for it became distant history. That happens again and again, I think, where new people come into a setting and develop something new, but unless the vision for that is maintained and nurtured it can be very sticky when things go wrong.

Closure

No organisation has an automatic right to continue, whatever the founder leader may think, and preparing for the future might mean being bold enough to decide it should close, and when:

I think too many charities try to carry on after a founder leader and should just close down. I'm talking to one now that needs to close down. The country they are working in was the 'sexy' country of thirty or forty years ago, but now it's a tourist destination, so why would anyone be interested in the kind of work they are trying to do there?

Much better to plan a good closure and celebrate what has been achieved rather than have it thrust upon you. The Christian youth festival, Soul Survivor, did that, announcing well in advance that the events in 2019 would be the last ones, and then making those into great celebrations alongside the challenge to young people that they had become known for.

Closing because of a crisis can leave a mess, and hurt staff and supporters in a way which can negatively affect other ministries in the same kind of work or same local area. A planned closure, marking what the charity has achieved, can challenge supporters and others to think about how they could help to fill any gap that is left, and also encourages those who have given to the charity that their support was not wasted.

Possible societal future trends

The charitable sector has a long and worthy history in the UK, with religious foundations as well as wealthy individuals and families deeply involved in supporting the poor, the sick and the needy. Living in York, I was fascinated to discover that one of the earliest charities still operating in this country is St Peter's School in York, founded in AD627, while the first recorded almshouse in England was established in the city by King Athelstan in the early tenth century. Many old churches, including my own, have boards listing giving to the poor in the seventeenth and eighteenth centuries. With my twenty-first century 'eyes' I find the oldest one amusing:

John Vaux, Alderman, Late Lord Mayor of York,
by his will dated ye 15th November 1641
Did give 10s every Lady-Day to the Minister of Huntington
For Preaching one Sermon.
And 10s to the Poor thereof who shall be
Present at said Sermon and to none else.[1]

The minister was to get ten shillings, a lot of money in those days, but the way I understand the statement is that the poor only got ten shillings between them – and then only if they turned up for the sermon!

Within half a mile of my home is New Earswick, a village built by the Rowntree family to provide housing and many facilities for the workers in their chocolate factory, and the legacy of that family continues today with the work of the Joseph Rowntree Foundation, which is well known for research into poverty and related social issues.

I don't have to look far to see evidence of how charity, and thus charities, have developed and changed over the centuries. The first significant charity legislation was the Charitable Uses Act of 1601, often referred to as the Statute of Elizabeth. The Charitable Trusts Act of 1863 established a national body to oversee charities but after that, charity law did not change significantly until 1950. Then a committee was commissioned by Parliament to produce a report on how to change both law and practice so that the community gained maximum benefit from charities' work. The report was the basis of the Charities Act of 1960.[2] Since then changes have gathered pace, so what changes are taking place now or may happen in the foreseeable future?

Increasing legislation

On my first foray into governance in the early 1980s there were relatively few things I needed to understand and learn that were not already part of my path to becoming a better leader. I discovered there was legislation affecting charities and trusts, but it was significantly less demanding than we now face. Since then there have been further Charities Acts in England and Wales, in 1992, 1993, 2006, 2011 and 2016; in Scotland in 2005 and Northern Ireland in 2008., The Charities Act of 2006 established the current structure and name of the Charity Commission and gave it stronger regulatory powers.[3] Their new emphasis on governance lies behind much of the recent tightening up of trustees' responsibilities and practice.

However, charities are not only affected by charity law: much other legislation applies to them, covering issues such as safeguarding, data protection, fund-raising and money laundering:

> *When I look at what's happened over the past few years, there's already been massive change. If I talk to colleagues, say at the cathedral where one of my friends was appointed a number of years ago, he told me that then there was little governance discussion, but now it is practically all they talk about in their meetings. In my role, we've seen a huge change in what is required. In the diocesan leadership team, we are constantly debating the speed at which we can introduce new things bearing in mind the balance between what is required and what PCCs can tolerate. One of the challenges is that we face people who think we've invented it when there's new legislation that they have to abide by, whereas in fact it's what we're required to do. It's a big issue, how we enable people to engage with all that.*

Some of the legislation has been brought in because of specific cases; for example, the death in 2015 of Olive Cooke, the Bristol poppy seller. There was a public outcry alleging she committed suicide as a result of being inundated with requests from charities for donations. Both her family and the coroner at her inquest denied that, but the emotion surrounding her case was a factor in new legislation regulating fund-raising.[4] Future scandals and crises in the charity sector may well lead to further legislation, while other concerns impinge on charities:

> *Other legal things are coming: I think there are going to be more issues around the influence on trustees, for example from large donors, and the money-laundering issues that might raise.*

There is a tendency to look on new legislation as a burden, a nuisance, yet another thing to cope with and get your collective head around. It certainly can feel that way, but it can have a positive impact as well as a negative one:

> *Increased regulation is a positive as well* [as a negative] *because it will force charities to become more professional where they can. I suppose the risk is that small charities and small churches will end up shutting because they can't manage the regulatory requirements — perhaps that's being a bit over pessimistic!*

Right at the start of the book I proposed that good governance is one way to demonstrate trustworthiness. As legislative requirements increase, I believe that will become more true.

Increasing scrutiny

The combination of more legislation and possibly (though hopefully not) more scandals in the charity sector and churches means it is not surprising that the Charity Commission and others want to keep a closer watch. In November 2018 the Charity Commission launched its new strategic direction, which was intended to challenge and support charities to raise their standards and practices.

Shortly afterwards Baroness Tina Stowell, the chair of the Charity Commission, gave a speech and the following is from a press release about it:[5]

> Charities must change their culture and behaviour so that it is more in line with what the public expects from charities, the chair of the Charity Commission warned last night ... Baroness Stowell warned about a lack of ethical standards in fundraising and too much focus on the pursuit of growth. She said charity 'in its purest form' is an expression of people's desire to help others and is 'about altruism and selflessness'. She said that in a 'country marked by divisions and disruption' charities have a 'unique potential to bridge divides and help us confront uncertainty with purpose and hope'. But to do this charities and the regulator need to change ... 'I urge charities, of all sizes, to recognise that they too must read the writing on the wall, and respond'.

How should charities and churches respond to increased scrutiny?

Charities are going to be under a lot more scrutiny and I think that's a good thing. Charities shouldn't be afraid of that. I think at times they've got away with things – for example, there are charities here in the UK that sit on multimillion reserve funds and I sometimes wonder whether it is legitimate for them to raise public funds when they've got all these reserves and don't use them. As Christians we should welcome the scrutiny and work within it well, not be overwhelmed by it, not be frightened into thinking we can't function any longer so we'll have to close the door and walk away because it's too hard.

Accepting scrutiny and responding to it with openness and integrity should be another mark of our trustworthiness.

Changes of governance
Governance matters are likely to have to take a higher priority because of the increasing legislation, greater scrutiny and tighter

reporting requirements. Charities which are already keeping abreast of issues are likely to take this in their stride. It will probably be more difficult for smaller charities and smaller churches as the threshold for registration reaches them, but there are ways to keep in touch with issues:

> We encourage the board to subscribe to the Charity Commission mailings. We also get some information through Global Connections – some of our departments are part of their specialist groups so they would get to know about things like changes in finance or regulation.

Some Trusts are considering changing their charitable status to become a CIO so that trustees' liabilities are limited:

> We're currently looking to change to CIO status, so the current chair is working through that, although very slowly. I have said that I will not remain a trustee if we buy a new building unless and until those liabilities are managed and we change status to CIO. Part of that is being sensible from my own perspective and part of it is because I don't have confidence in the management of the trustees at the moment.

For some charities and churches, a change of charitable status may lead to more people willing to take on the role of trustee because of the reduced liability. For other organisations such changes are being considered in order to separate out different functions:

> I think there will be a rise of two different things; one is parallel charities and the other is charitable companies. With the rise of CIOs I wonder if PCCs will be tempted where they have quasi-trading operations, or they want to do something new, into setting up another body. There is some published work but there isn't much out there about how to do it technically, and the relationships involved.

Setting up a separate organisation for an aspect of ministry, especially one which involves trading or which will be eligible for funding if it is legally separate from the original church or charity, may solve some problems, but it can create others, so it needs a great deal of care and prayer before embarking on such a course:

> However much you think you are reducing your risk by creating a separate legal entity, from the point of view of the community and the people who are employed by it, they are working for the church and therefore there is a moral question: 'If that fails, can we just let those people walk away with nothing?' We can wind it up and call in the administrators because it's legally a company, but that impacts on our mission as a church because the community sees that as our outreach. That raises a big question for trustees about whether it is a good thing to set up a parallel company or charity and what the best legal vehicle for it is. Sometimes it is the right thing to set up a trading company but it's important to make sure the relationship with the originating church works. That's another area where Christian charities need to think through the longer-term issues and risks.

Changes to what are acceptable Objects of a charity

Several people I talked to were concerned about the impact on charities of the changing religious scene in the UK, particularly that there might come a time when advancement of religion ceases to be an acceptable Object for charity, with serious consequences:

> I am quite nervous about the advice that's currently being given for charities to become CIOs. It's the best instrument for now, but if that Object is removed that charity would cease to exist because it would have no grounds for identity as a charity with the Charity Commission. If you're a Trust Fund you would still exist as a Trust Fund; if you're a company you would still exist as a company. I think ministries may need to find other formats in order to exist, rather than registering as a charity; for example, a Company Limited by Guarantee remains that whether or not it is also registered as a charity.

> There was a big fear about advancement of religion being ruled out as a charitable Object and it's difficult to know how the wind is blowing on this one now, because in the corridors of government there has been

this rise in a pluralist approach which has meant that religious charities have been somewhat looked down upon. There was a fear, possibly unfounded, and that still is in the firing line, which would make it very difficult for any charity which has purely religious Objects.

Because such a change would almost certainly affect churches as well as separate charities, it is unlikely to happen while there are still Church of England bishops in the House of Lords. But were the Church of England to cease to be the established Church, that could open the doors for a range of challenging changes in charity and other law. In the meantime, we need to make the most of the opportunities while they still exist.

Changing demographics

The demographic of churchgoers is older than the population, and some denominations are ageing more quickly than others. That has all sorts of implications, for example, sustainability. In a Church census we undertook at Christian Research[6] one response stuck in all our minds. When asked about the future of their church, the person who filled in the form wrote that there were only eight of them, all in their eighties, and they were just waiting to die. In parallel is the lack of younger adults in many churches, and those there are have less disposable income than previous generations had at their age because of the cost of housing, student loans etc:

We've got a population where the givers are dying out, the people who had the money. My kids' generation do not have disposable income like my generation had and I think we've got to be realistic. It's no good asking people for money who themselves don't have a lot of money and I think there's an integrity in there about 'asking, asking, asking' without thinking about 'How can we create wealth?'.

If you look at where our giving is at the moment, the fact that we have a church that's older than the population, with congregations of people who are mostly fifty plus, a lot of our giving is in that not-quite-

retired-yet, or the recently-retired-but-still-fit-and-active who have different kinds of pension schemes to those which are now emerging. These groups are the people with perhaps a little more capacity to give. I do suspect that some of the models we have of church will be challenged and whether or not we will be able to sustain paid staff in the way that churches have adopted.

It will be very interesting to see over the next few years how this plays out in the new resource churches which are growing and are very heavily staffed. If they have big staffs with the kind of congregations that will not have huge ability to give, then something's got to change. I do wonder whether we will see more self-supporting or hybrid ministry developing, and whether we will move away from thinking that the only way we can do church is to employ someone. Some of that is going to depend on what happens in employment more widely, because the reason why we need to employ people is because our congregations are time-poor so they're willing to pay for it. But if employment changes as the demographic changes and the nature of work changes, maybe people will have time again, even if they haven't got the money — it will be interesting to see.

Changing demographics may seem like a threat, but it could lead to some creative, entrepreneurial and exciting new ways to function.

Financial challenges

Changing demographics and employment patterns are factors which are likely to increase financial challenges, as they affect the ability or willingness of people to give financially to a church or charity. Another factor is the challenges associated with raising money from other sources:

I think it's a major challenge for charities, trying not to get too political, living in a day of austerity with a neo-liberal political structure which tends to put everything else at the service of money. It means that there will always be a growing marginalised sector and thus a growing demand on the charity sector and that is a challenge.

There's also the growth of what I might call a semi-charitable sector, where you have charities which are acting like contractors, getting contracts from government and carrying out work for government. They are structurally charities but in practice are subcontractors for government services. I don't know whether they are a threat to the pure charity sector because it's blurring the lines between commercial and non-commercial: commercial is for private benefit and non-commercial should be for pure public benefit. But when a charity becomes a contractor there is the danger of private benefit happening without being seen.

Sustainability is a challenge too: the days when a charity can be dependent on grants have long since passed:

We had a very good relationship with one particular Trust and the person who ran that wrote a book. In it he was saying that in the future Trusts will look at their money: a small amount they will not expect to get back, a larger amount they will expect to get back, and the rest they will expect to get back with interest. You're not going to have Trusts giving, giving, giving, because the Trusts can no longer do that. I don't think a lot of the Christian charity world has come to terms with that.

The demographic changes and financial challenges may well lead charities and churches to work out new ways to sustain ministry. Finding ways to generate income could be the answer for some. For others there may be a rise in self-funding: some leaders of BAME and independent churches are already employed elsewhere either full or part-time and do all their church work as volunteers, while the Church of England has a large number of non-stipendiary clergy.[7] Other denominations and independent churches may need to move in that direction.

International issues

For mission agencies which work internationally the challenges of trustworthiness and integrity are greater. The report by the Charity Commission into the scandal which rocked Oxfam made it very clear that a breakdown of behaviour overseas, which may not be illegal there, is nevertheless totally unacceptable. In responding to the report, Oxfam's chair of trustees, Caroline Thomson, said the charity accepted the findings, describing them as 'uncomfortable' and 'a terrible abuse of power and an affront to the values that Oxfam holds dear'.[8] As regulation tightens in the UK it will be an increasing challenge to maintain standards overseas on safeguarding and a range of other issues:

> *There are a lot of countries that don't have child protection laws whereas, of course, we have very strong child protection policies and screening of people, so I can foresee some problems in that sort of area. Then there's finance and accountability in the whole issue of transferring international funds and money-laundering laws, which are already starting to create problems.*

Trends in acceptability of Christian charitable work

There are two trends which seem to be heading in opposite directions: increasing secularisation of society but at the same time more local opportunities due to austerity. In recent years there has been a steady rise in the percentage of the population who describe themselves as having no religion. The annual British Social Attitudes survey has shown a rise in adults who say they have no religious affiliation, from 31% in 1983 to 52% by 2018, while nearly three-quarters (71%) of eighteen- to twenty-five-year-olds say they have no religion.[9] This is part of what is behind challenges by groups such as the National Secular Society, who would like to see the demise of any favour towards religious organisations. They campaign against, for example, Christian organisations being allowed into schools,[10] which could radically affect the possibility of bringing the Christian faith alive (as YoYo puts it) for the 95% of children who never go to church.[11]

On the other hand, the years of austerity and massive cutbacks in funding for Local Authorities have led many authorities to discover that Christians in their area are already doing some of the work that they can no longer fund. In York the local council encouraged churches and charities to add their activities which support the local community to a council website list. In my church, the local council-appointed neighbourhood coordinator has recommended our regular drop-in for adults to a number of lonely elderly people in the area. That is only one example from many across the city. It is a great opportunity, though it does not come without challenges:

> *The difficulty for us will be how do we fulfil our commitment to society in ways which are acceptable to people who don't come from a Christian persuasion and don't understand our issues. The 'law of unintended consequences' is at play here and I think some Christian work could be sidelined for utterly ridiculous reasons by people who don't understand our issues. Local authorities' senior managers usually understand it, but their middle management decision makers often don't and can run scared of giving funding to Christian organisations.*
>
> *On the one hand some of the new laws could give them further grounds for their decision-making that bypass us, but counterbalancing that is that austerity means authorities have to look more toughly at their budgets. There is good evidence for results from Christian projects, because many of them are not tick-box projects but build relationships, which local government can't do. So there's huge value for money in the Christian projects: there's a contradiction there but it takes good people to work their way through that.*
>
> *As Christians we need to be forceful enough and persuasive enough on the right issues so that the good of the work we're doing benefits the community that the local government also wants to see benefited.*

Working with local authorities and other statutory groups that are not normally interested in anything they perceive to be 'churchy' or 'religious' may open new doors of opportunity. Building relationships between churches and their local leaders is important, and where there is a strong network of church leaders it can be very helpful to have someone who can represent many churches in discussions.

Partnerships and umbrella organisations

One of the things which really frustrated me when I edited the *UK Christian Handbook* was new charities that were duplicating ones that already existed. That may become less likely in the future for a range of reasons:

> *A lot of charities get so caught up with 'our stuff' that they either replicate what someone else is doing, or they don't partner. We need to have the big kingdom picture, that we're all part of God's work here, and therefore we're subject to His authority and it's not our work but His, so that a charity is focused on the bigger picture than just its own operation. I think there is going to be less room for solo efforts. We're going to see a lot more charities, if they're not actually merging, at least going into partnerships in what they're doing.*

One reason for the development of more partnership could be to help retain a Christian identity. While a small, local charity might struggle to keep its Christian ethos and values, being part of a network or in partnership with other similar organisations helps with identity, and provides support in various ways, particularly at a legal level:

> *I think increasingly it will be important to have umbrella organisations which do the hard work legally and you sign up to what they've done and agree to fulfil their conditions – they have the framework in place, they have enough money to have experts, they have relationships that guide and direct them. I think that's the way forward for churches as well as charities.*
>
> *For churches there's a point where they come out of exemption – and that's gradually being extended to all of us – when that happens there's a wobble because suddenly the trustees have to pay attention and they're not sure they can do it. When it gets to the small churches of ten or twenty people I can imagine they'll just give up, they'll say, 'We'll stop because we don't want to go through that, we can't do it.' So sharing, umbrella groupings, economy of scale are going to be essential.*

This kind of networking and partnership already exists in a range of ways. For many churches it is their denomination, local or national commitments to Churches Together or membership of the Evangelical Alliance – or all these. It happens in the charity world also: YoYo is linked to Scripture Union while many evangelical mission agencies are members of Global Connections. In the future it may need to go much further. That may turn out to be very positive for witness and ministry as Christians are seen to work together rather than be in competition with one another, which is what many non-churchgoers think when they see different denominations and ministries!

As Christians we have a hope for the future which helps shape how we view the world. Every time we say the Lord's Prayer we pray, 'your kingdom come, your will be done, on earth as it is in heaven' (Matthew 6:10), and it is a joy as well as a responsibility to do all we can to further God's kingdom work through our churches and ministries. Like Daniel, we can ask God the question, 'What will the outcome of all this be?' (Daniel 12:8). Future-proofing our ministries as much as possible underlines that we believe there is a future, and doing it well will give the best opportunity for the work to continue after the current trustees, chair and staff have moved on.

Questions

Are there appropriate succession plans in place in your church or charity?

What are the particular challenges that your locality or kind of ministry present now? How might these change in, say, the next five to ten years?

In what ways do your preparations for the future demonstrate your trustworthiness?

14
Epilogue
Daniel's and Nehemiah's
Examples

My servant Caleb has a different spirit and follows me
wholeheartedly.
(Numbers 14:24)

The spiritually minded person does not differ from the materially minded
person chiefly in thinking about different things, but in thinking about the
same things differently.[1]

Daniel was not the only administrator for the various rulers he
served under, nor was Nehemiah the only person to build walls
round a city at that time in history. What they did was not so
different from what others were doing. What makes them
memorable, and amazing examples for us two and a half
millennia later, is the approach they had: they thought about
those things 'differently' and that affected their whole lives. God
commended Caleb, the person who, with Joshua, was sent to
spy out the land for the Israelites when they were still in the
wilderness. The two of them brought back a different report to
the other ten (Numbers 13:30), because they had looked at the

situation from God's perspective. That attitude remained with Caleb for the rest of his life.

I have found it fascinating to look at the stories of Nehemiah and Daniel from the perspective of what we as trustees can learn from them. Comparing their lives, their responsibilities, their faith is revealing and sets us an amazing example. Here, to conclude, are three ways in which they show similar traits, which we too need in our roles within churches and Christian charities.

Firm in faith

Daniel tells his readers his background: he was taken captive when Nebuchadnezzar conquered Jerusalem and carried off to Babylon as a young man. He was from the royal family or nobility and so was among those selected from the captives to be taught the language and literature of his captors (Daniel 1:1-5). We know nothing about Nehemiah's background, although it is very likely that something similar had happened to him. Neither of them had any say in what happened to them, but each found themselves in a responsible position in their new environment, Daniel as an administrator, Nehemiah as one of the servants closest to the king on a daily basis. Whatever our background and whatever age we are, God can use us for His purposes, which may include being a trustee.

Daniel's training would have included learning about the Babylonian gods, of which there were many. The new names he and his friends were given were linked to those gods, and as Babylon was the most powerful world force at that time, their gods were considered the most powerful too. Some of the exiles in Babylon were overwhelmed by their situation, as one of the psalms tell us:

> By the rivers of Babylon we sat and wept ... There on the poplars we hung our harps ... How can we sing the songs of the LORD while in a foreign land?
> (Psalm 137:1-4)

Neither Daniel nor Nehemiah succumbed to that despair. They were both able to hold on to their faith in God in a hostile world. They were surrounded by pressures to conform and to abandon worship of the God that their captors believed they had left behind in Jerusalem. They put God first, which shows in the way they reacted to situations, as we see from the very first chapters of their books. When Daniel and his friends were given royal food and wine, which had almost certainly been dedicated to the gods, they stood firm but in a gracious way rather than by confrontation (Daniel 1:8-16). When Nehemiah heard the news about the dreadful state of Jerusalem and its remaining residents, his reaction was to turn his concerns into prayer and then seek a way of doing something about it (Nehemiah 1-2).

In the UK we rarely face outright hostility but there is a steady marginalisation of Christian faith, values and ethics. As churches and Christian charities, we face issues thrown at us by society's increasing secularity. Is our first recourse to consider how God wants us to react, or have those attitudes pervaded our thinking to such an extent that we're in danger of becoming like those exiles who were overwhelmed by the anti-God pressures around them? As trustees, we hold responsible positions, and how we respond to testing situations can make the difference between succumbing to pressures or graciously standing firm in our faith and letting it be reflected in our work, witness, values and behaviour.

Fervent in prayer

Daniel had a lifelong habit of prayer. When the law was passed by Darius that no one should pray to any god or king other than himself for the next thirty days, what did Daniel do?

When Daniel learned that the decree had been published, he went home to his upstairs room where the windows opened towards Jerusalem. Three times a day he got down

on his knees and prayed, giving thanks to his God, *just as he had done before.*
(Daniel 6:10, emphasis mine)

That phrase is sometimes translated 'just as he had always done' (eg NLT). He prayed regularly and often, and given the situations he found himself in, his prayers were surely more than a meaningless repetition of the same words every day. When King Nebuchadnezzar had the dream which he refused to describe to his wise men, Daniel asked for time, and then

> ... returned to his house and explained the matter to his friends ... He urged them to plead for mercy from the God of heaven.
> (Daniel 2:17-18)

They must have done so, because God answered by revealing the mystery to Daniel that night. Whatever was going on around him, Daniel prayed!

Nehemiah's life also centred round prayer. When he first heard the dreadful news about Jerusalem, his response was:

> I sat down and wept. For some days I mourned and fasted and prayed before the God of heaven.
> (Nehemiah 1:4)

We have a record in chapter 1 of what he prayed, which is a great example of how to pray in a difficult situation. Towards the end of the prayer he makes it clear that he's not the only exile who still prays to the God of heaven:

> Lord, let your ear be attentive to the prayer of this your servant and to the prayer of your servants who delight in revering your name.
> (Nehemiah 1:11)

As well as the sustained prayer, which the dates in chapter 1:1 and chapter 2:1 show went on for some months, he also prayed the much-quoted 'arrow' prayer when he was challenged by the king:

> Then I prayed to the God of heaven, and I answered the king.
> (Nehemiah 2:4-5)

Scattered throughout his book we find several more of his prayers, as we considered in Chapter 3. For both of these men, prayer was not a duty or drudge, it was central to their lives. It shaped their attitudes to others and their response to the pressures, opportunities and opposition they faced. When we meet as trustees, it is so easy to rush into dealing with what may be a long agenda, giving at best a few minutes at the start and end to prayer. I somehow feel Nehemiah and Daniel would have approached things differently!

Faithful in their duties

As captives, neither man was able to choose their roles in their land of exile, though Nehemiah did choose to return to Jerusalem to tackle rebuilding it. If anything, they were more conscientious in carrying out their roles in exile because they recognised that God's honour was at stake. We can sometimes find ourselves thrust into a responsibility such as being a trustee, perhaps under pressure from others or because there is genuinely no one else to do it, but even if we did not choose to become a trustee, that should not diminish the effort we put into doing it as well as possible.

Daniel's responsibilities were lifelong – he was probably in his eighties by the time Darius appointed him one of his chief administrators, while Nehemiah had to leave Jerusalem and return to exile once the wall was complete, with only one further visit 'home' recorded (Nehemiah 13:6-7). Many trustees are older, retired people who have the time to give to the role. Knowing how long to continue and when to say 'No more' is not always easy: I have seen both – people determined to carry on when they were 'past it', and those who implicitly or explicitly say that they've worked hard all their lives and they don't want to take on responsibilities which might cut across the time or energy to enjoy themselves.

Charity best practice encourages a time limit for serving as a trustee, but there is no time limit on our service for God, and many people are trustees of more than one charity or take on a new trusteeship with a different charity when they have completed their time with one.

Conclusion

Nehemiah and Daniel both faced considerable opposition, and there is no guarantee that doing the right thing means that everything will go well. Christian charities do fail, churches do close, crises of all kinds do hit, but part of our Christian witness is how we react. Whether things are going well or not, there is a huge difference between acting with integrity in a godly, trustworthy and compassionate way and allowing God's work to be dishonoured by corruption or neglect. These attitudes leave evidence, just as animals in the snow leave tracks which show what passed that way.

While the work and legal requirements of trustees are very similar across the charity world, my prayer in writing this book is that God will enable you to be a trustworthy trustee and carry out your responsibilities in a way which honours Him and builds His kingdom.

Questions

What is the most important thing for your situation that you've learned from this book?

How would you summarise your experience of being a trustee? Has that changed as you've read this book? Could you encourage other trustees by telling them?

Postscript
Covid-19

Go, post a lookout and let him report what he sees ...
let him be alert, fully alert.
(Isaiah 21:6, 7)

The Covid-19 crisis is massively affecting charities.

If you look back to the end of chapter 13 (p255), which was on succession planning and possible future trends, you will find this conclusion:

> Future-proofing our ministries as much as possible underlines that we believe there is a future, and doing it well will give the best opportunity for the work to continue after the current trustees, chair and staff have moved on.

When I wrote that in the summer of 2019, little did any of us know what was about to hit us in 2020 as the world was engulfed by Covid-19. Now we need to add to that sentence '... for the work to continue after the pandemic', as well as after the current trustees, chair and staff have moved on. This book was already in the hands of Instant Apostle and due to be published by them in the autumn of 2020. It was soon agreed that the pandemic could not be ignored and so this postscript is being added close to printing, to be as up to date as possible.

During February and March, as more and more countries went into lockdown, it very quickly became clear that churches and charities were not immune from having their world turned upside down. The challenges and opportunities for churches and charities are changing frequently, so I offer here some reflections for trustees and leaders rather than detail, as we all move forward into what will inevitably be a different world for at least the foreseeable future.

What steps can we take?

Return to core vision
We examined the topic of vision in chapter 2, but the current situation demands that we look again at what is at the heart of our vision.

Cataclysmic change makes us go back to basics.

Over time it is easy to add a variety of peripheral activities and ministries to the core vision, but the virus stripped away many of those for both churches and charities.

- Charities. Some charities were unable to operate at all, while for others it was still possible to fulfil their core ministry, but it had to be done in a different way. YoYo's strapline is 'Bringing the Christian faith alive', and that had always been done face to face in schools, clubs and other settings. The trustees thought and prayed long and hard about whether to furlough the staff, but there was plenty of scope to help both schools that were open for children of key workers and parents who were home schooling. Working individually in their own homes was more difficult than working in teams and developing ideas and lessons together. But very quickly resources were created and posted online. YoYo's core vision is still being fulfilled, though in a very different way for the time being.

That is true of many other ministries. Carecent in York normally provides breakfast for homeless, unemployed or socially excluded people, but that had to stop. Homeless people were being housed temporarily in a local hotel with no provision of meals, so Carecent provided packed lunches for them and for some vulnerable people who continued to turn up at the centre's gates. The local food bank delivered parcels to people in self-isolation, as did York Neighbours. Anecdotally, this adaptability and use of social media was repeated by charities across the country. However, while some were able to find alternative ways to fulfil their vision, there were many others who could not.

- Churches. Churches faced similar issues, particularly about their evangelism or social action. Some of this outreach also had to stop, but where it could be carried out by alternative means, that helped embed witness and ministry in the community – and who knows what opportunities that might open up in the future?

The Charity Commission soon published guidance for trustees, encouraging them to continue to have an eye on the wider or longer-term impact of decisions on their charity and beneficiaries.

> We have advice for the many charities looking at how they can help the effort to tackle Covid-19 and whether they can do so within their existing objects.[1]

Good governance became even more important with the demands of the unprecedented situation, and a few weeks later the Charity Commission felt it necessary to warn some charities to pay attention to their governance.

At this stage nobody knows the long-term situation, but core vision is still being fulfilled by many churches and charities, even though peripheral activities have been stripped away. Wrestling with the issues and applying different methods provides an opportunity for new direction, which if it is not taken now may not come our way again for a very long time.

Reassess priorities

In the first week or two of lockdown, churches and charities had to quickly ask, 'What is most important to maintain?'

- Churches. Church is not the building; it is the people. Initially it felt like church as we had known it had disappeared, so how could that belief become reality with the building closed? Social media and video conferencing came to the rescue, though a bishop I talked to early on was inundated by conversations with vicars who had poor internet access or were unfamiliar with social media.

  There were soon widespread reports of much larger numbers of people 'attending' online than previously came to services (though not all watched for the whole time!). Some were chronically sick or disabled housebound people who were able to 'attend' church for the first time in many years; others were churchgoers 'visiting' other churches, or families watching together from different parts of the country so they could share the same experience. In spite of this, the majority of these extra 'attenders' are unknown and anonymous. How important was it to include those with no internet access? Delivering notice sheets or liturgy being used in streamed services was appreciated, as were phone calls, but nevertheless some felt abandoned as regular churchgoing ceased to be part of their lives.

  In the long term, what will be the right mix of face-to-face and online for services and activities, balancing the needs of the new online viewers, including the anonymous or housebound, with the needs of those without internet access?

  Forced out of comfortable familiarity and ritual, creativity was let loose in churches in a multitude of ways: Sunday services and daily prayers or mass became a spiritual and social lifeline for many churchgoers; youth groups moved on to mobile phones and activities such as Messy Church and toddler groups migrated to social media, sometimes with 'goody bags' of activities delivered to homes in advance. Can the creativity and flexibility which lockdown demanded be retained?

- Charities. Some of these observations apply to charities too: can they remain creative, and retain new people who have plugged into what they offer?

The key questions are what is most important for our church or charity to continue to do, what do we restart as and when we are able, and what should stop permanently? Trustee boards will need to be involved in such decisions, especially at a time when income has been drastically reduced, but the crisis allows, even demands, a major rethink.

Re-examine resources

One of the immediate effects of lockdown was that income all but dried up. Charity shops shut, national and local fund-raising events were cancelled, there were no offerings in church services, community groups were suspended and therefore also the rent they paid. Some donors were no longer able to give while others redirected their donations to charities focusing on the virus in some way. The situation was serious enough for the Charity Commission to respond (in the advice quoted above):

> We understand that many charities are currently very concerned about their financial position ... Reserves can be spent to help cope with unexpected events like those unfolding at present ... All decisions on such financial matters should normally be taken collectively, and significant decisions and action points noted in writing.

The guidance about reserves was helpful, though of course only if you had reserves beforehand! In the same guidance, permission was given for trustee meetings, and AGMs if necessary, to be held online even if this was not specifically permitted in the governing document. Will this blanket permission be extended long term or rescinded once social distancing requirements are eased? If it is withdrawn, it may be wise to seek to add it to a governing document, though that is a time-consuming process and it would be wise to get advice before starting down that route.

When considering resources, finance comes to mind first, but there are other aspects to consider alongside money.

- Fundraising. Many charities issued public appeals for support, and individuals plunged into fundraising, the iconic example of which was Captain Sir Tom Moore who set out to walk one hundred lengths of his garden before his one hundredth birthday. He captured the hearts of the nation as he raised nearly £33 million for NHS charities. As individuals, including some amazing children, followed his example, many charities benefited; nevertheless, most charities and churches faced a major shortfall in income.

- Cut back, or even close? There were various dire predictions about the likely resulting closure of charities and small churches, especially independent ones, and about the amount of money the charity sector might lose by the end of 2020. Charity trustee boards had to examine their finances carefully in order to decide whether to press on through the crisis, albeit perhaps with cutbacks, or reluctantly call it a day. Church trustees had to consider redundancies or furlough for staff and whether to reduce their giving. I suspect it will be a year or two before the full picture of closure and survival becomes clear.

- Merger or partnership? A devastating drop in income may lead charity trustees to conclude that they can no longer continue, but first consider what you can realistically do using the resources you have and then look at whether there are other options. Partnering, or even merging, with another organisation has already been suggested (see p254). This is a good time to seriously consider such action, which may be a positive way of combining limited resources and enabling ministry to continue in some form. Churches could consider whether they can invite local charities to move into unused space in their premises at a reduced rent, simultaneously helping the charity and bringing some income for the church.

- Volunteers. The wave of volunteering that swept across the country fuelled by employees on furlough filled many of the gaps created by volunteers who had to self-isolate because of age or medical conditions. But can people who have returned to work be encouraged to continue to volunteer? And what about the multitudes, especially young people, who have already been made redundant, doubtless with more to join their ranks in the months to come? Encouraging them to volunteer would help them gain experience and skills, as well as helping the charity. Will the changing employment scene lead to new ways of working, a possibility which was also raised earlier (see p250)?

If employment changes as the demographic changes and the nature of work changes, maybe people will have time again, even if they haven't got the money.

In the long term, the changes forced on charities and churches in the pandemic may not all be negative. It will be interesting to look back in, say, 2025 and see how it has all worked out.

The lookout

So how can we sum all this up other than by looking to the Bible again as we have done in every other chapter? This time I want to take you to one of Isaiah's prophecies, rather than to Nehemiah or Daniel. In chapter 21:6-12 Isaiah's prophecy against the then world-conquering power, Babylon, uses the metaphor of a lookout, or, as older versions translate it, a watchman.

Be alert

The Lord told Isaiah, 'Go, post a lookout and let him report what he sees ... let him be alert, fully alert' (vs 6-7).

In the first half of 2020 the situation regarding the pandemic changed repeatedly and there were regular pronouncements by the government and guidance from the Charity Commission and elsewhere. Issues that may have been peripheral previously may now be more important, such as mental health, poverty or fear. It is critical for trustees to be alert, up to date with not only what is happening but also how it affects their charity or church.

Keep it up

The lookout reported, 'Day after day, my lord, I stand on the watchtower; every night I stay at my post' (v 8).

This situation will affect what churches and charities can do and how they do it for a long time, so it may be worth giving one trustee specific responsibility to keep a lookout for relevant information.

Be ready for the unexpected

Babylon was a strong nation which had overwhelmed many others. The lookout saw 'a man in a chariot with a team of horses', but the news that man brought was probably unexpected for those who heard this prophecy, 'Babylon has fallen, has fallen! All the images of its gods lie shattered on the ground' (v 9).

The pandemic itself was unexpected by almost everyone. It has made us wake up to the possibility of sudden, radical change, and there is nothing to be gained by burying our heads in the sand! Risk assessments will need to be reconsidered, and this is an opportunity to think carefully about which activities to restart and which to stop permanently. We should also be ready to respond to other unexpected events, for example the sudden emergence of Black Lives Matter in the summer of 2020.

Realise God knows the situation

Israel was in a dire state after most of the people had been deported to Babylon (see p257), and here God describes them as 'crushed on the threshing-floor' (v 10).

It is a powerful description: what was left crushed on the threshing-floor was the chaff when the wheat grains had been removed, which is no doubt how the remnant felt. God had seen their situation, and he knows ours also. Much has already been written and said about God's role, or not, in Covid-19, and no doubt there will be much more, but one thing is certain: the pandemic did not catch God out, any more than the Black Death which devastated Europe and Asia in the mid 1300s or the Great Plague of 1655–66 in London.

Listen to God

The prophet went on to reveal that God had spoken to him: 'I tell you what I have heard from the LORD Almighty' (v 10).

There are many ways to listen to God, but as Christian trustees it is vital that we balance the challenges of what we see when we look around us with listening to God. What He says to us will be unique to our situation and therefore may change our perspective. Human logic or official advice may point one way, but God might give you the faith to believe and work towards a different outcome. The crisis of the pandemic may be an amazing opportunity to discern new avenues of ministry or new methods of fulfilling your vision. May how you respond to Covid-19 reveal tracks of trustworthiness which others can follow!

July 2020

Summary of Research Findings

Findings related to Section 1

- Separate charities were clearer about the Aims and Objects of their foundation document, whereas this was much less true of churches, especially in denominations where the whole denomination is registered as the overarching charity.

- When opportunities present themselves, some charities do not assess whether these are in line with their Aims and Objects or their vision, and can therefore unintentionally drift away from the reason they were set up.

- Most churches and charities are aware of their values but not many have written them down or use them when setting vision or evaluating projects and activities.

- Risk is most often related to finance or to specific issues such as safeguarding.

- Boards of Christian charities and churches can fall into one of two traps over risk: either they assume that God will provide for them and will protect them, so have no strategies or plans in place to manage risk; or they deal with risk at a human level without consciously praying for God's guidance and intervention. Finding the right balance is a challenge.

Findings related to Section 2

- Trustees of separate charities were much more likely to be aware that they are trustees than were those in churches who were trustees by virtue of being a PCC member, deacon, elder etc.

- When churches have had to register separately because their income is above the threshold for registration, their PCC / deacons etc have woken up to the fact that they are trustees, and sometimes been afraid of the responsibilities.

- Trustees can be appointed for inadequate reasons such as being a friend of a current trustee or someone who is known to have an interest in the work or time available. In churches people may be nominated for roles which involve trusteeship because they are popular or have their own agenda which they hope to impose on the church.

- Few churches or charities do a skills audit so that they can look for trustees who will bring needed skills to their board.

- One of the hardest roles to fill is treasurer. The workload can be substantial and the legal requirements feel onerous to people without an accountancy or similar background. Churches and charities seem mostly unaware that the treasurer does not have to be a trustee as long as the board takes overall responsibility for finances.

- The other hard role to fill is chair, especially for small, local charities. A trustee may be asked to take on the role because they are the longest serving member of the board or the person with the most time available, rather than because they have appropriate gifts or experience.

Findings related to Section 3

- Some charities and churches have a very clear vision but poor strategy to fulfil it, while others have a big programme of activities but no overarching vision to shape what they do.

- Small, local charities and independent churches are less likely to be aware of, or make use of, the resources available, such as the Charity Commission's regular emails and guidelines, external training, or online and printed resources.

- More collaboration between charities could help cut overheads, eg churches offering unused space as an office for a local charity, several charities in a local area agreeing to share the costs of employing a fund-raiser, or sharing 'back office' support, one treasurer serving several charities or churches.

- Finance is easier to raise for new projects and fresh vision, whether from individual giving, grant-making trusts or other sources of income. It is much harder to fund the day-to-day expenses. Especially in churches it is not easy to draw the line between mission and outreach and running costs.

- It is too easy for the availability (or not) of finance to control the vision and activities rather than the other way round.

- Charities and churches always in effect set a deficit budget and then exercise faith as well as practical action to see that money come in.

- Accountability is an important aspect of trustee responsibility, but it can be a thorny issue especially for churches with an ethos / theology of strong leaders who expect to personally make all the major decisions.

Findings related to Section 4

- Succession planning is easier in a charity than a church, but that does not mean it is regularly done.

- Trends in society and increasing legislation provide both challenges and opportunities for charities and churches.

Appendix 1
Definitions

These all apply to a church and charity unless otherwise stated.

Disclaimer – these definitions are in lay language. For full legal definitions see, for example, *Faith, Hope & Charity*.

Accountability	Being responsible to a person or body and giving honest accounts of actions, motives, decisions, activities, performance, finance.
Accounts	A record of the money received, spent or held. A full record must be made at the end of each financial year which must be audited or independently examined if more than £10,000.
Agenda	A list of items which will be discussed at a forthcoming meeting.
Aims and Objects	The reason the charity exists. These must be stated in the Governing Document. Often termed its mission (*see also* Objects).
Annual General Meeting (AGM)	A meeting once a year open to members. Normally includes election of trustees, presentation of accounts, report of the

	year's activities and how these met the Objects for the public benefit.
Annual Parochial Church Meeting (APCM)	An AGM held in a Church of England parish.
Annual Report	A report compiled by and agreed by the trustees. It covers the previous financial year and when combined with the accounts forms the Annual Return. An informal report created for members and/or supporters. Usually covers the calendar year between AGMs.
Annual Return	A report of the activities and finances for the previous financial year of a charity with an income of more than £10K. It should comply with SORP and be logged with the Charity Commission within ten months of the end of the financial year.
Articles of Association	*See* Governing Document.
AOB	Any other business. An opportunity at a meeting to raise items not listed on the agenda.
Audit / Auditor	An official check of the annual accounts carried out by a qualified Auditor. Required for charities with income of more than £1 million.
Beneficiaries	Those people who benefit from the charity's work, usually set out in the Governing Document.
Board	A collective term for the trustees or directors of a charity.

Budget	The projected spend for a period, usually a year, compiled annually in advance.
CEO	Chief Executive Officer. Senior employee, may be known by various other titles.
Chair (or chairman, chairperson)	The person appointed to lead the trustees and run the charity's meetings. In a church this is often the minister.
Charity	An organisation which is set up for charitable purposes for public, not private benefit and is registered with the Charity Commission. It may take one of several forms: Charitable company – also registered under the Companies Act Charitable Incorporated Organisation (CIO) Charitable trust Unincorporated charitable association.
Charity Commission	Set up by the Charitable Trusts Act in 1853. Current structure and name established by The Charities Act 2006. It registers charities and is independent of government.
Charity Governance Code	Guidance and principles for good governance. A collaborative document setting out best practice. Not a legal requirement.
Child Protection	Safeguarding of children; churches and any charity whose work involves children must have a Child Protection Policy.
Church Council	A local church's governing body in some non-conformist denominations.

Compliance	Ensuring all applicable laws are kept.
Conflict of interest	Occurs when a trustee, a relative of a trustee, or another organisation to which a trustee is linked could benefit from a decision.
Conflict of loyalty	Occurs when a trustee is a personal friend or relative of a person under discussion at a trustee meeting.
Constitution	*See* Governing Document.
Co-opt	When a board or committee votes that someone who has not been elected should join it because of their role or expertise.
Council of Reference	Well known people who support a charity, similar to patrons.
Directors	Trustees who hold office in a charitable company.
Disclosure and Barring Service (DBS)	Searches for information which may bar a person from contact with vulnerable children or adults; provides official clearance for such work.
Diversity	One of the recommendations of the Charity Governance Code.
Deacons / Diaconate	A local church's governing body in some nonconformist denominations.
Elders / Eldership	A local church's governing body in some nonconformist denominations.
Elders / Presbytery	A local church's governing body in Presbyterian denominations.
Equality	One of the recommendations of the Charity Governance Code.

Ex-officio	A person who has not been elected but whose role or office automatically makes them a member of a board or committee.
Expenditure	The money spent or given away by a church or charity.
Fiduciary	The responsibility of a trust or a trustee to act for the benefit of others, not personal gain.
Financial year	Twelve months of accounts. May be a calendar year or date from when a charity started.
Governance	Enabling and supporting compliance with relevant legislation and fulfilment of its vision.
Governing Document	Sets out what a charity exists to do and how it is to be governed. May be termed Articles of Association, Constitution, Conveyance, Trust Deed etc.
Governor	A trustee in some organisations eg schools, colleges.
Image	How the wider community perceives a charity or church
Income	The money received by a church or charity, whatever its source.
Independent Examination / Examiner	A less formal check of annual accounts acceptable for organisations with a turnover of less than £1 million and more than £10,000; the person who undertakes it.
Induction	A formal or informal process of introducing a new trustee to their role and the organisation.

Integral mission	Encouraging the restoration of people's relationships with God, each other and creation.
Job or role description	A document setting out what is expected of an employee, trustee etc.
Members	Membership as expressed by a denomination. An individual or organisation who has agreed to belong to a charity, as permitted and described in the Governing Document.
Minister	A person with the main leadership role in a church. May or may not be ordained or employed by the church.
Minutes	An accurate record of decisions made in a trustee meeting.
Objects	Defined under the Charities Act and refers to the thirteen permitted activities which are classed as 'charitable'.
Patron	A well-known individual who agrees to be publicly associated with a charity and speak up for it when appropriate.
PCC	Parochial Church Council, the local church's governing body in a Church of England parish.
Policies	Written documents setting out how to deal with particular situations, usually approved annually by trustees.
Quorum	The minimum number of trustees who must be present for decisions to be made, also the minimum number of members in attendance eg at an AGM.

	Usually stated in the governing document.
Reserves / reserves policy	The income which has not been spent or designated; a reserves policy sets out how much is held unspent against the event that income fails to meet expenditure.
Risk	The Charity Commission requires trustees to annually assess the risks to a charity and state how to respond to them.
Safeguarding	Protecting the health, well-being and human rights especially of children and vulnerable adults. Includes having in place appropriate policies.
Secretary	The person appointed to take the minutes. May also compile the agenda and the Annual Report.
SORP	Charity Commission's Statement of Recommended Practice for accounting and reporting by charities.
Staff	People employed by the church or charity.
Stakeholders	People who benefit from the work and who would miss it if it closed.
Stipend	The allowance Church of England clergy receive in lieu of salary.
Strategy	The means by which the vision will be achieved.
Statement of Faith	A formal document describing key theological beliefs. May or may not be part of the Governing Document.

Succession planning	Planning in advance for replacement of office holders, especially the chair or senior staff.
Supporters	Those who give to and / or pray for the work of a charity.
Treasurer	The person responsible for keeping accurate financial records, may not be a trustee.
Trust Deed	*See* Governing Document.
Trustees	People who are elected to control and manage the governance of a charity or church.
Values	The qualities deemed to be of importance in the way the work is carried out.
Vision	The goals and aims towards which work is focused.
Volunteers	Those who help in the work but are not employed.

Appendix 2
Resources

National organisations: note that some of these provide free information and advice, others are accessible on a payment or subscription basis.

ACEVO – Charity Leader's Network

acevo.org.uk

Network enabling charity leaders to connect with each other so they can share good practice, support and challenge each other.

AFVS – Advice for the Voluntary Sector

www.afvs.org.uk

Produces excellent summary documents, eg on the Charity Governance Code.

Distributes a free monthly bulletin (this is Daryl Martin's email, *see* Chapter 10) which summarises key issues occurring in the voluntary sector.

Association of Chairs

www.associationofchairs.org.uk

Supports chairs of charities and non-profit organisations so they can lead their boards effectively and thus enable the organisation's mission.

Centre for Charity Effectiveness

www.cass.city.ac.uk/faculties-and-research/centres/cce

Encourages organisations and individuals in the voluntary, community and social enterprise sectors to improve their performance.

Charities Aid Foundation
www.cafonline.org
Mainly enables giving to charities but also provides advice.

Charity Commission
www.gov.uk/government/organisations/charity-commission
Guidance and papers on a wide range of topics, many legally binding, including *The Essential Trustee* and other relevant papers and links.

Charity Governance Code
www.charitygovernancecode.org
A practical tool bringing together good practice to help charities and their trustees develop high standards of governance, including a diagnostic tool – not legally binding.

Civil Society
www.civilsociety.co.uk
Publishes *Civil Society News*, runs training events etc.

Global Connections
www.globalconnections.org.uk
Network of UK-based mission agencies; includes various useful papers such as *Models of Governance and Board Effectiveness*.

National Council of Voluntary Organisation (NCVO)
Local expressions in many English towns and cities as Council for Voluntary Service:

In England	ncvo.org.uk
In Northern Ireland	www.nicva.org
In Scotland	www.scvo.org.uk
In Wales	www.wcva.org.uk

NPC – charity consultancy
www.thinknpc.org
Charity experts who work with individuals and organisations in the charity sector to improve their effectiveness.

Small Charities Coalition
www.smallcharities.org.uk
Helps small charities access the skills, experience and resources they need to start up and achieve their aim.

Stewardship
www.stewardship.org.uk
Advice and support to help the Christian community, particularly by making giving easy and inspiring greater generosity but also providing other support, training etc to strengthen Christian causes.

The Chartered Governance Institute
www.icsa.org.uk
Trains, informs and represents the interests of charities and governance professionals.

Third Sector
www.thirdsector.co.uk
The UK's leading publication covering the charity and voluntary sector.

thirty-one:eight
thirtyoneeight.org
Provides advice, support and tools for churches and charities regarding Child Protection and Disclosure and Barring Service to enable the creation of safer places.

TrusteELearning
www.communityactionsuffolk.org.uk
An e-learning website providing self-paced training for trustees.

Publications

The following books are sources for various quotes in the book:

Back From the Brink, Heather Wraight & Pat Wraight (London: Christian Research and Goring-by-Sea: Verité, 2006).

The Charity Trustees Handbook, Mike Eastwood & Jacqueline Williams (London: dsc Directory of Social Change, third edition, 2017).

Eve's Glue, Heather Wraight (Carlisle: Paternoster Lifestyle, 2001).

Faith, Hope & Charity: The A to Z of governing a charitable organisation, Paul Martin (Milton Keynes: Malcolm Down, 2016).

God's Questions: Vision, Strategy and Growth, Peter Brierley (Tonbridge: ADBC Publishers, 2010).

The PCC Member's Essential Guide, Mark Tanner (London: Church House Publishing, 2015).

Rotas, Rules and Rectors: How to Thrive Being a Churchwarden, Matthew Clements (Leicester: Troubador Publishing, 2018).

For a range of other similar books see also:
PCC Resources section of Canterbury Press:
www.canterburypress.hymnsam.co.uk
PCC Resources section of Church House Publishing:
www.chpublishing.co.uk

Appendix 3
Models and Codes of Governance

The Seven Principles of Public Life (Nolan Principles)

1. Selflessness

Holders of public office should act solely in terms of the public interest.

2. Integrity

Holders of public office must avoid placing themselves under any obligation to people or organisations that might try inappropriately to influence them in their work. They should not act or take decisions in order to gain financial or other material benefits for themselves, their family, or their friends. They must declare and resolve any interests and relationships.

3. Objectivity

Holders of public office must act and take decisions impartially, fairly and on merit, using the best evidence and without discrimination or bias.

4. Accountability

Holders of public office are accountable to the public for their decisions and actions and must submit themselves to the scrutiny necessary to ensure this.

5. Openness

Holders of public office should act and take decisions in an open and transparent manner. Information should not be withheld from the public unless there are clear and lawful reasons for so doing.

6. Honesty
Holders of public office should be truthful.

7. Leadership
Holders of public office should exhibit these principles in their own behaviour. They should actively promote and robustly support the principles and be willing to challenge poor behaviour wherever it occurs.

For detail *see*: www.gov.uk/government/publications/the-7-principles-of-public-life

The following principles are extracted from two papers by Martin Lee: *Board Models and Effectiveness, Role of a Charity Chair*
See: Papers at www.globalconnections.org.uk

Policy Government (Carver Model)
Helps a board focus on ensuring that the goals of what they want to achieve (the 'ends') are met; it is not about the means of doing of them. There are four sets of policies, set within a Policy Circle.

1. Outcomes (Ends)
What good shall we accomplish, for whom, at what cost?

2. Executive Limitations
Constraints within which the CEO is required to deliver those results ensuring what they do is both ethical and prudent.

3. Board-Management Delegation
How the managing body interacts with the organisation through the CEO.

4. Governance Process
How the governing body fulfils its roles and responsibilities.

ACI framework (Responsibility Assignment ix)

roject management tool that helps in defining roles and ponsibilities

Я. What is the Board **Responsible** for doing?

A. What is the Board **Accountable** for?

C. What does the Board need to be **Consulted** about?

I. What does the Board need **Information** about?

Seven principles of the Charity Governance Code

1. Purpose
The board should be clear about the charity's aims and ensure these are being effectively delivered.

2. Leadership
Leadership should be strategic and effective in line with the charity's aims and values.

3. Integrity
The board adopts a culture and values appropriate to the charity's aims, being aware of the importance of public trust.

4. Decision-making, risk and control
These processes should be informed, rigorous and timely, with effective and appropriate delegation.

5. Board effectiveness
The board should be a well-functioning team with a good balance of skills, experience and knowledge.

6. Diversity
The Board should include trustees with different backgrounds and experience which supports its effectiveness.

7. Openness and accountability
Appropriate transparency and accountability are essential.

Ten Principles of the Relational Model of Governance

1. The organisation seeks a balance between the fulfilment of the needs of those being served and the personal fulfilment of the staff and volunteers.

2. The affirmation, involvement and servant leadership of every individual and group at every level in the organisation are vital to the success of the organisation.

3. Authority, responsibility and accountability are the primary components of all relationships. Limitations of authority and expectations of responsibility are the secondary components.

4. Circles of authority and responsibility are defined clearly and are maintained equal in size by negotiating limitations of authority or by expectations of responsibility.

5. The Board, acting on information from all stakeholders, is responsible for strategic planning: defining beneficiaries, services / needs, vision, mission and priorities, monitoring performance and measuring results.

6. The CEO is responsible for managing the delivery of services in accord with Board-stated priorities and for achieving the strategic goals within the limitations of the authorisation and resources available.

7. Each individual has a share in responsibility for creating, owning, understanding and implementing the mission of the organisation.

8. Decision-making proceeds from shared values, vision and mission, not unilaterally from the Board or the CEO. Decisions are made as close as possible to where they are implemented.

9. The organisation is results orientated. Indicators of results are identified. Strategic and tactical goals are set in balance with available resources. Results are measured.

10. Accountability is mutual. The source of authority is accountable to the recipient for providing adequate

authorisation and resources. The recipient is accountable to the source for achieving results.

The Top Drivers of Effective Governance (Compass Cass Governance Model)

Lists the fifty most important characteristics of effective governance under four key areas:

- Behaviours
- Meetings
- Processes
- Structures

Top drivers in order of importance:

1. Effective team work

2. Ensuring meetings deliver excellent governance

3. Having the required skills and experience

4. Focus on strategy

5. Operating with openness and trust

6. Having great diversity

7. Praising management

8. Providing robust challenge

9. Using committees effectively

10. Providing thorough induction.

Principles for Chairs of Charity Boards
1. Compliance
The chair needs to take a lead in ensuring that the board fulfils its function, legal duties and is well governed.

2. Governing

The chair needs to take responsibility for ensuring the board follows the governance model adopted and that the board does not stray into management tasks.

3. Meetings

The chair needs to ensure board meetings are chaired effectively and that meetings are based on a clear agenda and well-minuted.

4. Supporting the CEO

The chair needs to support the CEO and also ensure the CEO is held to account appropriately.

5. Liaison

The chair acts as a conduit between the board and the CEO (and possibly other senior staff).

6. Representation

The chair may need to represent the charity on occasions, but this needs to be in liaison with the CEO.

7. Arbitrator

The chair may act as a last point of call on behalf of the Trustees in disciplinary, grievance, whistle-blowing and complaints procedures.

Index

General index

Biblical index (excluding Daniel and Nehemiah)

Notes

Foreword
[1] Matthew Clements, *Rotas, Rules and Rectors: How to Thrive Being a Churchwarden* (Leicester: Troubador Publishing, 2018).

Acknowledgements
[1] Current edition: Paul Martin, *Faith, Hope & Charity: The A to Z of governing a charitable organisation* (Milton Keynes: Malcolm Down Publishing, 2016).

Introduction
[1] *Faith matters: Understanding the size, income and focus of faith-based charities,* New Philanthropy Capital, www.thinknpc.org, accessed 2nd March 2020. *See* also *What a difference faith makes* paper in resources section of website.
[2] Dr Peter Brierley, by email, 29th January 2019.
[3] Martin, *Faith, Hope & Charity.*

Chapter 1
[1] legislation.gov.uk (accessed 27th January 2020).
[2] Martin, *Faith, Hope & Charity*, p32.
[3] www.gov.uk/government/organisations/charity-commission.
[4] www.charitygovernancecode.org.
[5] Quoted in www.newworldencyclopedia.org (accessed 19th November 2018).
[6] There is confusion over the source of this saying, with many websites attributing it to C S Lewis. It is not by him – for discussion on the possible origin see www.whosaidthisquote.blogspot.com/ (accessed 14th April 2020).
[7] www.lausanne.org (accessed 3rd March 2020).

[8] Full extent of Church of England work to support local communities revealed, www.churchofengland.org, published 5th November 2018.
[9] Tearfund, Press Release, 5th May 2018.

Chapter 2

[1] Published in: Heather Wraight & Pat Wraight, *Back from the Brink* (London: Christian Research, Goring-by-Sea: Verité, 2006).
[2] Lesslie Newbiggin, *The Gospel in a Pluralist Society* (first published 1989, London: SPCK, 2004), p112.
[3] www.leadingyourchurchintogrowth.org.uk (accessed 7th January 2019).
[4] www.marysmeals.org.uk (accessed 4th March 2020).
[5] For detail *see*: Peter Brierley, *God's Questions* (Tonbridge: ADBC Publishers, 2010).

Chapter 3

[1] bbc.co.uk/news/uk-33788415 (accessed 14th January 2019).
[2] bbc.co.uk/news/uk-48593401 (accessed 12th June 2019).
[3] www.theguardian.com/world/2018/feb/20/oxfam-boss-mark-goldring-apologises-over-abuse-of-haiti-quake-victims (accessed 31st July 2020).
[4] *The Yorkshire Post*, 16th February 2018.
[5] www.thirdsector.co.uk, 15th March 2018 (accessed 1st July 2019).
[6] *Worldwide*, magazine of WEC International, January 2019.
[7] WEC Connected email (online version of *Worldwide*), January 2019.
[8] BAME – Black, Asian and Minority Ethnic.
[9] Charity Commission, *The Essential Trustee*, section 2, page 5, www.gov.uk/government/publications (accessed 27th January 2020).

Chapter 4

[1] Charity Commission, *The Essential Trustee*, section 2, page 5, www.gov.uk/government/publications (accessed 27th January 2020).

Chapter 5

[1] *The Essential Trustee*, section 3.3.
[2] Grace Davie, *Religion in Britain Since 1945: Believing Without Belonging* (Oxford: Blackwell, 1994).
[3] Heather Wraight, *Eve's Glue: The Role Women Play in Holding the Church Together* (Carlisle: Paternoster Publishing, 2001).

Chapter 6

[1] *The Essential Trustee*, www.gov.uk/government/publications.
[2] Mark Tanner, *The PCC Member's Essential Guide* (London: Church House Publishing, 2015).
[3] *Charity trustee: what's involved (CC3a)*, www.gov.uk/guidance/charity-trustee-whats-involved (accessed 27th January 2020).

Chapter 7

[1] *The Essential Trustee*, section 12.2.
[2] John Mason Neale, 1880-66, carol published 1853. Public domain.

Chapter 8

[1] Charles R Swindoll, *Hand Me Another Brick: Timeless Lessons on Leadership* (Nashville, TN: Thomas Nelson, 2006).
[2] Alan Redpath, *Victorious Christian Service: Studies in the Book of Nehemiah* (first published 1958; reprinted: The Redpath Family, CreateSpace Independent Publishing Platform, 2013).
[3] Tom Wright, *Paul for Everyone: The Prison Letters: Ephesians, Philippians, Colossians and Philemon* (London: SPCK, 2002), p97.

Chapter 9

[1] Gerard Arbuckle, *Out of Chaos: Refounding Religious Congregations* (Sydney, Australia: Geoffrey Chapman, 1988).
[2] For details of models and principles in this section *see* Appendix 3.

Chapter 10

[1] Carver Model (Policy Government), *see* appendix 3.
[2] Formerly Churches Child Protection Advisory Service, www.thirtyoneeight.org.
[3] For Daryl Martin's email *see* AFVS in appendix 2.

Chapter 11

[1] *UK Giving Report 2018,* Charities Aid Foundation, www.cafonline.org (accessed 18th May 2019).

Chapter 12

[1] Feba UK's magazine, *Voice*, Issue 3, 2018, p13.

Chapter 13

[1] All Saint's Church, Huntington, York.

[2] *Charitable organisations in the UK (England and Wales): overview*, Anne-Marie Piper, Philip Reed and Emma James, Farrer & Co, Thomson Reuters Practical Law, uk.practicallaw.thomsonreuters.com, article published 1st November 2018.

[3] *Ibid.*

[4] www.fundraising.co.uk (accessed 3rd June 2019).

[5] Reported in www.civilsociety.co.uk, 4th October 2018

[6] 2005 English Church Census, published in: Peter Brierley, *Pulling Out of the Nosedive: A Contemporary Picture of Churchgoing: What the 2005 English Church Census Reveals* (London: Christian Research, 2006) and Peter Brierley (editor), *UK Christian Handbook Religious Trends 6: A Contemporary Picture of Churchgoing: What the 2005 English Church Census Reveals* (London: Christian Research, 2006).

[7] In 2016 the Church of England had 3,230 self-supporting clergy, *Church of England Research and Statistics: Ministry Report 2016* (London: Research and Statistics, Church House, 2017).

[8] www.thirdsector.co.uk, 11th June 2019 (accessed 1st July 2019).

[9] Curtice, J, Clery, E, Perry, J, Phillips M and Rahim, N (eds) (2019), British Social Attitudes: The 36th Report, London: The National Centre for Social Research, *A Britain that is losing its religion, has faith in science and is adopting more liberal ideas about sex and relationships*, press release 11th July 2019 about British Social Attitudes Survey 2018, www.natcen.ac.uk/news-media/press-releases/2019/July (accessed 9th April 2019). *British Social Attitudes Survey 2018.*

[10] National Secular Society, www.secularism.org.uk/education (accessed 25th March 2020).

[11] *The 95 Campaign,* www.content.scriptureunion.org.uk (accessed 25th March 2020).

Chapter 14

[1] Archbishop William Temple, *Nature, Man and God* (Edinburgh: T & T Clark, 1934).

Postscript

[1] www.gov.uk, *Coronavirus (COVID-19) guidance for the charity sector*, 7th April 2020 (Accessed 8th April 2020).